Rumanian Air Force

The Prime Decade, 1938-1947

By Dénes Bernád
Color by Don Greer and Richard Hudson

squadron/signal publications

Don Greer

Căpitan aviator (Captain) Dan Vizante, flying an I.A.R. 81C (No. 344), shoots down a P-38J-15 Lightning of the 71st Fighter Squadron, 1st Fighter Group, over Popesti-Leordeni airfield, south of Bucharest, on 10 June 1944. Vizante, commander of *Grupul 6 vânătoare* (6th Fighter Group), was credited with two of the 23 P-38s claimed by *Grupul 6* pilots during the low-level American attack. Half of the 16 P-38s of the 71st FS that clashed with the I.A.R.s were actually shot down.

Acknowledgments

This book could not have been completed without the precious help offered over the years by veteran airmen, fellow aviation historians, and enthusiasts, as well as several Rumanian institutions. They are, in alphabetical order: *dipl.-arch.* Mihai Andrei, Dan Antoniu, *dr.* Valeriu Avram, Ion Becherete, *Maior rez.* Constantin Bujor (deceased), Răzvan Bujor, *dr. dipl.-eng.* Cristian Crăciunoiu, *C-dor. av. rez.* Ion Dobran, *C-dor. av. rez.* Ion Galea (deceased), *Gen. maior av. rez. dipl.-eng.* Vasile Gavriliu, *C-dor. av. rez. dipl.-eng.* Constantin Gheorghiu (deceased), *Cpt. c-dor. av. rez.* Tudor Greceanu (deceased), *dipl.-eng.* Ovidiu George Man, Cornel Marandiuc, Neculai Moghior, Mihai Moiscscu, *Cpt. c-dor* George Paul Sandachi, Ion Tarălungă, and Vasile Tudor. *Modelism International*, *Muzeul aviatiei*, *Muzeul militar national*, and *Muzeul de istorie al României* offered some assistance as well.

To all of them I express my gratitude: **multumesc**, thank you.

I would also like to thank the following colleagues and friends from all over the world for their co-operation (in alphabetical order):

Mark Axworthy (England)   Hans-Werner Neulen (Germany)
Jean-Pierre Brun (France)   James Perry (USA)
James Crow (USA)   Peter Petrick (Germany)
Hans-Peter Dabrowski (Germany)   György Punka (Hungary)
Fülöp family (Rumania)   Jean-Louis Roba (Belgium)
Manfred Griehl (Germany)   Matti Salonen (Finland)
László Jávor (Hungary)   Gyula Sárhidai (Hungary)
Karl Kössler (Germany)   Gerhard Stemmer (Germany)
Robert Michulec (Poland)   Ferenc-Antal Vajda (Belgium)
Péter Mujzer (Hungary)   Henry Larry de Zeng IV (USA)

Jason Long helped edit my English according to US standards.

The Author welcomes any comments, additions, and new information connected to the book. He can be reached at: denesbernad@sprint.ca (Internet e-mail address).

ISBN 0-89747-402-3

If you have any photographs of aircraft, armor, soldiers or ships of any nation, particularly wartime snapshots, why not share them with us and help make Squadron/Signal's books all the more interesting and complete in the future. Any photograph sent to us will be copied and the original returned. The donor will be fully credited for any photos used. Please send them to:

Squadron/Signal Publications, Inc.
1115 Crowley Drive
Carrollton, TX 75011-5010

Если у вас есть фотографии самолётов, вооружения кораблей любой страны, особенно, снимки времён поделитесь с нами и помогите сделать новые книг Эскадрон/Сигнал ещё интереснее. Мы переснимем фотографии и вернём оригиналы. Имена приславш будут сопровождать все опубликованные фотограф Пожалуйста, присылайте фотографии по адресу:

Squadron/Signal Publications, Inc.
1115 Crowley Drive
Carrollton, TX 75011-5010

軍用機、装甲車両、兵士、軍艦などの写真を所持しておられる方はいらっしゃ
ものでも結構です。作戦中に撮影されたものが特に良いのです。Squadron/Sig
において、このような写真は内容を一層充実し、興味深くすることができます
写真は、複写の後お返しいたします。出版物中に写真を使用した場合は、必す
させて頂きます。お写真は下記にご送付ください。

Squadron/Signal Publications, Inc.
1115 Crowley Drive
Carrollton, TX 75011-5010

Dedication

I dedicate this book for all Heroes of Air.
Dedic această carte tuturor Eroilor Aerului.

'Top Gun'. The Messerschmitt Bf 109G-6 was the ultimate aircraft Rumanian pilots flew during World War Two. They unequivocally praised it as the best fighting machine they had ever flown, whose only match was the respected P-51 Mustang. *'It fit me like a glove"* — a former ARR pilot remembers. *Locotenent aviator* (1st Lt) Tudor Greceanu of *Grupul 7 vânătoare* (7th Fighter Group) flew this Messerschmitt Bf 190G-6 (White 13) from 1 February to 23 June 1944. He scored three victories in this aircraft during 1944: an La-5 on 10 March, a P-39 Airacobra on 25 April, and an unspecified Yak on 20 May. Greceanu was one of the top Rumanian fighter aces with 18+ kills to his credit when he was shot down and wounded by a P-51 Mustang of the US 15th Air Force on 23 June 1944. (Greceanu)

Foreword

My research for this book began in 1983 while I was a freshman at the Technical University of Brasov. The city of Brasov was the core of the wartime Rumanian aviation industry. I met several retired airmen in Brasov who were veterans of Rumania's World War Two campaigns against both the Soviet Union *and* the Axis Powers. Some of these veterans reluctantly shared their wartime memories with me, although mentioning the officially denied anti-Soviet war was considered imprudent under the Communist regime. I realized that their stories must be preserved for posterity.

I am now able, after collecting the facts and photographs over 15 years, to assemble the story of the Rumanian Air Force in World War Two. Their story is a colorful and interesting one, filled with highlights and drama, as well as successes and failures. This unique story includes frequent historical and political turning points as well as the large variety of foreign and indigenous aircraft types operated by Rumania.

This book is a *première*, as it is the first comprehensive work published in English on the Rumanian Air Force. My task in compiling this book was difficult due to the scarcity of hard information combined with the occasional lack of co-operation by Rumanian historians. Some airmen and local historians refused to assist me, which considerably hindered my work.

Given the sensitivity of the recent history of Eastern Europe and the Balkans, I attempted to write this book in an impartial manner. I made every effort to discard stereotypes and look beyond the cliches perpetuated by all of the World War Two participants. Because I was born in Rumania, as a member of the Hungarian ethnic minority of Transylvania (i.e., I am not Rumanian), I am fluent in Rumanian and have first-hand knowledge of the Rumanian people's *psyché*. This knowledge has enabled me to avoid the prejudices present in many locally published writings. I have also worked to broaden my horizons by consulting documents and publications of *all* of the warring parties — a practice often overlooked by Rumanian historians.

In keeping with the impartial approach, I have attempted to preserve the status quo that existed at the time when the narrative of the book unfolds. Thus, except for quotations, I have avoided such controversial terms as 'liberation' of disputed territories, and epithets like 'Nazi', 'Communist', or 'Horthyist'. The senseless phrase 'Horthyist' is preferred by Rumanian historians when they refer to the Hungarian government and soldiers of World War Two. [Editor's Note: Rear Admiral Miklós Horthy was Hungary's regent during World War Two.] I have retained the orthography, official titles of institutions and military units, full military ranks, and place names of the period.

The place names issue was particularly difficult to deal with in multi-ethnic regions, with more than one name being used for localities and geographical terms. Places in Transylvania, for example, have both Rumanian and Hungarian names. Localities inhabited by *Volksdeutsche* (ethnic German people) had German names which often appeared in Luftwaffe documents. I therefore used the Rumanian name first for places in Southern Transylvania which remained within Rumania's borders throughout the war. Hungarian and German place names, if any, appear in brackets after the Rumanian name. For Northern Transylvania, which was returned to Hungary during August of 1940, the official Hungarian name is used first with the Rumanian (and German) version in brackets. I have similarly handled the cases of Southern Slovakia, returned to Hungary during November of 1938, and Bessarabia and Northern Bukovina, incorporated into the Soviet Union during June of 1940 and regained by Rumania the following year.

I have found apparent confusion when referring to the official title of the wartime Royal Rumanian Air Force. All sources published in Rumania and abroad so far have used *Fortele Aeriene Regale ale României* (FARR). Although this form *appears* authentic, the author did not come across any official Rumanian document using this form. Several documents and laws, including those published in the Rumanian State's official gazette, *'Monitorul Oficial'*, refer to the Air Force as *Aeronautica Regală Română*, or the Royal Rumanian Aeronautics. Accordingly, this title — abbreviated ARR for simplicity — is used throughout this book.

The limits of the software used to compile this book hindered my efforts to use all characters specific to the Rumanian language. Except for a couple of vowels, no other diacritical marks could be authentically reproduced here.

Finally, I have settled on using Rumania for the country's name, rather than the recently accepted Romania or the obsolete Roumania.

This is primarily because the reference English dictionaries still use this wording as the main form. Moreover, the languages of the major European powers with which Rumania has had historic connections (such as France, Russia, and Germany) all write or pronounce the country's name with a 'u'.

I sincerely hope I have managed to preserve the delicate balance and simultaneously present to the English language reader an overall and unbiased account. This account is of the men and aircraft of what was Eastern Europe's and the Balkans' largest and most colorful air force of World War Two.

Dénes Bernád
Toronto, Canada
June 1999

The statue *'Eroilor Aerului'* (For the Heroes of Air) was erected in Bucharest during July of 1935 and is dedicated to the memory of fallen Rumanian flyers. Artist Lydia Kotzebue, assisted by János Fekete, created this monument symbolizing past and present Rumanian aviation. Thirteen bronze plaques contain the names of 269 airmen killed between 1912 to 1938. Further hundreds have died since then, including an estimated 500 killed during WW II. (Bernád)

INTRODUCTION

A Blériot XI *La Manche* of *Liga Nationalã Aerianã* (LNA; National Air League) is handled by a ground crew at Bucharest-Bãneasa airfield in 1912. The early ARR insignia — a red, yellow, and blue roundel — is carried on the upper and lower wing surfaces. The rudder was vertically striped in the French pattern with the blue facing forward. Rumanian Blériots armed with machine guns quickly achieved air supremacy over Bulgarian aircraft during the Second Balkan War of 1913. (Bernád)

This I.A.R.-built Potez 25.14R (No. 93) crash landed during the early 1930s. Unit insignias such as this one representing the monogram of King Charles (Carol) were sometimes applied to the fuselage sides up to the mid-1930s. French designs were prevalent in Rumania during the inter-war period and included aircraft manufactured under license. (Moisescu)

Brief History of
Aeronautica Regalã Românã

Rumanians can claim a rich aviation heritage. The first flight from Rumanian soil took place on the morning of 18 October 1909 when famed French pilot Louis Blériot flew from Bãneasa hippodrome outside Bucharest. The following year, four aircraft — two Farman biplanes, a Wright Type B, and a Santos-Dumont *Demoiselle* — arrived from France to establish the nucleus of Rumanian military aviation.

On 1 April 1913, the Rumanian Parliament in Bucharest passed a law establishing an air arm within the Ministry of War. This air arm eventually evolved into *Aeronautica Regalã Românã* (ARR), or the Royal Rumanian Aeronautics. National markings were soon adopted in the form of a tri-color roundel consisting of a red outer ring, a yellow inner ring, and a blue center dot.

Two months after its establishment, ARR began operations against Bulgaria in the Second Balkan War. The Rumanian Kingdom entered World War One on 27 August 1916 after two years of uneasy neutrality. Rumania sided with the *Entente* (Allied Powers) and attacked her *de jure* ally, Austria-Hungary. Rumanian airmen flew French aircraft and were assisted by a large French military mission. Despite fierce fighting against German and Austro-Hungarian forces, Rumania was defeated in December of 1917. Rumania signed an armistice with the Central Powers on 9 December 1917.

Rumania re-mobilized its forces on 10 November 1918, just prior to the end of World War One, and again attacked Hungary. Rumanian troops, supported by ARR aircraft, defeated the demoralized Hungarian Red Army the following August and entered Budapest. Rumania annexed large amounts of territory as a result of the war with Hungary. These territories included all of Transylvania (in Rumanian: Ardeal or Transilvania; in Hungarian: Erdély; in German: Siebenbürgen). Rumania also annexed Northern Banat from Hungary, Bessarabia from Russia, and Bukovina from Austria. These were combined with the pre-war regions of Moldavia, Wallachia, and Dobruja to establish the so-called 'Greater Rumania'.

The war with Hungary resulted in abundant stocks of *matériel* for Rumania, including hundreds of aircraft and aircraft engines, captured from the Hungarians. These impressed aircraft, along with surplus aircraft purchased from France, allowed Rumania to field Eastern Europe's and the Balkans' most powerful air force during the inter-war era.

Restructuring and Rearming

ARR was a largely obsolescent air force by 1936, even while political and military tensions mounted in Europe. ARR headquarters responded to the threat to 'Greater Rumania' by initiating a restructuring plan. *Dipl.-Eng.* Nicolae Caranfil, the new head of *Subsecretariatul de Stat al*

Aerului (SSA; State Under-Secretariat of Air), proposed an ARR re-equipment plan during June of 1936. This plan called for the purchase of 406 combat aircraft to equip 36 new *escadrile* (squadrons) within the next two and a half years. The aircraft would consist of 60 reconnaissance machines, 132 observation and army co-operation aircraft, 150 fighters, and 64 bombers. SSA was dissolved and replaced on 13 November 1936 by *Ministerul Aerului si Marinei* (Ministry of the Air and Navy). The plan initially set forth by Caranfil was implemented by his successor, *Dipl.-Eng.* Radu Irimescu.

Repeated bribery scandals and lack of significant progress led to Irimescu's replacement by General Paul Teodorescu during April of 1938. A revised force modernization plan was issued by Teodorescu two months later. This new three-step plan was approved by the Supreme Council of the Army in July of 1938. The first step called for Caranfil's 1936 plan to be concluded by the end of 1938. Phase two envisaged purchasing a further 169 combat aircraft between 1 January 1939 and 1 April 1942. These aircraft would comprise 105 fighters, 24 bombers, and 40 observation aircraft — enough aircraft to create 13 new squadrons. The final step of Teodorescu's plan called for 96 additional aircraft (48 bombers and 48 assault aircraft) to be placed in service by 1 April 1944. No new fighters, except for attrition replacements, were to be acquired in phase three.

This ambitious plan was not smoothly implemented. On 10 October 1938, the ARR inventory showed a total of only 292 aircraft. This total comprised 72 fighters, 16 bombers, 120 short-range reconnaissance/army co-operation aircraft, 64 liaison aircraft, four transports, and 16 seaplanes. This small number of aircraft was considered inadequate for Rumania's critical situation with Hungary and the Soviet Union — both were seeking to recover the territories lost to Rumania at the end of WW I.

In light of the deteriorating political and military situation in Europe, the Rumanian military decided to purchase military aircraft from other countries. A large Rumanian delegation visited armament factories in France, the United Kingdom, and Germany during April of 1939. The delegation sought to purchase military hardware for rapid delivery and was successful in returning to Rumania with substantial equipment orders. This success was mainly due to Rumania's strategic location in Southeastern Europe and to the country's important oil and grain resources.

The Rumanians were able to sign contracts with both the British and Germans for significant amounts of military hardware. The French, however, turned down Rumanian requests for aircraft citing their need to quickly re-equip their own air force, *L'Armée de l'Air*. Besides aircraft, Rumania successfully acquired Oerlikon anti-aircraft guns, ammunition, and special machine tools from Switzerland, and a contract was signed in Belgium to install Browning machine guns in Rumanian-built aircraft. Germany's invasion of Poland on 1 September 1939 halted many of these deliveries before most of these contracts could be fulfilled.

The ARR's inventory increased dramatically in September of 1939

An I.A.R. 38 of *Flotila 2 informatie* (2nd Information Flotilla) and a German Hs 126A of 4./(H)13 are parked on a Rumanian airfield during early 1941. The I.A.R. 38 carries a narrow yellow band on the fuselage. From the late 1930s, narrow colored squadron stripes were painted on the mid-fuselage and wing center sections. Narrow yellow stripes were retained on some ARR aircraft during the 1941 campaign against the Soviet Union. (Petrick)

A Messerschmitt Bf 109E-3 (Yellow 37) assigned to *Grupul 7 vânătoare* (7th Fighter Group) flies near Bucharest-Otopeni airfield during late April of 1941. This aircraft is painted olive green over light blue and has the yellow band on the aft fuselage and yellow cowl associated with Axis aircraft in the east. The earlier mid-wing yellow stripes have been retained on this aircraft. (via Faucard)

due to the arrival of nearly 300 Polish military and civilian aircraft. These aircraft had fled Poland to avoid capture by the German Wehrmacht (Armed Forces). Among the Polish aircraft that arrived in Rumania were approximately 50 P.Z.L. fighters and a like number of P.Z.L. bombers. These aircraft were welcome additions to the ARR's combat strength, however, the increasing number and variety of aircraft and engine types further complicated the already considerable maintenance problems facing Rumanian technicians.

By the spring of 1940, the arrival of just over 160 contracted military aircraft gave Rumania the largest and most modern air force in the region apart from the Soviet Union. During June of 1940, the *Ipoteza 32* (Hypothesis 32) Order of Battle listed 556 first class aircraft in the ARR inventory. These included 92 fighters, 113 bombers, 35 long-range reconnaissance, 214 army co-operation aircraft, 28 seaplanes, and 74 liaison and transport machines. ARR had another 371 aircraft on order, primarily from indigenous companies. The wide range of aircraft types continued to hinder efficiency. Spare parts shortages reduced serviceable aircraft totals by 20 to 30%.

The summer of 1940 was a turbulent time for Rumania. Combat capability of the Rumanian Army and Air Force was reduced by one-third following the loss of Bessarabia and Northern Bukovina to the Soviets. Rumania also lost Northern Transylvania to Hungary and Southern Dobruja to Bulgaria during this period. This was also the time that General Ion Antonescu rose to power as *Conducător* (Leader) of the 'National Legionnaire (Iron Guard) State of Rumania'. Antonescu forced King Charles II to abdicate in favor of his 18 year old son, Prince Michael. King Michael I possessed only a ceremonial role, however, since Antonescu held the country's real power.

Rumania's armed forces were reorganized during the summer of 1940. *Subsecretariatul de Stat al Aerului* (SSA) was reformed as part of a new *Ministerul Apărării Nationale* (Ministry of National Defense). SSA replaced the Ministry of Air and Marine, and was responsible for all aviation and anti-aircraft defense matters. This organizational structure was retained throughout World War Two.

General Antonescu sought to modernize Rumania's armed forces and strengthen his country's ties with the surging Third Reich by inviting a German military mission to Rumania. The first German units arrived in the country on the morning of 12 October 1940. All assigned Luftwaffe (German Air Force) units had occupied their designated airfields and command posts by mid-November. Commanding the Luftwaffe element in Rumania was Lt Gen Wilhelm Speidel. Luftwaffe units were directed to protect the vital oil fields from a possible Soviet attack, as well as help train ARR personnel and improve the ARR's combat capability. ARR was reorganized from the French pattern of mixed aircraft groups and regiments to a German-style structure. This structure meant units would have a single primary mission and were equipped — if possible — with a single aircraft type. A small Italian military mission, which included several instructor pilots, arrived in Rumania on 14 October 1940 to balance the German presence. The Italian influence on the

Rumanians, however, was minimal.

Although Rumania joined the Axis Powers on 23 November 1940, it did not accept Adolf Hitler's invitation to participate in the German invasion of Yugoslavia during April of 1941. Luftwaffe units, however, were allowed to stage attacks on Yugoslavia from Rumanian bases, notably Deta, Arad, and Bucharest-Pipera. During this time, ARR aircraft began to conform to Luftwaffe regulations by having the engine cowlings painted Chrome Yellow — the Axis aircraft recognition color in Eastern Europe. Rumania adopted a new national marking in mid-May of 1941 which further conformed to the Axis line. This marking, known as 'Michael's Cross', consisted of four white-bordered blue 'M' letters arranged in a cross pattern and filled with yellow. (M stood for *Mihai*, or Michael, King of Rumania.) A smaller version of the earlier red-yellow-blue roundel was placed in the center of the cross. In some cases, a blue 'I' was inserted between the legs of the four 'M's, symbolizing King Michael the First.

The national markings further departed from the old style by being applied in six positions: the upper and lower wings as well as fuselage sides. Rumanian military and civil aircraft received a yellow band around the aft fuselage, while yellow was also applied to the under surfaces of the wing tips. Rarely, on non-German aircraft, the upper surfaces of the wing tips were also painted yellow to cover the narrow blue-yellow-red striping applied previously. By the summer of 1941, yellow cowlings, aft fuselages, and wing tips were mandatory for all Axis aircraft operating on, or in the vicinity of, the Eastern Front.

Rumanian aircraft retained their camouflage schemes of olive green over light blue-gray which had been standardized in June of 1940. Beginning in early 1941 new aircraft, manufactured by I.A.R.-Brasov or purchased from abroad, began to receive large segments of earth brown (*terra cotta*) over the olive green upper surfaces. Dark green was also used occasionally in lieu of the earth brown. British and Polish aircraft in Rumanian service retained their original camouflage finish until standard ARR camouflage was applied during their first general overhaul. Individual serial numbers were applied to each ARR aircraft on the fin instead of the fuselage side, as before. These numbers were usually in white, although some were painted in yellow or red. German-built fighters delivered to Rumania had their serial numbers applied on the fuselage, usually between the national marking and the yellow fuselage band. There were no mandatory squadron emblems in effect, however, several units had their own insignias, often inspired by Walt Disney characters. The aircraft marking regulations were fully implemented by early June of 1941, just in time for the Axis Powers' 'crusade' against the Soviet Union.

The Bessarabian Campaign

Selected Rumanian fighter and bomber groups, equipped with the most advanced aircraft were transferred to *Gruparea Aeriană de Luptă* (GAL - Combat Air Grouping) in mid-June of 1941. GAL was incorporated into Germany's *Luftflotte 4* (4th Air Fleet) and represented the ARR's main offensive element in the anti-Soviet campaign. GAL com-

Heinkel He 111H-3 (No. 5) was assigned to *Grupul 5 bombardament* (5th Bomber Group) and painted with the new national markings adopted during May of 1941. The new 'Michael's Cross' was applied to the wings and fuselage. The cross replaced the earlier roundel which was carried only on the wings. The wing tips and aft fuselage band are painted yellow. The earlier mid-wing stripes were overpainted with a darker color. An additional 'I' is barely visible between the stylized legs of the wing insignia's four 'M's. (Crow)

prised nearly all of the available ARR bomber force which was composed of five groups with 11 squadrons. Three fighter groups, totaling eight squadrons, were also included in GAL. A total of 253 aircraft (of which 205 were serviceable) with 208 crews were under the GAL's command on 21 June. The designated area of operation for the Rumanians was Southern Bessarabia, between the Rivers Prut and Dnester, south of the Dubossary (Dubăsari)-Iasi (Jassy) line. The GAL's mission was to support the Rumanian 4th Army, the main element of the 'General Antonescu Group of Armies.'

ARR fielded a total of 672 aircraft to cope with this assignment and to perform home defense duties. Luftwaffe strength in the same sector totaled nearly 420 aircraft. The combined Rumanian-German air forces faced approximately 1750 V-VS (*Voyenno-Vozdushniye Sily*; Soviet Air Force) aircraft as follows: 950 of the Southern Front, covering the area between Kamenets-Podol'skiy and the Danube delta; 624 of the Black Sea Fleet; and 350 of the Long-Range Air Force (only some 176 of this latter unit was dispatched against Rumanian targets). Apparently, the numerical superiority was on the Soviet side (1:1.6 ratio), however, technical superiority belonged to the Axis since three quarters of the Soviet fleet was considered obsolete.

The primary task of GAL during the first 11 days of the Bessarabian Campaign was to destroy Soviet tactical targets — aircraft and airfields, fortified positions, matériel depots, motorized columns, and artillery positions. On 3 July GAL switched from interdiction to close support missions. This move coincided with the Royal Rumanian Army's crossing of the River Prut. The ARR's lack of a dedicated assault aircraft type became apparent during this phase of operations.

The capture of Bessarabia, the immediate objective of the war, was achieved by Rumanian and German troops on 28 July. After a ten day lull, Rumanian forces began their drive on Odessa, a strategic harbor and communications center on the northwestern coast of the Black Sea. Odessa fell on 16 October after a bitter struggle — a successful end to the ARR's first campaign.

Fighters assigned to Rumania's home defense were kept on constant vigil during the Bessarabian Campaign. These fighters engaged V-VS bombers and fighters which attacked Rumania almost daily. Soviet aircraft struck key Rumanian targets from the first day of the war. These targets included the harbor of Constanta, Cernavodă bridge, oil fields in the Ploiesti area, as well as the capital city of Bucharest. Rumanian and German fighter pilots claimed an impressive number of kills without significant losses.

GAL aircraft flew 2405 missions totaling 7857 sorties during 118 days

of fighting, with the entire GAL fleet flying only 84 of those days. GAL airmen claimed 266 Soviet aircraft destroyed for a loss of only 40 Rumanian aircraft. The entire ARR flew a total of 17,368 sorties totaling 29,638 flight hours during the campaign.

To complete the overall picture, during the same time period the V-VS of the Southern Front reported 32,000 sorties (5000 during the first 18 days, 19,000 from 11 July to 30 September, and 8000 during the defense of Odessa). Additionally, the Black Sea Fleet flew 22,000 sorties by mid-October and some 1100 sorties of the Long Range AF were dispatched against targets in Rumania. Thus, the overall number of V-VS sorties exceeds 55,000.

ARR pilots took part in 217 air engagements over Bessarabia, Trans-Dnestra (*Transnistria* in Rumanian), or over Rumania proper. These pilots claimed 332 Soviet aircraft shot down and another 150 aircraft destroyed on the ground. Rumanian anti-aircraft defenses added a further 115 Soviet aircraft destroyed for a total of 597 V-VS aircraft claimed by Rumanian forces.

The majority of these reports appear to be overclaims since the Soviets operated no more than 250 to 300 aircraft on that particular area of the Southern Front during that time. It is believed that Rumanian pilots and gunners claimed up to three times as many aircraft destroyed than was actually the case. These claims do not take into account German claims for Soviet aircraft destroyed. (This was not a unique occurrence. According to a notable British researcher, Royal Air Force flyers filed five claims for one actual Luftwaffe combat loss during June of 1941.)

Soviet airmen also reported large numbers of Axis aircraft destroyed in air combat while diminishing their own losses. The Soviets regarded Rumanian fighter pilots as less dangerous than those of the Luftwaffe. A Soviet source stated: *"Luckily for pilots of OdVO (Odessa Military District), the majority of their opponents were Rumanians. They had been found not as skilled and dangerous as their German colleagues — veterans with extensive combat experience — and could not take advantage of the existing drawbacks of the Soviet Air Force. The obsolescence of several Rumanian aircraft types — such as the P.Z.L. P.11 and P.24, similar to our I-15 — had also shown in detriment."* ARR actually lost 136 aircraft in the four-month-long campaign.

Next Stop: Stalingrad

Most ARR units returned to Rumania following the capture of Odessa. A long overdue restructuring of ARR was soon implemented. Older and obsolescent matériel, primarily the Polish aircraft, but also some German and Italian machines, were relegated to training duties. The gap in modern aircraft could not be filled, however, by the small number of aircraft from Germany or the Rumanian aviation industry. Attempts to order large numbers of military hardware from Germany and Italy were largely unsuccessful. Only a few new squadrons could be raised as a result. These squadrons were primarily formed by reorganizing the existing units or by equipping with indigenous types produced by I.A.R.-Brasov.

ARR units conducted little activity on the Soviet Front between 17

A *celulā* (cell, a two-aircraft element) of Heinkel He 112Bs assigned to *Escadrila 52 vânātoare* escorts a *patrulā* (patrol, a three-aircraft bomber element) of Potez 633 B2s assigned to *Escadrila 75 bombardament* at 1100 hrs on 22 June 1941. These aircraft were flying to attack Soviet airfields at Bolgrad and Bulgãrica, in Southern Bessarabia, during the first day of fighting on the Russian Front. Three of the 13 Potez 633s launched that day were lost to enemy anti-aircraft fire and fighters. (Antonlu)

October 1941 and 1 August 1942. Operations during this time primarily consisted of transport, courier, and reconnaissance missions supporting the Rumanian 3rd Army in the Crimean Peninsula. Occasional fighter and close support missions were also flown. ARR units during these nine and one-half months conducted a total of 3439 sorties totaling 6638 flight hours. The break-down consisted of 1380 sorties by reconnaissance and army co-operation aircraft, 1021 by fighters, and 1038 sorties for liaison aircraft. ARR pilots claimed seven Soviet aircraft shot down and three others destroyed on the ground. Rumanian anti-aircraft gunners claimed an additional 111 V-VS aircraft destroyed during the same period.

ARR personnel casualties (including ground and anti-aircraft crews) totaled 862 from 22 June 1941 to 1 August 1942. Of these, 383 were killed, 414 wounded, and 65 were missing in action. This toll was tremendous given the low number of personnel involved in combat operations.

The United States declared war on Rumania on 5 June 1942 (in a belated response to Rumania's declaration of war on 12 December 1941). One week later, on 12 June, 13 B-24 heavy bombers attacked the oil fields of Ploiesti for the first time. This mission, code-named OPERATION HALPRO, was the first US Army Air Forces (USAAF) combat operation in Europe. Although damage to the oil fields was negligible, the surprise American raid alerted the Germans and Rumanians to the possibilities of further large-scale attacks. A strong air defense was subsequently built up around Ploiesti and other strategic areas of Rumania. This effort included installing radar stations throughout Wallachia, Southern Rumania. (These defense measures were almost complete by 1 August 1943 when the USAAF mounted the next raid on Ploiesti, OPERATION TIDAL WAVE.)

The 1942 Stalingrad campaign was Rumania's major commitment to the Axis effort on the Russian Front. *Comandamentul Aviatiei de Luptā* (CAL; Combat Aviation Command) was formed on 6 September and headquartered in Rostov. CAL included *Regiunea Aerianā Înaintatā* (RAI; Forward Air Region) which was headquartered at Oblivskaya. RAI components included *Flotila 2 vânātoare* (2nd Fighter Flotilla), *Flotila 2 bombardament* (2nd Bomber Flotilla), and *Grupul 1 recunoastere îndepārtatā* (1st Long-Range Reconnaissance Group). Several non-combat squadrons with spotting, transport, and liaison missions, as well as *Brigada 4 artilerie antiaerianā* (4th Anti-Aircraft Artillery Brigade) were also attached to CAL. CAL controlled 30 squadrons — eight fighter, seven bomber, three reconnaissance, six spotting/army co-operation, four liaison, and two transport. The 272 aircraft comprising CAL were put under the command of *Luftflotte 4*.

ARR units selected for front line service began arriving in the Stalingrad area during the first week of September 1942. Their primary mission was to support German and Rumanian troops in their attack on the city. This support was rendered by bombers flying tactical missions against railways, marshaling yards, trains, and selected targets within Stalingrad itself. Fighters performed interdiction missions and low-level attacks on targets of opportunity, including enemy troop columns and artillery positions. Rumanian aircraft averaged 70 to 80 sorties per day during this period.

Comandamentul Aviatiei de Luptā (CAL) was renamed *Gruparea Aerianā de Luptā* (GAL; Combat Air Grouping) on 10 October and placed under the command of *General de escadrā aviator* (Major General) Ermil Gheorghiu. The following combat units were assigned to the new GAL: the 2nd BF (headquartered at Tatshinskaya) with *Grupuri 1* and *5 bombardament*; the 2nd FF (HQ at Morozovskaya) with *Grupuri 6* and *8 vânātoare*; the 1st LRRG, and *Escadrila 113 legāturā* (113 Liaison Squadron). *Grupul 7 vânātoare*, equipped with Messerschmitt Bf 109Es, was temporarily transferred to German command.

The Soviet counter-offensive against Axis forces at Stalingrad began on the night of 19/20 November 1942. The Red Army's major efforts were directed towards the 4th Rumanian Army north of Stalingrad and the 3rd Rumanian Army south of the city. These attacks prompted GAL to mount close-support missions. The Soviets broke through the Rumanian lines, and encircled the bulk of the two armies. The Red Army also surrounded several forward-based GAL air units, along with 7th FG based at Karpovka airfield. GAL was able to reorganize by the end of November when the front stabilized to some degree. This reorganization resulted in the December recall of several squadrons to Rumania. These units were primarily equipped with obsolescent non-German aircraft which the Luftwaffe could not service. Surviving I.A.R. 80/81 fighters and Savoia J.R.S./J.I.S. 79B bombers were later sent home. A mixed fighter-bomber group, equipped with Bf 109Es and He 111Hs, remained at the Stalingrad front for several more weeks. This ad hoc unit was then disbanded during late February of 1943 and the surviving aircraft and crews were returned to Rumania.

GAL units flew approximately 4000 sorties in the Stalingrad area between October of 1942 and January of 1943. This number completed the 1000 sorties previously reported by CAL. Rumanian airmen claimed at least 61 Soviet aircraft destroyed, including 39 destroyed in air combat. [By comparison, *Major* Hermann Graf, *Staffelkapitän* of 9./JG 52, shot down 62 enemy aircraft (victories 141 to 202) in the Stalingrad

The wreckage of a Soviet Ilyushin DB-3F (Il-4) bomber was displayed on a street in Bucharest during the summer of 1941. This aircraft was shot down by anti-aircraft fire during the evening of 14-15 July 1941 while attempting a raid on the capital. The Soviets sent unescorted bombers on day and night attacks against Bucharest, Ploiesti, Constanta, and other strategic Rumanian targets. Most of these bombers were shot down by ARR and Luftwaffe fighters and anti-aircraft gunners. (Nicolescu)

King *Mihai* (Michael) I, wearing an Air Marshal's uniform and dark sunglasses, speaks with an ARR officer while visiting an airfield. Michael was a passionate flyer who received his pilot's license during 1944 when he was 23. Former (and largely still royalist) ARR airmen remember Michael as an outgoing and friendly King, who often visited airfields accompanied only by his personal aide. In 1997, King Michael returned to Rumania — fifty years after his forced abdication and subsequent exile. (Avram)

area during September of 1942. *Kapitan* Ivan Kozhedub, the top scoring V-VS ace, made 62 kills during his entire career.] Total GAL losses amounted to 538 personnel (killed, wounded, or missing) and 79 aircraft, between 16 October 1942 and 15 January 1943. Only 26 of the aircraft lost were shot down by flak or fighters, the remaining 53 were destroyed in accidents or left behind on hastily abandoned airfields. An additional 12 CAL aircraft lost up to 15 October 1942 can be added to the overall total.

Rumanian anti-aircraft gunners achieved one of their most important successes while defending Morozovskaya and Tatshinskaya airfields. These gunners claimed 65 aircraft shot down. A single-day high of 16 aircraft victories was achieved at Morozovskaya on 8 December. The gunners brought down various aircraft, including DB-3 bombers and I-26/Yak-1 fighters. Rumanian anti-aircraft defenses claimed 199 enemy aircraft during 1942. These victories included 65 between the rivers Donets and Dnepr, four between the rivers Dnepr and Bug, and 35 in the Caucasus. Rumanian gunners brought down five Soviet aircraft over

Two He 111Hs and an I.A.R. 39 are parked in front of a fabric hangar at a Bessarabian airfield during the summer of 1941. The I.A.R. 39 wears a rare four-color camouflage scheme with overpainted mid-wing stripes. The wooden ammunition boxes near the hangar are only partially covered with tree boughs due to the low risk of V-VS strafing attacks at this stage of the war. (Bernád)

Rumania (not including Bessarabia and Trans-Dnestra) and 90 others over the 3rd Rumanian Army's area of operations.

Re-equipping

The need to overhaul the ARR's aircraft inventory became paramount after the Stalingrad campaign ended during February of 1943. This need was apparent from the obsolescent and fatigued state of the existing aircraft. Lack of spare parts for the large variety of aircraft and engines — some long out of production — lowered serviceability rates. The increased quality of Soviet aircraft encountered over the front also played a role in the ARR's modernization plans. In addition to the re-equipment plan, ARR also desired to restructure and consolidate the combat squadrons' aircraft inventories.

Any Rumanian procurement decisions, however, hinged on German assistance. Hitler regarded Rumanian participation in the Third Reich's war against the Soviet Union as vital. Additionally, German aircraft production had increased without a corresponding increase in trained Luftwaffe aircrews. Since there was no shortage of Rumanian aviators, a political decision was made in the spring of 1943 to re-equip ARR with modern German aircraft similar to current Luftwaffe types. These new aircraft would replace all but a few old Italian, Polish, French, British, and German machines. The Germans either loaned these aircraft to Rumania, restricting their use to the front lines, or exchanged them for oil, food, and raw materials. Earlier in the year, the reformed *Regiunea Aeriană Înaintată* (RAI; Forward Air Region) was renamed *Corpul 1 Aerian Român* (C1AR; 1st Rumanian Air Corps). C1AR, under the command of *General de escadră aviator* Ermil Gheorghiu, became the ARR's main combat element deployed to the Soviet Front.

During March of 1943 the Luftwaffe transferred new-generation Messerschmitt Bf 190G-2 fighters to *Grupul 7 vânătoare* at Tiraspol airfield in Trans-Dnestra. These 'Gustavs' replaced the unit's elderly Bf 109 'Emils'. One hundred thirty-two aircraft were handed over to the Rumanians by 16 June 1943. These aircraft comprised 31 Bf 109G-2/G-4s, 12 Ju 88D-1s, 25 Ju 88A-4s, 29 Ju 87D-3s, and 35 Hs 129B-2s. All of these units were ready for action, except for the Hs 129-equipped assault group. The assault unit was slower in learning to operate their aircraft than the other units in C1AR. Nevertheless, C1AR was declared combat-ready on 16 June.

Several new Bf 109G-2s first saw action with the Rumanians over Ploiesti on 1 August 1943 when 177 B-24s of the US IX Bomber Command conducted a full-scale attack on the oil fields. These Bf 109G-2s were assigned to *Escadrila 53 vânătoare* which had previously been equipped with Hurricanes. This squadron was temporarily incorporated into JG 4 as a fourth *Staffel* at the time of the attack. The American raid on 1 August resulted in heavy US bomber losses, but only yielded mediocre results. OPERATION TIDAL WAVE, however, was the precursor of the devastating attacks conducted on Ploiesti during the summer of 1944.

The majority of C1AR's units, assigned to *Luftflotte 4*, arrived on the Eastern Front during June of 1943 to participate in the ARR's third campaign. C1AR was assigned to a zone in southern Ukraine, north of the Sea of Azov, between the rivers Mius and Donets. The Corps was tasked with supporting Wehrmacht forces engaged south of Kharkov

with the numerically superior Red Army. C1AR, headquartered at Mariupol, fielded 22 squadrons with just over 200 aircraft. All these aircraft were new German types, except for I.A.R. 80/81 and Fleet F-10Gs.

The re-equipped ARR was again at its peak effectiveness early in this campaign. Rumanian units performed at high levels due to new and plentiful aircraft combined with prompt service and replacements provided by the Germans. C1AR flew a high number of missions and claimed several Soviet aircraft without major loss to itself. This battle was an uphill struggle for the Rumanians, however, since the Red Army's advance could only be slowed. Rumanian units were forced to gradually retreat to airfields in Trans-Dnestra and Bessarabia by the end of 1943.

The Luftwaffe replaced C1AR aircraft losses as quickly as possible, however, keeping the Rumanian units at their theoretical 12 aircraft per squadron with three to six in reserve was not sustainable. C1AR's strength gradually declined as a result with only 60 aircraft available for service by early March of 1944. The remaining aircraft saw continuous action, with dive bomber and assault crews averaging three to four sorties per day.

Rumanian anti-aircraft gunners claimed 32 USAAF aircraft during 1943, including 17 confirmed during OPERATION TIDAL WAVE. These gunners also brought down 84 V-VS aircraft that year. Forty-three Soviet aircraft of that total were shot down between the rivers Volga and Dnepr, 15 between the rivers Dnepr and Bug, and 26 over Rumanian territory.

Defending the Homeland

The Second World War reached Rumania's northeastern frontiers during mid-March of 1944 when the first Soviet troops reached Rumanian soil. Rumania was confronted with a situation many Rumanians had believed would never happen. 'The Russian steamroller', as the Red Army was called by wartime propaganda, was now at the gates of Moldavia.

This Soviet advance prompted the ARR Headquarters to concentrate all of its available resources into the battle. *Corpul 1 Aerian Român* units relocated to Bessarabia and Moldavia during April of 1944 and regrouped to face the advancing Russians. Other ARR units — previously kept in reserve — were assembled into the new *Corpul 2 Aerian Român* (C2AR; 2nd Rumanian Air Corps) on 1 April. Most aircraft assigned to this corps possessed limited combat capability. Beginning on 25 April, C2AR's 25 squadrons, composed of just over 180 serviceable aircraft, were sent into battle alongside the elite C1AR.

Rumanian air activity increased even though Rumania's fortunes grew increasingly desperate. Fighters and bombers flew three to six combat sorties daily. These aircraft were engaged in defending Rumanian airspace or striking tactical targets 6.2 to 31.1 miles (10 to 50 km) behind the front line. From 4 April, USAAF and RAF aircraft appeared regularly over Rumania — joining the Soviet aircraft already sweeping over the country. US bombers made daylight attacks, while British bombers struck Rumania at night under the Allies' 'round the clock' bombing campaign. Both Rumanian and German day and night fighters, combined with strong anti-aircraft defenses, fiercely resisted the Allied air

raids. The air battles of 1944 were the most demanding clashes fought by Rumanian airmen and both sides absorbed heavy losses in men and equipment. The ARR's fourth campaign, the homeland defense between April and August of 1944, proved to be the most difficult for Rumanian airmen.

During June of 1944, ARR took advantage of a temporary halt in the Soviet onslaught to reorganize their units. ARR Headquarters allowed all units, except for fighter squadrons on home defense duties, time to rest and rebuild. In July, C2AR was withdrawn from the front and replaced by units of Germany's *Luftflotte 4*. The main unit was renamed *Corpul 3 Aerian Român* (C3AR; 3rd Rumanian Air Corps), and redeployed to Dobruja to defend the seacoast and Danube delta from the Soviets. The balance of German and Rumanian combat aircraft was nearly equal during this time, although the Luftwaffe had the larger number. On 26 June, for example, the Germans fielded 538 aircraft (not counting seaplanes). Total ARR combat strength on the same date was slightly less than 500 aircraft.

C1AR celebrated its first anniversary on the front on 16 June 1944. The Corps had flown 18,074 sorties over southern Ukraine and Bessarabia/Moldavia and had dropped 8055.3 tons (7312.4 metric tons) of bombs during that time. C1AR aviators and anti-aircraft gunners claimed 401 Allied aircraft destroyed.

ARR fighter units were overstretched by having to face superior numbers of higher quality Allied aircraft and pilots on two fronts. V-VS units assigned to OPERATION JASSY-KISHINEV outnumbered their Rumanian opposition by two and a half to one. After the morning Soviet attacks, the Rumanians had to face USAAF bombers and their fighter escorts. The obsolescent I.A.R. 80/81 fighters were completely outclassed by their American opposition. This prompted *Subsecretariatul de Stat al Aerului* (SSA) during early July to prohibit these Rumanian fighters from engaging American fighters. The I.A.R. 80/81s were reassigned to the less demanding Moldavian front where their capabilities against Soviet opposition were more or less equal. The ARR's two Messerschmitt Bf 109G equipped *grupuri de vânătoare* (fighter groups) assumed the difficult home defense duties. They were joined by similarly equipped Luftwaffe *Jagdgruppen*.

According to the author's research, 42 daylight air raids were conducted by USAAF units during 1944, while the RAF mounted at least 23 night attacks. Rumanian documents state that the US 15th Air Force lost 223 bombers and 36 fighters during these raids. Fifty-six of the bombers were shot down by fighters, 131 were brought down by anti-aircraft fire, and 36 were lost to other causes. The Americans lost 15 fighters to aeri-

An I.A.R. 80A (White 130) assigned to *Grupul 9 vânătoare* is parked at Bucharest-Pipera air base during the summer of 1942. The aircraft has been draped with camouflage netting and displays the Group's early green four-leaf clover insignia on the fuselage. The I.A.R. 80 was one of the world's best fighters at the time of its first flight on 20 April 1939. By 1944, however, the I.A.R. 80 had become obsolescent. Production delays and a lack of further improvements and suitable powerplant caused the aircraft to be outclassed by superior Allied and Luftwaffe fighters. (Bernád)

Capt Alexandru Serbănescu, the top pro-Axis ARR air ace, links arms with a Luftwaffe pilot during February of 1944. The Luftwaffe pilot is believed to be Lt Ludwig Neuböck, a former JG 52 pilot with 32 kills. Neuböck served as liaison officer to *Grupul 9 vânătoare*. ARR and Luftwaffe airmen enjoyed warm relationships with each other during their common war on the Eastern Front. This relationship lasted up to Rumania's about-face of 23 August 1944. (Antoniu)

al combat, one to anti-aircraft fire, and 20 to other causes. The British lost 48 bombers on their night missions over Rumania. A total of 286 Allied aircraft crashed on Rumanian soil, while several other aircraft fell into inaccessible areas or bodies of water. Other aircraft, damaged on raids over Rumania, crashed on the way back to their bases.

Prior to the end of the war against the Allies, Rumanian anti-aircraft gunners claimed 245 USAAF and 82 V-VS aircraft shot down during the first eight months of 1944. The Soviet aircraft destroyed included 18 over the Crimea, eight over Trans-Dnestra, and 56 over Rumania.

The total US and British attrition rate over Rumania was approximately seven percent, compared to an average 3.5 percent rate over Western Europe. Total US and British Commonwealth casualties — killed, wounded, and prisoner — amounted to 2200 men. From this casualty figure, 1095 American and 52 British airmen were repatriated in early September of 1944. OPERATION REUNION also saw two Dutch officers, five Yugoslav officers, and two British civilians flown out of Rumania. Fifty-six B-17 Flying Fortress bombers flew the Allied prisoners out of the country under the noses of the advancing Soviet troops. Soviets were also eager to take custody of their allies which they considered valuable bargaining chips in high-level diplomacy.

During the same period, ARR lost over 80 fighter aircraft in combat. The combined Rumanian/German air forces lost 225 aircraft and 121 pilots. Rumanian casualties on the ground between 4 April and 19 August 1944 totaled 15,140. This total included 7444 killed (6716 civilians and 728 soldiers) and 7696 wounded (6979 civilians and 717 soldiers).

The temporary lull on the Moldavian front ended early on 20 August when the Soviet offensive in the Iasi-Chisinău (Jassy-Kishinev) area began. This offensive was aimed at overrunning Rumania and forcing

her out of the war. The Red Army had built up their reserves and V-VS aircraft flew only a minimum number of missions before launching the offensive. The Soviet campaign, OPERATION JASSY-KISHINEV, began with support from the 1952 aircraft of the 5th and 17th Air Armies. Russian armor penetrated the weak Rumanian and German defense lines within hours, despite the harassment of ARR and Luftwaffe aircraft. One hundred sixty-one Rumanian aircraft took part in sorties against the Soviets on 20 August. The number increased to 304 on 21 August with 305 flying the next day. The numerically superior Soviet forces, however, could not be stopped. Soviet sources put the total number of their aircraft losses during the ten-day Jassy-Kishinev Offensive at 111. At least 25 ARR aircraft were shot down between 20 and 23 August, mainly by newer generation V-VS fighters. Rumania's fate was sealed during the four days of this Soviet offensive.

By 23 August it became clear to the Rumanian Government and to King Michael that the front would not hold and that Soviet troops would reach Bucharest within days. The war against the Allies was lost.

Turning the Arms against the Luftwaffe

During the evening of 23 August 1944, King Michael I spoke on Rumanian national radio. The King declared an immediate cease-fire with Allied (Soviet) troops, broke political and military ties with the Axis, and requested an armistice. The surprised German forces in Rumania, however, did not cease to fight. German forces within Rumania followed Hitler's direct orders and tried to remove the 'traitor' government and King. Luftwaffe level and dive bombers struck Bucharest, including the Royal Palace, over the next two days. Rumania responded to these attacks — and Soviet pressure — by declaring war on Germany on 25 August. The Rumanian government later declared war on Hungary. ARR pilots suddenly found themselves at war with their former comrades-in-arms.

Both sides were confused by the fast pace of events. Although Rumanian and German aircraft clashed, initially the general desire by both sides was to avoid conflict. This situation, however, rapidly deteriorated. From 25 August, Rumanian anti-aircraft gunners and ARR pilots began shooting at Luftwaffe bombers attacking the capital. The Rumanians also began shooting at transport planes carrying reinforcements to Wehrmacht troops fighting in and around Bucharest. Those German land and air units which avoided capture retreated by the end of August through passes in the Carpathian Mountains and Transylvanian Alps into northern Transylvania in friendly Hungary, or south of the Danube to not-so-friendly Bulgaria.

The last USAAF bombing attack on Rumania occurred on 26 August. Some 230 B-24 Liberators of the 15th Air Force attempted to help Rumanian troops fighting the Germans around Bucharest. Poor coordination with the Rumanians, however, led some B-24s to drop bombs on advanced positions of *Batalionul 4 parasutisti* (4th Paratrooper Battalion) in Băneasa and Otopeni.

ARR documents recorded a total of 126 combat missions during the initial week-long hostilities against the Axis forces. These missions consisted of 336 sorties totaling 451 flight hours. Sixty-four of these missions — 246 sorties and 320 hours — were performed in Wallachia, south of the Transylvanian Alps. The remaining missions were flown over southern Transylvania. Claims were filed for 84 Luftwaffe aircraft destroyed in the air or on the ground. The real number, however, is less than 25 and this does not count anti-aircraft victories. German pilots also made exaggerated victory claims. Rumanian troops captured 228 German aircraft from combat units or repair shops throughout Rumania. The peace treaty between the Rumanian Kingdom and the Allied Powers expressly stated that all captured equipment and personnel be handed over to the Red Army. ARR, however, retained over 150 ex-Luftwaffe aircraft which were hastily repainted in Rumanian markings and quickly issued to various ARR units.

Official ARR combat losses consisted of four aircraft shot down and another 30 destroyed on the ground. The total number lost, however, is believed to be approximately 50 machines. The majority of these were set on fire at airfields. Luftwaffe personnel destroyed hostile Rumanian aircraft and seized a number of German-built Rumanian aircraft. These

Chattanooga Choo Choo, a B-24D-95-CO (42-40782) assigned to the 389th Bombardment Group, was shot down near Ploiesti on 1 August 1943. The USAAF lost nearly 300 aircraft over Rumania during the war. ARR fighters and anti-aircraft gunners initially claimed 277 American aircraft from that total. These 277 claimed victories were probably double the number of actual kills, as Luftwaffe airmen and flak crew claimed a similar total of kills. (Gheorghiu)

aircraft included Ju 87Ds and Ju 88As which had been lent to their former ally for sole use on the Soviet Front. Germany deployed these aircraft against the Rumanians or flew them to safety. The bulk of the ex-C1AR aircraft remained firmly in Rumanian hands, however, and were later employed against their former owners.

All aircraft were grounded by ARR Headquarters on 1 September 1944 according to strict Soviet orders. The new political situation also imposed a change in Rumanian national insignia. The pre-May 1941 roundel — red-yellow-blue — was reinstated on 3 September 1944. The roundels were now applied in six positions instead of four as per pre-war regulations. These roundels were usually painted over the outdated Michael's Cross insignia. The yellow Axis identification color painted under the wing tips and around the rear fuselage was overpainted in white. White was the recognition color of the Soviet 5th Air Army under the command of Gen-Col S. K. Goryunov. The upper wing tips and the underside of the engine cowling were also ordered painted white, although this was not accomplished on all aircraft. Rumanian Air Force elements were placed under Soviet 5th Air Army command on 7 September. Aircraft serial (tail) numbers and other unit insignias were not affected by these changes.

After 1 September 1944, the fighting shifted from southern and eastern Rumania to the northwest across the Transylvanian Alps and into Rumanian-owned southern Transylvania. Surviving Luftwaffe air and ground elements retreated into eastern Hungary (northern Transylvania). Rumanian Army intelligence reports estimated the Axis had assembled 240 aircraft in eastern Hungary. After this redeployment the *Jagdfliegern* carried out low-level attacks against tactical targets in Rumania proper. These targets included airfields, railway stations, and radio transmission towers. The Luftwaffe was able to take advantage of the power vacuum caused by the temporary grounding of ARR units and the absence of V-VS units from the new front zone. Low level German attacks were unchallenged by aircraft and only slightly hindered by anti-aircraft fire. These strafing missions destroyed 161 ARR aircraft during the first five days of September. Not all Rumanian aircraft, however, were destroyed by the Luftwaffe. Some strafing was done by USAAF aircraft who were not aware of the exact location of the Transylvanian borders between 'hostile' Hungary and 'friendly' Rumania. This was the heaviest short-period loss suffered by ARR during its existence. The majority of the destroyed equipment, however, consisted of obsolete fighters and bombers relegated to training roles and assembled in previously quiet areas. Force parity with the Axis became more balanced once Rumanian and Soviet aircraft arrived in the area.

The 'Western Front'

The ARR inventory at the time of Rumania's about-face on 23 August 1944 stood at 1692 aircraft in 61 squadrons. These included 527 combat aircraft, 22 seaplanes, 12 gliders, and 1131 training aircraft. This number decreased by over 200, however, during the following two weeks. A 20-squadron strong expeditionary air unit was assembled from this force. The unit was composed of 210 aircraft, of which approximately half were German-made machines. The expeditionary air unit was formed to assist the ground troops in fighting the Germans and Hungarians on the new anti-Axis 'Western Front'.

The once-again reformed *Corpul 1 Aerian Român* (C1AR) was deployed to airfields in southern Transylvania on 7 September. These airfields were shared with V-VS aircraft, which included A-20 Boston attack bombers, Il-2 Shturmovik assault aircraft, and Yak-7B and Yak-9 fighters. The uneasy alliance between the until-recently-sworn-enemies led to repeated skirmishes when Soviet fighters and anti-aircraft artillery fired indiscriminately on Rumanian aircraft. These incidents caused substantial losses in Rumanian lives and equipment.

The first days in the new theater of war passed without notable encounters between the two sides. This situation changed on 11 September, when ARR and Luftwaffe aircraft clashed. Several engagements took place from 11 September around Kolozsvár (Cluj/Klausenburg), the capital of Transylvania. The majority of Rumanian aircrews were veterans of the anti-Soviet war, however, they were no match for the experienced Luftwaffe *Jägern*. The fighting

peaked on 23 and 25 September, when up to 50 fighters clashed above Turda (Torda/Thorenburg). The engagements ended disastrously for the Rumanians, with 13 ARR aircraft shot down. Most of the lost aircraft were obsolescent I.A.R. 80 and I.A.R. 81 fighters. ARR pilots filed four claims which were not fully substantiated by Luftwaffe loss records. After 25 September 1944, the I.A.R.s were withdrawn from fighter duties and redeployed as fighter-bombers.

The first month of the 'Western Front' — the ARR's fifth and final campaign — was the most intensive month of the anti-Axis war. At least 25 Rumanian aircraft were shot down in 17 engagements. Only four Axis aircraft were claimed shot down, while five were claimed destroyed on the ground. This heavy attrition led to C1AR being reorganized between 5 and 10 October. Parts of the decimated fighter and bomber units were recalled to the homeland, while other *escadrile* were consolidated to keep up the minimum number of required aircraft per squadron. A Savoia-'Jumo'-equipped J.R.S 79 group arrived at the front to strengthen the Corps' strike capability.

The 174-aircraft strong C1AR was restructured into 15 squadrons and moved to forward airfields in pursuit of Axis troops retreating deeper into Hungary. During October and November, air activity on both sides decreased significantly due to unfavorable weather conditions and water-logged airstrips. These conditions were the major reason for the low number of combat missions and a high number of accidents.

C1AR aircraft performed their first combat mission over northern Hungary on 20 December 1944. The Soviet High Command ordered all available aircraft assembled for this operation, including some 50 ARR machines. These aircraft would be sent to strike the railway station and marshaling yard at Losonc (today Lucenec, Slovakia). The Soviets sought to paralyze this important communications hub in northern Hungary with one blow. The results of the bombing mission were satisfactory, however, the station was not completely destroyed. C1AR continued to fly extensive combat missions during the last two weeks of December.

C1AR flew 792 missions consisting of 2541 sorties between 7 September and 31 December 1944. These aircraft dropped 508 tons (460.9 metric tons) of bombs in that period and fought 21 engagements with German and Hungarian aircraft. Forty Axis aircraft were claimed destroyed in combat, with 23 of these confirmed. Of the 40 aircraft claimed, Rumanians aircraft shot down four in air combat and destroyed five aircraft on the ground. Anti-aircraft gunners claimed the remainder. C1AR lost 64 aircraft during its four months of operations. Twenty-six aircraft were shot down in air combat, 17 were lost to anti-aircraft fire, six were destroyed on the ground, five force-landed in enemy territory, and the remaining ten were scrapped for miscellaneous reasons. Additional aircraft were damaged in combat or accidents. These aircraft were sent back to repair shops in Rumania effectively withdrawing them from the combat units. C1AR suffered 60 personnel killed — 21 officers, 21 NCOs, one technician, and 17 enlisted men — in the fighting during late 1944.

The Last Year of War

C1AR began 1945 with only 152 aircraft organized into 14 squadrons. The Corps was part of the Soviet 5th Air Army, which had a total of 655 aircraft. The Rumanians provided almost one-quarter of the Allies' air strength deployed to the northeastern Hungarian front. This front was aimed at capturing Budapest. The burden of combat sorties was taken up by the mixed dive bomber-assault group equipped with Ju 87Ds and

This I.A.R. 37 (White 40) has had the Axis era 'Michael's Cross' hastily overpainted with the pre-war roundel of blue (center), yellow, and red. A white band has been painted on the aft fuselage. Rumania defected from the Axis on 23 August 1944 and ARR aircraft were sent to the new front fighting alongside the Soviets. Despite being prone to accidents, the I.A.R. 37 army co-operation aircraft remained in active service until the end of the war. (Greceanu)

This Savoia J.R.S. 79B bomber force-landed on a field in Hungary following an engagement during late 1944. The propeller spinners of many ARR aircraft were painted with a white spiral beginning in late July of 1944. ARR aircraft retained such pro-Axis signs as the *Spiralschnauze* following the *coup d'état* of 23 August 1944. The pro-Axis markings led to confusion among German air and ground units, however, this did not prevent Luftwaffe fighters from shooting down 'traitor' Rumanian aircraft when presented with the opportunity. (Avram)

Hs 129Bs. Twin-engine Ju 88 and Savoia bombers struck strategic targets, while I.A.R. 80/81s strafed enemy columns and positions. The sole Messerschmitt Bf 109G-6-equipped fighter group provided air cover.

ARR Headquarters augmented C1AR's waning numbers and met increasing Soviet demands by moving six new squadrons and replacement aircraft from Rumania to the front. These units were made up of captured Luftwaffe fighters, as well as repaired and refurbished aircraft. The infusion increased C1AR's strength to 20 squadrons and 239 aircraft by 20 February.

The last major operation performed by ARR aircraft took place on 25 February 1945. The aircraft supported a joint Soviet/Rumanian ground offensive to capture Zvolen (Zólyom/Altsohl), Slovakia. C1AR sent all available light, heavy, and dive bombers to support the ground troops, along with fighters to provide air cover. Although the Luftwaffe seldom appeared over Slovakia in 1945, this major operation prompted them to reappear over what had been considered a secondary battle zone. Several engagements developed between German and Rumanian aircraft. German participants included Bf 109G/Ks of JG 52 and JG 53 and Fw 190A/Fs of SG 2 and SG 4, while the Rumanian aircraft consisted of Bf 109Gs, Ju 88As, and Savoia bombers. ARR aircraft conducted 148 sorties that day and dropped 42.4 tons (38.5 metric tons) of bombs during 188.6 flight hours. The last encounter between Rumanian and German aircraft occurred on 25 February 1945. The ARR claimed two Luftwaffe fighters — a Bf 109K and an Fw 190F. Both aircraft claims remained unconfirmed, although the Fw 190 kill by Cpt Constantin 'Bâzu' Cantacuzino — the top ARR ace with 56 confirmed victories — appears authentic. ARR lost seven aircraft in the encounter: four Bf 109G-6s, two Savoia J.R.S. 79s, and one Ju 88A-4. One Rumanian pilot was killed.

In the following period, ARR aircraft were able to conduct a growing number of missions due to the Luftwaffe's virtual disappearance from Slovakian skies. Axis anti-aircraft fire, however, remained deadly until the last days of the war.

By March of 1945, the number of missions increased to 10 to 15 per day. These missions were primarily tactical sorties flown by assault aircraft, dive bombers, and fighter-bombers. Peak days included 26 April, when C1AR aircraft flew 75 missions consisting of 192 aircraft sorties totaling 134 flight hours. These aircraft dropped 36.4 tons (33 metric tons) of bombs on targets near Uhersky Brod. The commander of the Stuka squadron led his unit in all nine of his unit's missions that day.

C1AR achieved its last victory on 7 May when gunners from *Bateria 147 Rheinmetall* (147 Rheinmetall Battery) shot down a Luftwaffe aircraft attacking the V-VS airfield at Brno (Brünn). This victory was the 1110th aircraft shot down by Rumanian anti-aircraft crews during the war. ARR suffered their last combat loss on 8 May, when an I.A.R. 39 flown by an unidentified Lieutenant was shot down near Voderady, north of Brno. The pilot was the last victim of the long war fought by the ARR against four of the most powerful air forces in the world: the Soviet Union, the United States, Great Britain, and Germany.

C1AR Headquarters summed up the combat activity in the Czechoslovakian Campaign after the war ended in Europe. The Corps flew 4981 aircraft sorties in 2578 missions between 21 December 1944 and 12 May 1945. C1AR aircraft flew 6303 hours and dropped over 1042.1 tons (946 metric tons) of bombs on the retreating Germans. Two enemy aircraft were shot down by ARR pilots, while anti-aircraft crews brought down an additional five aircraft. C1AR lost 62 aircraft during this same period, primarily to enemy flak and accidents. Air corps personnel killed totaled 200, including 59 aircrew. C1AR strength at the end of hostilities consisted of 189 aircraft organized into 20 squadrons.

ARR flew 4307 combat missions between 24 August 1944 and 12 May 1945. These missions consisted of 8542 sorties totaling 11,384.5 hours. The Rumanians expended 1498.2 tons (1360 metric tons) of bombs and 59 tons (53.6 metric tons) of ammunition. ARR aircraft consumed 2.7 million tons (2.45 million metric tons) of fuel and 169.3 tons (153.7 metric tons) of oil during those eight and one-half months. Rumanians claimed at least 101 Axis aircraft in the Western Front fighting with the majority being downed by anti-aircraft gunners. ARR also captured 228 Luftwaffe aircraft when Rumania joined the Allies in late August of 1944.

Rumanian aircraft losses during the last eight and one-half months of World War Two totaled 337 aircraft. One hundred seventy-six of these were destroyed in combat or captured by German forces. These aircraft represented over one third of the aircraft committed to combat against the Axis. The remaining 161 aircraft destroyed during this period were training aircraft set on fire during early September of 1944. ARR also lost 106 anti-aircraft batteries and suffered 865 personnel casualties in the Western Front conflict. These casualties included 273 aircrew, 83 anti-aircraft gun crews, and 509 ground crewmen.

Although Rumania's Army and Air Force made a substantial effort for the Allies in the last eight and one-half months of WW II, the Allied Powers still regarded Rumania as a member of the defeated Axis. Eventually, Rumania was treated as a defeated nation by the Allies.

It should be briefly mentioned, that a pro-Axis Rumanian government-

A Bf 109G of *Magyar Királyi Honvéd Légierö* (Royal Hungarian Air Force) displays battle damage following air combat during late 1944. All Rumanian war documents unanimously identify aircraft engaged on the 'Western Front' as German or simply 'fascist'. Rumanian and Hungarian pilots were unfamiliar with each other's national markings. Hungarian airmen also reported encounters with I.A.R. aircraft or *"strangely painted Bf 109Gs that acted hostile"*. (Hemmert)

A Bf 109G-6 assigned to *Grupul 1 vânătoare* is parked on a snowy runway in Slovakia during February of 1945. This airfield is probably Piest'any (Pöstyén) and was used by both Rumanian and Soviet units supporting the campaign against the Axis forces in Slovakia. These Rumanian airmen wear German Model 1944 field caps, sheepskin flying jackets, and airmen's boots. Such attire often caused problems for ARR pilots landing in Soviet held territory, particularly in German-made aircraft. The Soviets often considered the Rumanians to be the 'fascist' enemy and handled them roughly. (Bernád)

in-exile was formed in Austria shortly after the *coup d'état* of 23 August 1944. The so-called 'Rumanian National Government of Vienna' included a Ministry of Defense headed by Brig Gen Platon Chirnoagă. Several Rumanian aviators either voluntarily accepted, or were forced to join this organization. These included ARR personnel studying in Germany, prisoners of war, and defectors from the pro-Allied government in Bucharest. The last of these defectors flew to the German side as late as March of 1945. The government-in-exile aviators, however, were not organized into a flying unit due to a lack of available aircraft, fuel, and, mainly, trust. Instead, most of these airmen were used as ground troops and thrown into the face of the Russian juggernaut surging into Poland during early 1945.

Life in Troubled Peacetime

ARR Headquarters ordered *Corpul 1 Aerian Român* and the attached *Divizia 1 Artilerie Antiaeriană* (1st Anti-Aircraft Artillery Division) to return to Rumania on 5 July 1945. All ARR units returned from the front by 1 August to officially end the 'Western Campaign'. A military parade was held in Bucharest on 23 August to mark the first anniversary of Rumania's defection from the Axis to the Allies.

The harsh reality of post-war life under Soviet occupation came into being after the speeches were given and the cheering stopped. ARR and the Army had to revert to a peacetime organization. The number of combat aircraft was to be reduced to 150 machines under the strict terms of the peace treaty. This treaty also forbade Rumania any bombers. The existing aircraft inventory was consolidated into ten scaled-down *flotile* (flotillas, restyled regiments at this time). Personnel were also reduced at the same time. These reductions were not enough, however, to satisfy the Allied (i.e., Soviet) Control Commission. ARR Headquarters ordered a further restructuring on 15 June 1946. This reduced the number of regiments (formerly flotillas) from ten to four. The four regiments consisted of fighters, close support aircraft, reconnaissance aircraft, and a mixed formation of miscellaneous types. These regiments were augmented by a transport group. The ARR's inventory shrank from 1607 machines at the end of 1944 to 1316 aircraft in 1945. Further force reductions brought the aircraft totals to 935 in 1946 and 361 in 1947.

The final reorganization of ARR took place during August of 1947. The force structure was reduced to four regiments of two groups each.

Aircraft totals were reduced to 168 first-line aircraft and 108 training and auxiliary aircraft. The first large-scale discharges of ARR personnel also took place during this time. Total personnel was reduced to 13,000. Most of the World War Two veterans, particularly those who had fought against the USSR, were discharged from ARR with virtually no support from the government. Morale among Rumanian airmen hit rock bottom and many of them defected to neutral Turkey or Cyprus.

King Michael was forced to abdicate and the People's Republic of Rumania was proclaimed on 30 December 1947. Nothing now stood in the way of 'progressive' (i.e., Communist) political forces from virtually destroying the 'imperialist' ARR. These political forces would create a new 'democratic' air force that was closely based on the Soviet pattern of political and military education and control. The obsolete 'Royal' appellation was deleted from the official title of the air force. ARR thus became *Aeronautica Română*. The air force was renamed *Forțele Aeriene ale Republicii Populare Române* (Air Forces of the People's Republic of Rumania) in 1949. The prime decade of the most powerful air force in Eastern Europe and the Balkans had come to an inglorious end.

Rumanian air cadets study a damaged I.A.R. 27 trainer at an aviation school near Bucharest on 3 September 1948. This aircraft has the white wing tips and aft fuselage band applied after Rumania's defection to the Allies on 23 August 1944. The remains of several other ARR aircraft, including a rare Focke-Wulf Fw 189A, are scattered in the background. The aircraft in this scrapheap would be replaced with the so-called 'new Soviet technology' designs such as the Polikarpov Po-2 biplane. (MMN)

ARR AIRCRAFT AND AIRMEN

Fighters

ARR hosted an International Fighter Contest at Pipera airfield (Rumanian military aviation's main base) near Bucharest in June of 1930. The goal of this competition was to select a new fighter to equip the ARR's *escadrile de vânătoare* (fighter squadrons).

After extensive tests, the Polish-built, gull-winged P.Z.L. P.1 was declared the winner. The Polish entry had good overall performance characteristics, including a top speed of 189 mph (304 kmh). Foul play was suspected, however, by the losing manufacturers who considered the commission to be biased towards the 'generous' Poles. (This practice was not uncommon in the Balkans.) Regardless of these allegations, the result defined the shape of the ARR's fighter force for the next decade. Despite its apparent success, the P.1 was not put into production. Eventually, ARR selected the superior P.11 which first flew in August of 1931 and entered ARR service during 1934.

In early 1937, an important measure was undertaken to consolidate the front-line fighter groups into a single main unit. This unit, designated *Flotila 1 vânătoare* (1st Fighter Flotilla) and based at Bucharest-Pipera airfield, consisted of the ARR's most experienced fighter pilots.

Rumania was faced with both an increased arms race and a deteriorating political situation in Europe during the late 1930s. The Rumanian military decided to speed up efforts to purchase foreign aircraft in order to meet the planned number of aircraft required by ARR Headquarters. The Air Force required 216 fighters, however, only 144 first-line fighters were theoretically available during March of 1939. In fact, less than 100 fighters were serviceable. These fighters were all P.Z.L. P.11s, which Rumanian Prime Minister Armand Călinescu described in his diary as *"bad matériel"*. A large Rumanian military delegation visited arms factories in France, the United Kingdom, and Germany during April of 1939. The Rumanians returned home with some success, ordering 50 Hurricane Mk Is from Britain and 30 off-the-shelf Heinkel He 112Bs from Germany. Germany also promised 50 Messerschmitt Bf 109Es. Rumania's request for significant numbers of Bloch and Morane-Saulnier fighters from France was denied. The French cited an urgent need for these aircraft to equip their own air force, the *Armée de l'Air*.

ARR reported a total of 121 fighters in service on 12 August 1939. These included 98 P.Z.L.s, the first 11 He 112s, and 12 Hurricanes (under delivery). Among Rumania's 556 first-line aircraft the following June were 122 fighters. These fighters included 30 P.Z.L. P.24Es, 30 He 112Bs, 20 Bf 109Es, 12 Hurricanes, and 30 indigenously produced I.A.R. 80s. The first batch of I.A.R. 80s was still in the factory, however, undergoing pre-delivery acceptance tests. Therefore, they were part of the ARR's strength only on paper. The older P.Z.L. P.11bs had been relegated to the training role. All front-line fighter squadrons were equipped with modern first-class aircraft by mid-1940. Rumania led her neighbors in fighter force quality. The wide range of aircraft origins and types, however, seriously hindered maintenance efficiency. Spare parts shortages decreased the number of serviceable ARR aircraft by 20 to 30%.

The withdrawal of surviving Polish Air Force units to Rumania during mid-September of 1939 increased the ARR's inventory by over 250 aircraft. These Polish aircraft included approximately 60 P.Z.L. fighters, however, only some 30 P.11cs were deemed to have any combat value. The increased number of aircraft further complicated the already difficult maintenance and supply problems.

The Rumanian aircraft industry began making significant progress beginning in the late 1930s. Notable successes were achieved by the I.A.R. (*Industria Aeronautică Română*; Rumanian Aeronautical Industry) Works in Brasov. The I.A.R. design team, unable to secure orders for their early fighter designs, came up with the I.A.R. 80 project during late 1938. This aircraft, based partly on the Polish P.Z.L. 24 already in production at I.A.R., incorporated modern features including a low-wing monoplane configuration, all-metal structure, and retractable undercarriage. The I.A.R. 80 prototype, however, remained 'old fashioned' in some respects by retaining an open cockpit, lacking a radio, and being armed with only two rifle-caliber .312 inch (7.92mm) machine guns in the wings.

The prototype first flew on 20 April 1939 and surpassed all expectations. Following extensive trials, the Ministry of Air and Marine ordered 100 I.A.R. 80s on 18 December 1939. The first 20 early series examples, however, were not delivered until the last days of 1940. This situation was due to various production problems which included a temporary lack of specific materials, armament availability, repeated undercarriage failures, and engine problems. The early I.A.R. 80s were intended to equip two squadrons — *Escadrile 59* and *60 vânătoare* — assigned to the newly formed *Grupul 8 vânătoare* (8th Fighter Group).

Following the delivery of the first I.A.R. 80 fighters, the remaining 30 Messerschmitt Bf 109Es arrived in the spring of 1941. (German sources mention 11 new E-3s delivered in 1940 and 39 refurbished E-3s shipped in 1941.) The Bf 109Es were delivered to the elite *Grupul 7 vânătoare* (7th Fighter Group), which was formed on 1 June 1940. These machines increased the available ARR fighter strength to just over 200 first-line aircraft. This force increase came just in time to take part in the invasion of the Soviet Union.

Battle for Bessarabia and Trans-Dnestra

Selected fighter groups, equipped with the most modern aircraft, were transferred to *Gruparea Aeriană de Luptă* (GAL; Combat Air Grouping) in mid-June of 1941. GAL was the main ARR unit supporting the Rumanian and German armies in their planned invasion of the southeastern Soviet Union.

The fighter groups assigned to GAL consisted of:
1. *Grupul 8 vânătoare* (*Escadrile 41, 59, & 60*), equipped with I.A.R. 80/80As (part of *Flotila 2 vânătoare*, or 2nd Fighter Flotilla).
2. *Grupul 5 vânătoare* (*Escadrile 51 & 52*), equipped with Heinkel He 112Bs.
3. *Grupul 7 vânătoare* (*Escadrile 56, 57, & 58*), equipped with Messerschmitt Bf 109Es (both latter units were part of *Flotila 1 vânătoare*, or 1st Fighter Flotilla).

The GAL inventory consisted of the following fighters

ARR departed from traditional French aircraft and ordered 50 P.Z.L. P.11b fighters from Poland in 1933. The P.11b shaped the Rumanian fighter arm during the early 1930s. Aviation technology advances were unprecedented and new aircraft were tested and introduced into service each year during this time. The P.11b was powered by a 515 hp Gnome & Rhône K.9 engine which gave the aircraft a top speed of 211 mph (340 kmh) at 14,764 feet (4500 m). The P.11b was armed with two 7.92mm machine guns. This aircraft was subsequently manufactured by I.A.R under license as the P.11F. (Bernád)

(available/unavailable) on 22 June: 23/1 I.A.R. 80, 23/5 Heinkel He 112B, and 30/6 Messerschmitt Bf 109E.

The 8th FG, equipped with the indigenous I.A.R. 80, was assigned the pure fighter role, while the latter two groups — flying superior German aircraft — were employed primarily as fighter-bombers. These assignments were probably due to the strategy developed by the joint German-Rumanian headquarters. This strategy reserved the fighter role to the more experienced Luftwaffe *Jagdgruppen* (fighter groups). The Hurricane-equipped *Escadrila 53 vânâtoare* was temporarily transferred from *Grupul 5 vânâtoare* to *Comandamentul Aero Dobrogea* (Air Command Dobruja). This command was assigned to the defense of the Black Sea coast, including the vital harbor of Constanta and the strategic Cernavodă rail bridge across the Danube.

Serving alongside the coastal defense Hurricanes were three secondary fighter groups equipped with P.Z.L. fighters. These groups were not incorporated into GAL and were assigned to protect the rear zone and capital. The three groups consisted of:
1. *Grupul 6 vânâtoare* (*Escadrile 61 & 62*), equipped with P.Z.L. P.24Es (part of *Flotila 2 vânâtoare*, or 2nd Fighter Flotilla).
2. *Grupul 3 vânâtoare* (*Escadrile 43, 44, & 45*), equipped with P.Z.L. P.11Fs.
3. *Grupul 4 vânâtoare* (*Escadrile 46, 49, & 50*), equipped with P.Z.L. P.11Cs and Fs (both latter units were part of *Flotila 3 vânâtoare*, or 3rd Fighter Flotilla).

The Bucharest-Otopeni based 6th Fighter Group was successful in defending the capital and claimed 37 victories within a few days. The 3rd and 4th Fighter Groups, however, were equipped with the obsolete P.11Cs and Fs, and primarily conducted fighter-bomber missions using small 4.4-6.6 lb (2-3 kg) grenades mounted under the wings. GAL had 76 fighters and fighter-bombers available on 22 June 1941. An additional 12 aircraft were unserviceable. These fighters comprised 35% of GAL inventory. Outside of GAL, 102 P.Z.L. fighters were in service and 22 additional P.Z.L. aircraft were unserviceable. These were augmented by the 13 Hurricanes, although three of these were unavailable. The fighters and fighter-bombers amounted to approximately one third of ARR aircraft participating in the fighting.

Rumanian fighter pilots performed well during the first day of fighting — a day which proved to be one of the fiercest ones of the entire Second World War. These pilots scored ten confirmed victories. At least four Rumanian aircraft were damaged, although all of them were repairable. One of the first Rumanian fighter pilots to score a pair of victories was *Sublocotenent aviator* (2nd Lieutenant) Teodor Moscu of the He 112B-equipped *Escadrila 51 vânâtoare*. He claimed two I-16 'Ratas' and a probable over nearby Bulgărica airfield. The pilot of one of Moscu's kills, *Lejtenant* Grilyuk of the 67 IAP (Fighter Aviation Regiment), managed to abandon his burning I-16 in time. The other Soviet pilot's fate is unknown.

The pace of operations lessened on 23 June, although the fighters were active over the front and in home defense. The most successful unit on the home front was the Hurricane-equipped 53rd FS. *Locotenent aviator* (1st Lieutenant) Horia Agarici shot down two Soviet DB-3 bombers near Constanta harbor and claimed a third over the sea. The Rumanian airmen's luck ran out on the second day. Two Rumanian fighters were destroyed and two others damaged on 23 June. The first Rumanian fighter pilot killed in action during World War Two was *Adjutant aviator* (Warrant Officer) Anghel Codrut of the 5th FG. His He 112B (No. 12) was shot down by Soviet fighters over Bolgad airfield in Southern Bessarabia. *Kapitan* Piotr Kozachenko of the 249 IAP was one of the most experienced V-VS pilots of that time, having achieved 15 victories over Japanese and Finnish aircraft. He led a formation of seven I-153s which intercepted 12 He 112s strafing Bolgrad airfield. Kozachenko shot down Codrut's aircraft and the I-153s returned to base without loss.

The primary mission of Rumanian fighters during the first two weeks of the Axis air offensive was protecting bombers and reconnaissance aircraft as well as performing ground attack missions. The joint German-Rumanian offensive across the Prut River began during the evening of 2/3 July. Luftwaffe and ARR aircraft were involved in direct air support of their troops. The increase in ground support missions coincided with a decrease in air superiority and fighter sweep missions. The decrease was due to the almost complete lack of Soviet air activity following the first days of combat. Russian anti-aircraft defenses nevertheless gained experience and improved their effectiveness. Veteran Rumanian pilots recalled that during the first campaign of the 'anti-Bolshevik' war the main threat came from anti-aircraft fire rather than from Soviet fighters. Rumanian bomber crews also shared this opinion.

The battle for Bessarabia reached its peak on 12 July. Nine waves of bombers totaling 59 aircraft struck Soviet targets east of the Fălciu bridgehead between 0850 and 1940 hours. Russian troops, vehicle columns, and armored vehicle formations were continuously bombed and strafed. *Sublocotenent aviator* (2nd Lieutenant) Vasile Claru of the 8th FG allegedly shot down three out of six I-16s over the front. Claru, running out of ammunition, reportedly rammed his I.A.R. 80 (No. 23) into another enemy fighter. Both aircraft were destroyed in the collision and Claru was killed, although it is not known if this was a deliberate act or an accident. Claru's four kills were not officially confirmed. Nevertheless, this action was picked up by Rumanian propaganda and served as an example of supreme sacrifice for 'King and Country'. Rumanian fighter pilots claimed three other kills that day. One claim was made by *Sublocotenent aviator* Ion Zaharia of the 52nd Fighter Squadron. He shot down one of four I-16 'Ratas' that flocked around a P.Z.L. P.37B bomber (No. 218) in the Lărguta area.

The territory between the Prut and Dnestr Rivers was completely secured by Rumanian forces on 28 July. Bessarabia and Northern Bukovina were now considered by the Rumanians as 'liberated' from Soviet rule and reintegrated into the Rumanian Kingdom. [Editor's Note: Under the terms of the 1939 German-Soviet Non-Aggression Pact, the Soviet Union was allowed to annex Bessarabia and Northern Bukovina during the spring of 1940.]

The first statistics on the air campaign were compiled after the immediate goal had been achieved. During the single month of fighting, ARR airmen had claimed 88 enemy aircraft in air combat. The majority of these were brought down by fighters. An additional 108 aircraft were destroyed on the ground, while anti-aircraft gunners shot down 59 aircraft. Rumania lost 58 aircraft in combat. The *vânâtori* (fighters) flew 2162 sorties out of the total of 5100 sorties flown by GAL. Eighteen Rumanian fighter pilots were killed in action.

This I.A.R. 14 served as a fighter trainer with *Scoala militarã de pilotaj si antrenament* (Military Piloting and Training School) at Tecuci during the late 1930s. One of the few female pilots is surrounded by a group of airmen and soldiers. The I.A.R. 14 was the first series produced Rumanian fighter. Twenty I.A.R. 14s were delivered in 1934 for evaluation by ARR in the fighter role before relegation to training duties. The aircraft was powered by a 450 hp Lorraine Dietrich radial engine and had a maximum speed of 183 mph (294 kmh). The I.A.R. 14 was armed with two 7.7mm (.303 in) Vickers machine guns. (Bujor)

Rumania purchased 50 P.Z.L. P.11bs from Poland and also acquired license production rights for this aircraft. The I.A.R. Works of Brasov manufactured a re-engined version designated P.11F with the first aircraft delivered to ARR in early 1937. White 70 features a high-gloss upper surface paint finish and asymmetrically-placed wing roundels which follow the Polish pattern. (Avram)

Combat did not cease once the Dnestr River had been reached. The next objective was the capture of Odessa — the main communications hub on the northwestern coast of the Black Sea. This target, however, was well beyond the range of Rumanian-based aircraft. Consequently, the majority of ARR combat units were deployed to new forward air strips in order to reduce flying time. These deployments also had the effect of lengthening the ARR supply routes. These airfields were formerly used by the V-VS or were newly established in Southern Bessarabia and Trans-Dnestra. Several fighter units were reorganized and restructured at this time. The badly mauled *Grupul 5 vânãtoare* was reduced to a single squadron — the 51st — on 13 August. The 52nd Fighter Squadron transferred their He 112Bs to the sister squadron and was merged with the similarly battered 42nd Fighter Squadron. This mixed squadron was renamed *Escadrila 42/52 vânãtoare* and re-equipped with new I.A.R. 80As. This unit was relegated to the *apãrarea teritoriului* (Home Defense) role.

The fighter units, in addition to redeploying to new forward bases, also requested additional aircraft to replace losses. ARR could not rely on replacements from Germany, however, since the Luftwaffe was not required to provide attrition replacements to their allies. For this reason, only *Grupul 8 vânãtoare* and *Escadrila 42/52 vânãtoare* — both equipped with I.A.R. 80s — received new aircraft. Several P.Z.L. equipped squadrons also began converting to the I.A.R. 80.

The battle for Odessa began on 8 August 1941. Air activity on both sides gradually escalated with engagements becoming more frequent than during the initial Axis offensive. Both the Soviet Union and the Axis claimed an impressive number of air victories. I-16 pilots of the 69th IAP that evening reportedly shot down nine out of twelve Bf 109s encountered over Odessa. (No Rumanian '*Emil*' was downed that day and only two Luftwaffe Bf 109F-4s were reported damaged in combat on the entire Soviet Front.) The next day, the pilots of the same V-VS fighter regiment filed claims for five out of 20 P.Z.L. P.24s engaged. The Soviets reported two of their own aircraft lost with a third aircraft damaged. Despite the Soviet pilots' claims, ARR reported only one P.Z.L. P.11F of *Escadrila 46 vânãtoare* being damaged in combat that day. The Rumanian P.Z.L. pilots claimed three Soviet aircraft shot down. The 69th IAP claimed a further seven Axis aircraft on 19 August while the 9th IAP of the Black Sea Fleet reported shooting down eight Axis aircraft the same day. V-VS Headquarters was inundated with inflated kill reports, yet Axis records do not substantiate most of these Soviet claims. Although the Rumanians also overclaimed, they appear to have been to a lesser degree than those of the Soviets.

Several Bf 109Es of the 7th FG clashed with a Soviet formation over Dalnik during the afternoon of 21 August. This formation consisted of 12 Ilyushin Il-2s escorted by some 20 fighters identified by the Rumanians as Yakovlev Yak-1s. The Group commander, *Locotenent comandor aviator* (Major) Alexandru Popisteanu, ordered the commander of the 57th FS, *Cãpitan aviator* (Captain) Alexandru Manoliu, to engage the low-flying Shturmoviks. (This Rumanian squadron included three Italian volunteers, the Prince Ruspoli brothers, flying Macchi MC 200s.) The remaining 10 Bf 109E-3s of Popisteanu's command climbed to intercept the Yaks circling at 6562 ft (2000 m). The Soviet fighters, contrary to Popisteanu's expectation, did not wait for the Rumanians and dived into the ARR formation while it was still trying to gain altitude. Popisteanu's lead Bf 109 was hit in the fuselage and cockpit on the

A Red Army soldier guards the wreckage of a Heinkel He 112B (Black 18, W.Nr. 2049) after it was shot down on 2 July 1941. The pilot, *Adjutant stagiar aviator de rezervã* Aldea Cerchez, was captured by the Soviets after belly landing his damaged aircraft. The He 112B was the first new generation fighter in ARR service. Thirty He 112Bs were delivered to ARR during 1939 and 1940. The aircraft featured all-metal construction, a high level and dive speed, powerful armament, and an enclosed cockpit. The Heinkel was vulnerable to enemy fire, however, due to a lack of armor protection. Armament consisted of two 20mm cannons and two 7.92mm machine guns. (Petrick)

Only 12 of 50 Hawker Hurricane Mk Is ordered from Great Britain had eventually reached Rumania. The Hurricane's eight wing-mounted .303 in (7.7mm) caliber machine guns were greatly appreciated by the *vânători* (Rumanian fighter pilots). The Hurricane-equipped *Escadrila 53 vânătoare* (53rd Fighter Squadron) was responsible for large numbers of Soviet bombers shot down while attacking Rumanian targets early in the war. This independent squadron operated mainly over Rumania's Black Sea coast. (Bujor)

Yaks' first high-speed pass. The wounded Maj Popisteanu attempted to land his stricken fighter near Marienthal, but died in the ensuing crash. Popisteanu's group reported shooting down six Yaks in the engagement, however, these victories did not balance the loss of their commander. According to V-VS reports, nine I-16s of the 96th IAP clashed with five Bf 109s on 21 August. Two of the Bf 109s were shot down west of Karpovo and between Vigoda and Palyevo, respectively. Only one I-16 was damaged in the brief fight. The commander of *Flotila 1 vânătoare*, *Căpitan comandor aviator* (Lieutenant Colonel) Mihail Romanescu, took personal command of the 7th FG the next day. The appointment of Romanescu, dubbed 'The Lion' for his strong character, was meant to boost the morale of the Group's pilots.

The battle for Odessa reached its climax during the evening of 21/22 September when Soviet troops formed a bridgehead at Chebanka-Grigorievka. This move endangered the right flank of the Rumanian 4th Army. GAL Headquarters ordered all available aircraft into the zone to engage the Soviet bridgehead. Ninety-four Rumanian aircraft, 62 of which were fighters, were sent to the area on 22 September. Nine V-VS aircraft were reported shot down during more than ten hours of air activity. One additional aircraft

Yellow 31, a Bf 109E-3, was an aircraft from the second batch delivered to Rumania. This aircraft retains the early roundels and the yellow engine cowling, however, the yellow band has not yet been applied to the aft fuselage. Although Hitler badly needed the Messerschmitt Bf 109 *'Emil'* for his own Luftwaffe, he used the aircraft to secure Rumanian oil supplies that were vital to the German war machine. (Galea)

Sublocotenent aviator de rezervă Ioan Di Cesare sits in the cockpit of his Bf 109E *Hai fetito!* (Come on little girl!) during the summer of 1942. Five bars representing his kills during 1941 are painted ahead of the cockpit. Di Cesare served in *Grupul 7 vânătoare* and was one of the first airmen awarded the prestigious *'Mihai Viteazul'* ('Michael the Brave') Order, 3rd Class. Di Cesare, now in his 80s, serves as chairman of a Rumanian veteran airmen's association. (Bernád)

An early production I.A.R. 80 displays the pre-May 1941 markings. Until 1943, the I.A.R. 80 fared well against V-VS aircraft due to its maneuverability and adequate armament. The fighter was obsolete by the time USAAF aircraft appeared over Rumania in the spring of 1944. It was withdrawn from home defense duties after suffering severe losses to American fighters. (Moisescu)

downing was unconfirmed. The Soviets claimed to have destroyed over 20 enemy aircraft, however, only one P.Z.L. P.11F was downed over Dalnik. ARR lost four other aircraft to anti-aircraft fire and strafing Soviet fighters. The efforts of the Rumanian aircrews seriously hindered the Soviet push which gradually lost ground. The battered Soviet bridgehead finally collapsed and the Russians withdrew from Chebanka-Grigorievka during the evening of 4-5 October.

I.A.R. 81 'dive' bombers (a fighter-bomber variant of the I.A.R. 80 fighter), assigned to the 59th FS, 8th FG, made their combat debut at this time. The six available I.A.R. 81s were ordered to strike Soviet supply vessels in the Black Sea using 496 lb (225 kg) and 110 lb (50 kg) bombs. The Rumanians mounted these attacks in concert with German Ju 87 Stukas.

Several Rumanian ground attacks against Odessa were repulsed by the Soviets at heavy cost to both sides. The fortress city finally succumbed on 16 October. The capture of Odessa marked the end of the first Rumanian campaign in the Soviet Union.

GAL reported a total of 858 missions comprising 4739 fighter sorties between 22 June and 16 October 1941. These included 329 escort missions for ARR aircraft, 193 missions for short-range reconnaissance, 113 for airfield protection, and 112 providing air cover against enemy intruders. The mission totals also included 80 free hunting, 24 low level attack, and seven surveillance missions. There were only two additional missions flown by I.A.R. 81s. All branches of GAL reported destroying 266 Soviet aircraft in the air or on the ground. (Only 215 Soviet aircraft claims were eventually confirmed.) GAL officially acknowledged losing 16 fighters during 118 days of action (of which 104 had favorable flight conditions for fighters). The real loss figures, however, are believed to be much higher, exceeding 46 fighters. The top ace of the 'Bessarabian Campaign' was *Locotenent aviator de rezervă* Nicolae Polizu of the Bf 109E-equipped *Grupul 7 vânătoare*. Polizu scored eight confirmed air victories. He was closely followed — and eventually surpassed — by *Adjutant sef aviator* Andrei Rădulescu of *Escadrila 53 vânătoare*. Rădulescu posted seven confirmed and four unconfirmed victories while flying a Hurricane Mk I.

Overall, the ARR fighter force flew a total of 8514 sorties during the first campaign. *Flotila 1 vânătoare* reported 145 confirmed and 18 unconfirmed aircraft

Sublocotenent mecanic (Technical 2nd Lt) Remus Marin stands in front of an *'Emil'* of *Escadrila 56 vânătoare* at Pipera-Bucharest airfield during 1942. A make-shift mirror has been installed on top of the Bf 109E's windshield. The propeller spinner has been painted 1/4 white and 3/4 black according to German *Luftflotte* (Air Fleet) *4* regulations. (Greceanu)

An ARR pilot sits in the cockpit of White 6, a P.Z.L. P.11b. The basic two-tone green camouflage has been overpainted with wavy bands of terra cotta, a red-brown color. Only the top third of the rudder displays the blue-yellow-red striping. The stripes were usually applied to the entire rudder on ARR aircraft. (Bujor)

A Ukrainian defector flew this MiG-3 fighter to Melitopol airfield in early December of 1941. The aircraft was repainted in Rumanian markings and evaluated at Brasov. The E.19 on the vertical stabilizer referred to *Escadrila 19 observatie* (19th Spotting Squadron), which was based at Melitopol during late 1941. Soviet troops seized this aircraft from their new allies — the Rumanians — during September of 1944. (Moisescu)

destroyed in the air and another 47 destroyed on the ground. *Flotila 2 vânătoare* claimed 102 Soviet aircraft shot down and 24 destroyed on the ground. *Flotila 3 vânătoare* scored 57 kills. The *vânători* reported a total of 322 air and 71 ground victories during their first campaign against the Soviets.

Rumanian losses in both combat and accidents reached 59 fighters by the end of 1941. These losses included: 20 I.A.R. 80/81s, 18 P.Z.L. P.11Fs, nine Bf 109Es, five He 112Bs, 3 P.Z.L. P.24Es, two P.Z.L. P.11cs, and two Hurricanes. This loss figure represented 18%, or almost one in five, of the total number of fighters available on the first day of the war or received as replacements. At least 40 fighter pilots were killed in action or accidents during the four months of combat. The Rumanian airmen were recalled to Rumania for rest, reorganization, and re-equipment after the fall of Odessa.

Rumanian fighter activity was low between 17 October 1941 and 1 August 1942. Only 1021 sorties were flown, mainly to observe Soviet activity on the Black Sea. The rare scrambles were primarily directed against Soviet reconnaissance aircraft. This low activity is the reason for Rumanian fighter pilots only claiming seven V-VS aircraft destroyed in combat. Three more Soviet aircraft were claimed destroyed on the ground or on the water.

Following the reorganization of the ARR's fighter arm, the bulk of the P.Z.L. fighters was withdrawn from front-line duty. These aircraft were relegated to the training role. The majority of squadrons operating P.Z.L. fighters received the I.A.R. 80 — the only fighter available in any numbers. *Grupul 3 vânătoare* (43, 44, and 45 FS) of *Flotila 3 vânătoare* converted to the I.A.R. 80 at Galati. The first I.A.R. 80 unit, *Grupul 8 vânătoare* (41, 59, and 60 FS), simultaneously replaced their early series I.A.R. 80s with the newer 80A and B series fighters. I.A.R. 80As and Bs also replaced the Hurricanes of the independent *Escadrila 53 vânătoare*. On 19 April 1942, a new fighter group was formed within *Flotila 1 vânătoare* to take advantage of the availability of I.A.R. 80s. This new unit, *Grupul 9 vânătoare*, was composed of *Escadrile 47* and *48*. *Grupul 6 vânătoare* received I.A.R. 81 dive bombers and was renamed *Grupul 6 bombardament în picaj* (6th Dive Bomber Group), abbreviated *Gr. 6 bopi*. ARR did not receive any brand new fighters from abroad, however, 15 second-hand Messerschmitt Bf 109E-7s (Nos. 51-65) were taken on strength along with a reported three ex-Yugoslav Hurricanes.

Stalingrad

The Stalingrad campaign was Rumania's major commitment to the Axis war effort on the Eastern Front during 1942. The Rumanian air element of their expeditionary force was designated the *Comandamentul Aviatiei de Luptă* (CAL; Combat Air Command). Attached to CAL were two fighter groups: the Bf 109E-equipped *Grupul 7 vânătoare* (56, 57, and 58 FS) and the I.A.R. 80A and '80B-equipped *Grupul 8 vânătoare* (41, 42, and 60 FS). ARR also sent *Grupul 6 bopi* (*Escadrile 61* and *62*), a dive bomber group equipped with I.A.R. 81s. Total ARR fighter and dive bomber strength in the Stalingrad area amounted to slightly less than 100 aircraft in the fall of 1942.

CAL Headquarters moved to the front zone during early September of 1942 and was soon followed by its subordinate combat units. *Grupul 8 vânătoare* was the first fighter group to begin operations at the front, followed by *Grupul 6 bopi*. Both *grupuri* (groups) were deployed to Tuzov airfield, some 12.4 miles (20 km) from the front line. *Grupul 7 vânătoare*, under the command of *Căpitan aviator* Grigore Crihană, arrived on 8 September. The Group was originally based at Tuzov before transferring to Karpovka one week later. On 16 September, the Messerschmitt pilots began flying combat missions in support of German and Rumanian troops advancing on Stalingrad.

From September to November of 1942, the fighters' primary mission was to provide air cover for Luftwaffe and ARR bombers. Fighters also flew airfield protection, free hunting, and weather reconnaissance missions. Takeoffs became a struggle when temperatures fell below 0° F (-17.8° C) and wind speeds topped 62 mph (100 kmh). Nevertheless, the fighter pilots continued to fly their missions regardless of weather conditions.

Between 7 and 10 September, I.A.R. fighters of the 8th FG shot down three Pe-2 bombers which had attacked Tuzov daily. Soviet attacks on Tuzov airfield had killed airmen and technicians, and destroyed several aircraft on the ground. Rumanian fighter pilots also reported shooting down several MiG-3 and Yak-1 fighters during the first week of operations at the front. The I.A.R. 81-equipped *Grupul 6 bombardament în picaj* lost several aircraft and pilots on operations while achieving only limited success. Two I.A.R. 80 pilots had been killed in a mid-air collision on a ferry flight to the Stalingrad front.

The Karpovka-based 7th Fighter Group shared the airfield with Luftwaffe fighter and reconnaissance units and was under virtual

Mechanics work on the engine of an I-16 Type 29 captured by Rumanian forces during July of 1941. This aircraft, White 1, was the first intact Soviet fighter captured by the ARR. *Cpt. av.* Popescu-Ciocănel usually flew this 'Rata' in mock combat against ARR and Luftwaffe aircraft. This I-16 was destroyed in a hard landing by 1st Lt Ivanciovici at Iasi in September of 1941. Although obsolete, I-16s accounted for approximately two-thirds of the V-VS (Soviet Air Force) fighter strength when the USSR was invaded on 22 June 1941. (Kössler)

The P.Z.L. P.24E served as an advanced fighter trainer following a brief career in home defense during 1941. This aircraft was intended to replace the earlier P.11 in front-line fighter service, however, the P.24E was already obsolete by 1941. This aircraft is painted in a two-tone green camouflage scheme. The P.24E is marked with the Michael's Cross and yellow fuselage band, however, no tricolor stripes have been applied to the rudder. A P.W.S. 26 and an I.A.R. 27 are parked in the background. (Bujor)

German command and supply conditions. The Messerschmitt pilots flew, weather permitting, four to five sorties per day. This group flew escort, reconnaissance, and free hunting missions similar to those of the I.A.R. 80-equipped units. Sporadic air combat yielded few victories, however, the group lost *Escadrila 47 vânătoare*'s commander *Căpitan aviator* Alexandru Manoliu on 12 September. The squadron was then temporarily commanded by *Căpitan aviator* Alexandru Serbănescu, the future top pro-Axis ARR ace of WW II. One of the first victories claimed by ARR Bf 109 pilots at Stalingrad occurred at 0610 hours on 14 September. *Adj. av.* Constantin Ursachi shot down a Yak fighter 6.2 miles (10 km) from the city.

CAL was renamed GAL (*Gruparea Aeriană de Luptă*; Combat Air Grouping) during early October of 1942. The Red Army's Great Winter Offensive in the Stalingrad sector began on 19 November. The offensive first struck the Rumanian Third Army's sector, while the area held by the Rumanian Fourth Army was attacked the next day. The focus of GAL air operations shifted over to ground support for the isolated Rumanian troops and escort for transport aircraft. The transports were attempting to bring vital supplies including ammunition, food, and fuel to the surrounded troops.

Rumanian forces continued their retreat through the beginning of 1943. This reversal prompted GAL fighter units to evacuate their threatened airfields. The I.A.R. 80/81 equipped groups (the 6th DBG and 8th FG) were withdrawn to Rumania in mid-January. The 7th FG remained in theater, however, reinforced with German-provided replacement aircraft. These fighters were merged with the few surviving Heinkel He 111H bombers into a mixed fighter-bomber group. This unit was named

Grupul mixt Locotenent comandor aviator Iosifescu after Maj Nicolae Iosifescu, the group's commander. The ad hoc unit consisted of ten Bf 109Es and six He 111Hs. Reduced numbers of serviceable aircraft limited air activity for the unit, which was finally evacuated to Rumania during late February of 1943.

The fighter units flew 1345 sorties between 16 October 1942 and 15 January 1943. These sorties represented approximately one quarter of total CAL/GAL activity during the Stalingrad Campaign. Sixteen Bf 109Es were lost from 1 September — including 12 abandoned at Karpovka at the end of November. At least 12 I.A.R. 80/81s were also lost, primarily due to Soviet ground fire and spare parts shortages. The reluctance of V-VS pilots to engage Axis aircraft resulted in only 39 Soviet aircraft being claimed by Rumanian fighter pilots during this campaign.

Re-Equipment

The obsolescence of Rumanian aircraft became clear to ARR as well as Luftwaffe officials by the spring of 1943. This state of affairs had been further reinforced by the appearance of new and more advanced Soviet aircraft along with an expansion of ARR missions. Consequently, Germany decided to equip their most important eastern European ally with modern aircraft.

The potent Bf 109G was delivered to Rumania with the first aircraft going to *Escadrila 43 vânătoare*. This squadron, which had previously operated P.Z.L. P.11Fs, was transferred from the 3rd Fighter Flotilla to strengthen the 7th Fighter Group. Less experienced pilots in the 7th FG also trained on the Bf 109G. These pilots were followed by all of the 9th FG. Bf 109G transition training for both groups took place at Tiraspol airfield in the Trans-Dnestra region. Experienced German pilots of *Jagdgeschwader* (JG) 52 assisted in training the Rumanians. Among these instructors was the future fighter ace *Leutnant* Helmut Lipfert of the 6th *Staffel* (Squadron). The first six aircraft — two Bf 109F-4s and four Bf 109G-2s — arrived at Tiraspol on 8 April for ARR pilot familiarization. Rumanian P.Z.L. and I.A.R. 80 pilots greatly appreciated the superior Bf 109 'Gustav', which they dubbed '*Gheu*' (pronounced '*Ghae-oul*'). The Bf 109G-2s were used to train ARR pilots for the Bf 109G-4s which they would fly in front-line service. Assisting the con-

This Bf 109F of III./JG 52 bellied in near Tiraspol during the spring of 1943. This German aircraft, believed to be coded White 6, was a Bf 109 *'Friedrich'* flown by pilots from *Grupuri 7* and *9 vânătoare* during their transition training from the Bf 109E to the Bf 109G. Unlike the Bf 109E and G models, the Bf 109F did not enter operational ARR service. (Bernád)

Top aces of *'Deutsch-Königlich Rumänischen Jagdverband'* (German-Royal Rumanian Fighter Unit) talk with Minister for Air *General de escadră aviator* Gheorghe Jienescu (right) at Kramatorskaya air base in April of 1943. Gen Jienescu is with (left-right): *Căpitan aviator* Alexandru Serbănescu; *Leutnant* Eberhard von Boremski, commander of this joint unit; and (probably) *Locotenent aviator* Nicolae Polizu. The Bf 109G (White 6) in the background was flown by 1st Lt Tudor Greceanu while escorting He 111Hs to Kurgan on 29 May 1943. (Greceanu)

version process were four surviving Heinkel He 112Bs from the decimated *Grupul 5 vânătoare*.

During this time 20 experienced *Grupul 7 vânătoare* pilots were temporarily transferred to JG 3 *'Udet'*, one of the Luftwaffe's elite fighter units on the Eastern Front. These pilots flew to Dnepropetrovsk-South airfield in two He 111H transports on 11 March. German and Rumanian officials attempted to achieve two goals with this personnel assignment. One goal was to train the Rumanians to fly the Bf 109G, while the other was for the Rumanians to learn combat tactics first-hand from experienced German pilots.

The Rumanian pilots were loaned 40 Bf 109G-2 and G-4 aircraft by the Luftwaffe. These fighters were equipped with either of two *Rüstsatz* armament equipment packages. *Rüstsatz R2* consisted of an underfuselage ETC 50 VIId rack for four 110 lb (50 kg) splinter bombs. *Rüstsatz R6* comprised two underwing gondolas each housing a single 20mm MG 151/20 cannon. These Bf 109Gs were painted with the Rumanian 'Michael's Cross' insignia although they were technically German property.

The Rumanians and Germans formed a joint fighter group named *'Deutsch-Königlich Rumänischen Jagdverband'* (German-Royal Rumanian Fighter Unit). This unit was led by well-known Luftwaffe *Experte* pilot *Leutnant* Eberhard von Boremski. Initially, Rumanian Bf 109G missions were flown from Pavlovgrad, the home of III./JG 3.

The first Rumanian Bf 109G combat mission took place on 29 March. This mission ended badly for the Rumanians with the loss of the Rumanian commander, *Căpitan aviator* Gheorghe Radu, to Soviet fighters. Radu had logged many hours as a flight instructor, however, he lacked combat experience. The Rumanians achieved a single victory that day when *Adjutant aviator* Ion Panait reported shooting down an Il-2. The German-Rumanian unit moved to Kramatorskaya airfield — closer to the front — during April. The unit then moved northeast to Chasoviar-Krivorotovska, approximately 311 miles (500 km) north of the Sea of Azov. More fighter missions followed in quick succession and both victories and casualties increased. One major loss was that of *Locotenent aviator de rezervă* Nicolae Polizu-Micsunesti, bearer of the prestigious *'Mihai Viteazul clasa a III-a'* order. Polizu-Micsunesti had been the top-scoring ARR fighter pilot during the 1941 Campaign and

was shot down on 5 May 1943 (2 May according to another source). His colleagues avenged his death the following day by shooting down seven Soviet fighters. Three of the fighters were LaGGs downed by *Ofiter echipaj clasa a III-a aviator* (Deputy 2nd Lt) Ion Milu. Milu would finish the war as the ARR's third-ranking fighter ace with 45 confirmed victories.

The *Deutsch-Königlich Rumänischen Jagdverband* participated in a military parade on 5 June 1943 in Kirovgrad. The personnel marched in front of King Michael I and Marshal Ion Antonescu, along with several high ranking Luftwaffe officers. The day also marked the activation of *Corpul 1 Aerian Român* (1st Rumanian Air Corps). Soon after the parade ended, the German-Rumanian fighter unit was dissolved to the regret of both Luftwaffe and ARR pilots. The Rumanians had flown 583 fighter and fighter-bomber sorties over the front between 29 March and 1 June. These Bf 109Gs dropped 32,187 lbs (14,600 kg) of bombs and claimed 28 Soviet aircraft for a loss of three pilots killed.

The Rumanians rejoined the 7th FG and arrived at Tiraspol on 6 June wearing the badge of *'Jagdflieger der Udetgeschwader'* (Fighter Pilot of the *'Udet'* Wing). The German-trained Rumanian pilots were soon joined by pilots fresh from Bf 109G conversion training in Rumania. *Grupul 7 vânătoare* was then ordered into action for the campaign on the Rivers Donets and Mius.

The Third Campaign

The headquarters of *Grupul 7 vânătoare* moved to the large airfield at Mariupol on 12 June 1943. This base also served as the headquarters of *Flotila 1 vânătoare* and was located on the northern shore of the Sea of Azov. The *vânători* were principally tasked with providing escort and air cover for Rumanian and German level and dive bombers, assault, and reconnaissance aircraft.

C1AR began flying combat missions at the southernmost part of the Eastern Front where ground and air combat was intense. The veteran pilots were able to take advantage of their experience and mastered their Bf 109G-2 and G-4 aircraft to near perfection. Opening the impressive list of air victories on 24 June was the 47th FS's commander, *Căpitan aviator* Alexandru Serbănescu. Serbănescu shot down a Yak on his way to becoming the ARR's top pro-Axis air ace. *Adjutant aviator* Cristea

Two rows of Bf 109G-2/G-4 fighters are readied for a parade held at Kirovgrad on 5 June 1943. These fighters were loaned by the Luftwaffe to *Corpul 1 Aerian Român* for use on the Eastern Front and have been repainted in ARR markings. The *'Gustavs'* in the front row appear to wear a three-tone gray camouflage scheme of RLM 74, 75, and 76. The uppersurfaces of the Bf 109 at left, however, were oversprayed with RLM 71 Dark Green over the three-tone gray scheme. (Prien)

Two Bf 109G-2s of *Escadrila 53 vânătoare*, assigned to the joint German-Rumanian I./JG 4, are parked at Mizil, east of the Ploiesti oil fields. White spirals have been painted on the black propeller spinners and the 'Riding Mickey Mouse' emblem of *Grupul 7 vânătoare's* Bf 109Gs is painted on the cowlings. White 1 in the background was flown by *Adjutant aviator* Dumitru 'Mitrică' Encioiu against American bombers attacking Ploiesti on 1 August 1943. Encioiu downed a B-24 which crashed near Albesti railroad station. (Bujor)

Chirvăsută, Serbănescu's wingman, also shot down a Yak on 24 June. Less experienced pilots were lost in action beginning in the first week of this campaign. A Bf 109G-4 *celulă* (a two-ship formation) consisting of

Locotenent aviator Ion Bârlădeanu of *Escadrila 45 vânătoare, Grupul 4 vânătoare*, receives a last-minute order from an ARR general prior to taking off from Târgsor airfield, west of Ploiesti, during 1943. Two of the three vertical bars beneath the I.A.R. 80C's cockpit represent Bârlădeanu's victories over two B-24 Liberators on 1 August 1943. Bârlădeanu was killed near Clejani during a dogfight with USAAF fighters on 31 May 1944. (Bernád)

squadron commander *Căpitan aviator* Octav Penescu and *Adjutant aviator* Mircea Hlusac became lost flying over the endless Russian plains. Incorrectly reading their compass, the Rumanians flew on until fuel exhaustion forced a landing on a Soviet rear airfield. Penescu and Hlusac soon were joined in captivity by *Adjutant aviator* Laurentiu Catană. Catană was forced to bail out over Soviet territory after colliding with a Soviet Spitfire during a dogfight on 26 June. These three aviators were not repatriated to Rumania until well after the war.

The 7th FG flew nine missions comprising 48 sorties on 18 July. Eight engagements were fought in the Kuybyshev-Uspenskaya-Slavyansk area with Rumanian pilots claiming a record 20 kills against V-VS aircraft. ARR Headquarters confirmed 15 of these kills and listed the other five as probables. Three of the confirmed victories were by *Cpt. av.* Alexandru Serbănescu. This single-day tally would only be surpassed twice by ARR. The first such occurrence was on 16 August. Rumanian pilots, in 40 sorties, were credited with 22 confirmed and 5 probable victories against three losses — their most successful single day against the Soviets. These victories over Soviet LaGG, Yak, and P-39 Airacobra aircraft took place over Izyum, Kramatorskaya, Dolina Golaya, and Bogoroditnoye. The top scoring ARR pilot that day was *Ofiter echipaj clasa a III-a aviator* Ion Milu with five confirmed victories — a single-day record. (The ARR's other outstanding single-day score would come on 10 June 1944, when Rumanian pilots claimed 28 USAAF P-38 Lightnings. The US confirmed losing 23 P-38s on that day over Rumania.)

Nine 9th FG pilots were transferred to the 7th FG on 14 August 1943 in order to replace personnel losses. These pilots had completed their Bf 109G transition training at Tiraspol and were then ordered to Kramatorskaya — only 10 miles (16 km) from the front. This base was long known to the Soviets and was subjected to nightly raids. V-VS bomber and assault aircraft dropped their bombs at random on Kramatorskaya. These aircraft included ancient U-2 biplanes (nicknamed 'Kukurzniy' — approximately 'corn grinder' — by the Rumanians). Although these raids caused little material damage, the harassment attacks sapped energy from the German and Rumanian aviators. The 7th FG engaged Soviet bomber and assault aircraft formations during daylight with a corresponding rise in victories. Many of the veterans wearing the 'Udet' badge continued to add to their victory scores.

The skill, experience, and courage of the Rumanian pilots was sometimes not enough against the overwhelming Soviet numerical supremacy. Six Rumanian Bf 109s (three G-2s and three G-4s) were damaged in combat on 17 August — a single-day record. Only one fighter was a total write-off, the one flown by *Sublocotenent aviator* Costin Georgescu of the 43rd FS. Georgescu was escorting Henschel Hs 129Bs when his Bf 109G-4 (No. 28) was shot up in combat with 15 Yak fighters. Georgescu was gravely injured in the dogfight and was forced to crash land his aircraft in friendly territory near Slavyansk. 2nd Lt Georgescu's left arm was amputated in the hospital, thus ending his flying career. He had flown 50 combat missions on the Bf 109G after flying 45 missions in the P.Z.L. P.11F.

On 20 August, *Ofiter echipaj clasa a III-a aviator* Ion Milu and his wingman, *Adjutant aviator* Vasile Firu, were escorting Hs 129Bs of *Grupul 8 asalt* (8th Assault Group). This was Milu's first mission since being awarded the '*Eisernes Kreuz, I. Klasse*' (Iron Cross, 1st Class) by Field Marshal Wolfram von Richtofen, commander of *Luftflotte* 4. (Also receiving this award during the ceremony were *Căpitan aviator* Constantin Cantacuzino and Dan Scurtu.) The two pilots were ambushed over the target at Dolina Golaya by at least ten Yakovlev fighters. Milu immediately engaged these aircraft and soon faced eight Soviet Lavochkins who had joined the fight. Milu's Bf 109G-4 received a cannon hit from a LaGG-3 and he was forced to crash land his stricken aircraft in friendly territory near a German unit. He returned to his base after counting eight cannon and 13 machine gun hits in his Bf 109's fuselage.

Rapidly advancing Soviet armor forced the Rumanians to evacuate Kramatorskaya airfield in early September of 1943. Those fighters still fit for combat were sent to Dnepropetrovsk and Mariupol, while those requiring maintenance went to Melitopol. The 7th FG went to Genichesk later in September, where they received their first Bf 109G-6s from the Luftwaffe.

The Rumanian *vânători* suffered one of their worst days on 10 October, when three fighters in a four-ship *patrulă* were shot down by Soviet fighters near Molothnoye Liman, near the Sea of Azov. One of

those aircraft brought down was that of Cpt Serbănescu, then the top scoring ARR ace. Serbănescu crash landed his burning aircraft in friendly territory and was rescued. Serbănescu returned to the air five hours later. One of the other victims, *Slt. av.* Liviu Muresan, was less fortunate. Muresan, a five-victory ace, was fatally injured in the wreckage of his Messerschmitt. Soviet propaganda immediately asserted that these air victories marked the virtual destruction of *Grupul 7 vânătoare*. Reportedly, a Rumanian aircraft counteracted this radio announcement by flying over the nearest Soviet airfield. The pilot dropped a note to the Soviets inviting a V-VS delegation to visit the Rumanian base under immunity to meet Serbănescu in person. The Soviets did not take up this offer — the time of aerial chivalry was long gone.

The freshly trained pilots of *Grupul 9 vânătoare* and its three subordinate squadrons — *Escadrile 47, 48,* and *56* — arrived from Tiraspol on 23 October. These three squadrons relieved the exhausted *Grupul 7 vânătoare*, although some pilots of the 7th FG did stay to work with the 9th FG pilots. The rest of the 7th FG returned to Rumania after five months of front-line duty.

An American Interlude

While *Grupul 7 vânătoare* was locked in the deadly air battles against numerically superior V-VS aircraft over the USSR, ARR fighter pilots in Rumania were enjoying a relatively quiet period. The fighter pilots continued their transition training to German aircraft at the Luftwaffe fighter schools at Galati and Tiraspol.

ARR Headquarters decided to form a night fighter unit to counter sporadic Soviet night bombing missions as well as the expected 'Anglo-Saxon' air raids. Eleven pilots were sent to Tecuci air base to prepare for night fighter training in September of 1942. The Rumanians were trained by experienced Luftwaffe personnel and received their first Bf 110Cs during the spring of 1943. Due to the majority of these pilots having served with *Escadrila 51 vânătoare*, the new unit was named *Escadrila 51 vânătoare de noapte* (51st Night Fighter Squadron). The squadron was based at Bucharest-Pipera and commanded by the veteran *Căpitan aviator* Marin Ghica. A Luftwaffe night fighter group, IV./NJG 6, was formed alongside the Rumanian squadron. The Rumanian unit was put under the command of the German group after their two other squadrons (Nos. 10 and 11) arrived in Bucharest. *Escadrila 51 vânătoare de noapte* was later renamed 12./NJG 6 by the Luftwaffe and *Escadrila 1 vânătoare de noapte* (1st Night Fighter Squadron) by ARR. The Germans flew the more advanced Bf 110Fs with modern radar sets, while the Rumanians initially flew obsolescent Bf 110Cs, Ds, and Es.

Sunday, 1 August 1943, began as a quiet weekend day and both military personnel and civilians enjoyed the warm summer weather throughout Rumania. These included the few ARR pilots and other personnel on their airfields who were on or off-duty. The quiet was broken at 1300 hrs, when a large, loose formation of four-engine bombers penetrated Rumanian airspace from the southwest at low level. These bombers were bound for the Ploiesti oil production and refining complexes, however, they were detected by the German 'Freya' chain of radar stations. These stations, located throughout Wallachia (Southern Rumania), picked up the bombers in time to warn German and Rumanian fighters and anti-aircraft artillery units of the imminent attack.

German and Rumanian aviators thought at first the air raid warning sirens were part of another drill. The pilots scrambled and headed toward the zone indicated by *'Tigrul'* ('The Tiger') — the code name

A pilot warms up the engine of his *Grupul 6 vânătoare* I.A.R. 81C prior to take off from Bucharest-Pipera airfield on 13 August 1943. The heavy stain on the front fuselage was due to spilled 87-octane gasoline. (MMN)

for the fighter control center at Pipera. The pilots reached the zone at 16,404 ft (5000 m) as ordered by *'Tigrul'*, however, they failed to locate the bombers. The fighter pilots soon detected thick smoke columns rising from and around the Ploiesti area along with the deep sound of an intense flak barrage. The German and Rumanian pilots were still searching the sky when one of their comrades suddenly shouted over the radio, *"Down! Look Down!"* A large formation of American B-24 Liberator bombers flew at less than 492 ft (150 m) — just over the top of the oil refineries and storage tanks. The German and Rumanian fighters dived into the bombers. Shouts, commands, and curses filled the air in English, German, and Rumanian. The ensuing battle lasted for approximately one hour and was fierce and bloody for both sides. At least 36 of the 130 Liberators that reached Ploiesti fell victim to German and Rumanian air defenses.

The defenders were able to count their victories and losses after the battle ended. ARR fighters, according to Rumanian statistics, achieved ten confirmed and two probable victories. These fighters included Bf 109Gs of *Escadrila 53 vânătoare*, attached to the mixed German-Rumanian I./JG 4 (previously designated *'Ölschutzstaffel Ploesti'*, Oil Protection Unit Ploiesti). Also involved were I.A.R. 80/81s assigned to *Escadrile 61 & 62* of *Grupul 6 vânătoare* and *Escadrila 45* of *Grupul 4 vânătoare* as well as the Bf 110C equipped 51st NFS. ARR lost one I.A.R. 80B and one Bf 110C with one airman killed and two wounded in the engagement. The Luftwaffe claimed seven victories, while losing a Bf 109G and a Bf 110E and suffering the loss of two airmen. The strong anti-aircraft defenses were credited with 17 bombers from the 35 initially claimed, with a loss of 15 personnel. More Liberators were severely damaged over Rumania and subsequently were shot down over Bulgaria and Greece, or crashed or force-landed en route back to their bases in Libya.

Although USAAF officials declared OPERATION TIDAL WAVE a success, the attack was only a 'Pyrrhic victory'. The Ploiesti oil refineries were only moderately damaged and production resumed within a few weeks. The USAAF paid a heavy price for this limited result. This raid also resulted in the reorganization and reinforcement of the joint Rumanian-German air defense of Bucharest, as well as of the vital Prahova Valley oilfields. US and British aircraft re-entered Rumanian airspace in early April of 1944 to encounter well-organized and effective fighter and anti-aircraft defenses. These defenses caused the USAAF and RAF to suffer one of its highest loss rates in the European Theater of Operations (ETO).

The Hot and Bloody Summer of 1944

New Year's Day 1944 found the Rumanian fighter force engaged on two fronts. Some squadrons were fighting the Russians on the Eastern Front, while the bulk of the force was based in the homeland in anticipation of increased Allied — primarily US — bombing raids.

Grupul 9 vânătoare was the main ARR fighter element in the East. On 10 January, the *grup* was ordered to withdraw from Nikolayev to Lepetika airfield due to the shifting front. The unit was then recalled to Dalnik (near Odessa) in early March. *Grupul 9*'s combat strength fell to

Sweet Clara II, a P-51B-15-NA, s/n 43-24857 (No. 90), rests at Bucharest in early September of 1944. This checkertail Mustang was flown from Foggia, Italy, by *Cpt. av.* Constantin Cantacuzino after the successful completion of a diplomatic mission to Italy. This particular Mustang had been flown by Major Robert M. Barkey of the 319th Fighter Squadron, 325th Fighter Group, when he claimed at least one ARR Bf 109G. Prince Cantacuzino's personal Fleet F-10D, another US-designed aircraft, is parked in the background. Rumanian fighter pilots considered the P-51 their deadliest opponent in the air. (Bernád)

one squadron due to combat losses, bad weather, inadequate maintenance facilities, and insufficient spare parts and supplies. On 30 March, the Group reported a mere 13 Bf 109Gs ready for operations.

Soviet advance units reached the outskirts of Odessa on 10 April. Tiraspol, the capital of the Rumanian-administered Trans-Dnestra region, fell to the Soviets two days later. The 9th FG withdrew from Tiraspol on 6 April and relocated to Tecuci air base in Moldavia. *Grupul 9 vânătoare*, in concert with other ARR combat units, was tasked with stopping the Soviet steamroller from penetrating into northeastern Rumania.

Rumanian fighter pilots became more ambitious and pugnacious at home, being filled with determination to defend their homeland. They were defending not only against what Rumanian propaganda called the 'Bolshevik menace', but from the 'American sky terrorists' as well. The latter label was bestowed on USAAF airmen after the first large-scale attack of 1944 came against the main Bucharest railway station on 4 April. A large portion of the bombs, intended for 'Gara de Nord' and

Chitila railroad stations and marshaling yards, fell onto a nearby housing district. The bombs killed 2736 people and wounded 2341 others in less than one hour — the largest single loss in the Rumanian capital during the war. The dead were buried in a new cemetery named '4 April' which was established in the Giulesti district of Bucharest. Ninety one German and 81 Rumanian fighters scrambled against the unescorted bombers and downed 11. (The USAAF listed eight B-24Hs lost over Rumania: one over the Mediterranean, and another over Italy for a total of ten bombers lost on this raid.) The pilots of the two I.A.R. 80/81 groups were credited with 28 confirmed and 12 probable air victories* against a loss of only two aircraft out of 57 scrambled. One pilot from these groups was killed and another was wounded. Nine B-24Hs and two B-17Fs & Gs were reported by the USAAF to have been lost over Ploiesti on 5 April. (Rumanian sources mention 14 bombers shot down.) I.A.R. 80/81 pilots of the 6th FG were credited with 15 confirmed and two probable air victories without loss. The similarly equipped 1st FG reported downing three enemy aircraft (only one being confirmed) and damaging two others against the loss of two of their own.

Complementing the daylight raids of the US 15th Air Force were night missions carried out by the RAF's 205 Group. These missions were primarily bombing and mine laying sorties along the Danube. The British bombers were met by a well-organized German defense which usually claimed several bombers during each raid. Rumanian night fighters were not involved in combat, however, since the Germans believed that the Rumanian pilots would only complicate matters due to their lack of experience.

Soviet aircraft bombed Rumanian cities and other strategic targets alongside the Americans and British. Bombs fell on Cetatea Albă (Byelgorod/Akkermann) and Bugaz during the night of 8/9 April. Long-range V-VS bombers attacked Constanta harbor on 11 April, while other Soviet aircraft laid mines in the Danube. Soviet bombing attacks were considered insignificant and inflicted only minor damage compared to the massive strikes by the Western Allies.

Combined Allied bombing missions over Rumania became regular events from April to August of 1944. ARR initially sent the Messerschmitt Bf 109Gs of the experienced 7th FG (53, 57, & 58 FS) to engage the intruders. *Grupul 7 vânătoare* was augmented by the I.A.R. 81C-equipped *Grupul 6 vânătoare* (59, 61, & 62 FS), and occasionally

*During early 1944, ARR headquarters began awarding fighter pilots with three victories for each four-engine bomber shot down. Two victories were awarded for each two-engine aircraft destroyed and only one was given for a single-engine aircraft. ARR Headquarters made this move in order to boost the morale of the *vânători* facing the new and tougher enemy. This revised scoring method meant that 27 air victories were awarded for nine B-24s actually shot down by ARR fighter pilots.

German and Rumanian pilots gather by the port wing of an I.A.R. 80A for a propaganda exercise. Among the Luftwaffe pilots in this exercise is *Hptm.* Wilhelm 'Willi' Steinmann, *Staffelkapitän* of 1./JG 4. The Rumanian pilots are wearing field caps and were assigned to *Escadrila 53 vânătoare, Grupul 7 vânătoare. Adj. av.* Valeriu 'Bimbo' Buzdugan is seated on the wing, while *Lt. av.* Horea Pop (left) and *Lt. av.* Ion Galea stand with the Germans. The I.A.R. 80A (White 109) in the background displays the Group's 'Riding Mickey Mouse' emblem, however, the replacement rudder lacks the blue-yellow-red striping. (Pop)

joined by *Grupul 1 vânătoare* (43 FS equipped with Bf 109Gs and 63 & 64 FS flying I.A.R. 81s). These three groups totaled no more than 30 Bf 109Gs and 70 I.A.R. 80/81s. The Rumanians were reinforced by 60 to 80 Luftwaffe Bf 109Gs and a few Fw 190s and Bf 110s. The number of serviceable fighters was usually less than half of the existing inventory. Consequently, Allied airmen arrived over Rumania in the hundreds to face approximately 100, or often less, Axis fighters.

The Soviet threat to Rumania's northeastern borders had grown each day by mid-April. To meet this threat, *Grupul 7 vânătoare* was transferred from Bucharest-Pipera to southern Moldavia in order to reinforce the overwhelmed 9th FG. The 7th FG flew morning missions against the Soviets before being put on alert after 1000 hrs to meet the expected American bombers. The relatively inexperienced *Grupul 2 vânătoare* (65, 66, and 67 FS), which had formed only three months previously on I.A.R. 80/81s, replaced *Grupul 7* at Pipera. Thus, only two I.A.R. 80/81-equipped *grupuri* defended the capital during April and May. These units fought well against a technically and numerically superior enemy. According to Rumanian statistics, for example, the 6th FG engaged USAAF aircraft 12 times between 4 April and 6 June. The 363 I.A.R. 80/81 sorties launched claimed 60 confirmed and 10 probable victories (this amounted to 35 to 40 aircraft). Only seven pilots were killed in action, however, one of them was *Adjutant aviator* Florian Budu. Budu was one of the leading I.A.R. 80 aces when he was killed on 31 May.

One of the bloodiest engagements between USAAF and ARR aircraft took place on Saturday, 10 June 1944. Forty-six bomb-laden P-38 Lightnings of the 82nd Fighter Group escorted by a similar number of Lightnings from the 1st FG took off from Foggia, Italy. The P-38s were sent to seriously damage the Ploiesti oilfields. The Americans took off before dawn, at 0500 hrs, two hours earlier than usual. The Lightnings attempted to enter Rumanian airspace undetected, however, the 'Freya' and 'Würzburg' radar chains detected the incoming formation before it reached Rumania. This early warning enabled 'The Tiger' fighter command post (jointly commanded by *Oberst* Eduard Neumann of the Luftwaffe and *Căpitan comandor aviator* Gheorghe Miclescu of ARR) to alert both Rumanian and German fighters of the imminent attack. All combat-ready I.A.R. 80/81s were sent into the air, while non-combat aircraft were ordered to disperse to secondary airfields.

The low-flying USAAF fighters reached Popesti-Leordeni airfield, home of *Grupul 6 vânătoare*, however, the airfield was empty when the Lightnings arrived. I.A.R. fighters then bounced the P-38s by diving from a higher altitude. Several Lightnings fell to the Rumanians in the first pass. Other P-38s hit the ground with their wings or collided in mid-air while trying to maneuver at low altitude. Anti-aircraft gunners fired indiscriminately at all of the aircraft. Two I.A.R. 81Cs collided in mid-air, while others were hit by their own aircraft or anti-aircraft fire. Nevertheless, the 6th FG came away the clear winner of the mêlée. The 23 I.A.R. pilots involved in the battle claimed 23 P-38s while

Bf 110C, (2Z+FW/W.Nr. 973), suffered a collapsed main landing gear while landing at Zilistea on 13 March 1944. This aircraft was assigned to *Escadrila 51 vânătoare de noapte*, or 12./NJG 6, an experimental night fighter squadron raised by ARR during late 1942 in anticipation of Allied night raids. This Bf 110 is camouflaged in overall light gray and oversprayed with wavy lines of dark gray, which are barely visible on the port wing and fuselage side. Rumanian night fighters did not achieve any victories. (Stoenescu)

Barefoot Rumanian peasant boys guard a pair of oxen next to *Nina*, an I.A.R. 81C assigned to *Grupul 2 vânătoare* during the summer of 1944. The pilot's leather flying helmet is hanging out the side of the cockpit. This aircraft is believed to have been named for the pilot's girlfriend. (Bujor)

Two Heinkel He 112Bs, formerly assigned to *Escadrila 52 vânătoare*, serve as advanced trainers during 1944. Despite lacking armor protection, the He 112Bs performed well during the ARR's first campaign against the Soviet Union in 1941. The aircraft in the background is painted overall light gray — a scheme usually worn by the He 112Bs assigned to *Escadrila 51 vânătoare*. (Matthiesen)

Grupul 6 vânătoare pilots scramble to their I.A.R. 81Cs parked on the grass at Bucharest-Pipera airfield during 1944. They have been alerted of an approaching USAAF bomber formation. This Group, led by *Căpitan aviator* Dan Vizante, destroyed several P-38 Lightnings during the Americans' ill-fated 'surprise' low-level mission of 10 June 1944. A Bf 109G (White 7) is parked in the background. (Antoniu)

Red 9 was an early production Bf 109G believed to have been assigned to *Escadrila 56 vânătoare* during the early summer of 1944. In early 1944, ARR began to follow the *Jagdwaffe* practice of using colored tactical numbers to distinguish the squadrons and group staff members. The high fuselage color demarcation indicates this Bf 109 was possibly one of 48 G-1/G-2 aircraft (series 200) assembled and painted at I.A.R.-Brasov during early 1944. The fuselage drop tank mounted on this fighter was rarely seen on Rumanian Bf 109Gs. (Antoniu)

losing three of their own and having one pilot badly wounded. The group's commander, *Căpitan aviator* Dan Vizante, added two Lightnings to his tally. Vizante became the top ARR ace flying I.A.R. 80/81s. This was probably the finest hour for the sleek, but increasingly obsolescent I.A.R. 80/81s.

The other part of the American attack plan that day would not fare better. Rumanian and German Bf 109Gs engaged the low-flying P-38s before the Lightnings could reach the large *'Româno-Americană'* refinery near Ploiesti. *Grupul 7 vânătoare* claimed five Lightnings and Luftwaffe *Jagdfliegern* (notably I./JG 53 and III./JG 77) claimed 15 others. One German pilot was lost in the battle. The anti-aircraft defenses at Ploiesti reported shooting down five P-38s, while other Rumanian gunners claimed another three. The Rumanian and German claim of 51 P-38s destroyed was more than twice as much as those actually lost on this mission. Nevertheless, the destruction of 23 USAAF fighters — approximately one-fourth of the strike force — was indeed a major loss. This loss ratio was the highest for any mission involving significant numbers of Lightnings during World War Two. The American pilots claimed 33 confirmed and six probable air victories as well as eight aircraft damaged and ten locomotives destroyed. The Rumanians actually lost 14 aircraft, primarily non-combat types surprised by US aircraft while dispersing to other airfields or destroyed on the ground.

The Allies shrugged off these losses and returned to Rumanian skies on 11 June. This time the Americans sent four-engine bombers with fighter escort in two separate formations. One formation was launched from Italy and approached Rumania from the south. The second formation came from the north and was the return leg of the first 'shuttle raid'. The northern formation was the start of OPERATION FRANTIC, which involved US bombers striking Axis targets while flying to and from the Soviet Union. Luftwaffe and ARR fighters met both formations and claimed 15 aircraft shot down. The Germans bagged ten of these, while the five Rumanian victories included a B-17 Flying Fortress shot down by *Cpt. av.* Alexandru Serbănescu. This victory was one of Serbănescu's three that day and his 45th kill of the war.

The successes posted by the *vânători* would not last, however, since the Rumanians faced greater numbers of technically superior US aircraft. Rumanian losses began to mount.

This ex-ARR Bf 109G-2 (White 8) is looked over by *Örnagy* (Major) Aladár Heppes, the commander of *5/I. 'Puma' vadászosztály* (5/I. 'Puma' Fighter Group), MKHL (*Magyar Királyi Honvéd Légierö*; Royal Hungarian Air Force). This aircraft was reportedly left behind in a German *Werft* (repair shop) at Genitchesk airfield on 28 October 1943. The fighter was then transferred to Hungary by the Germans. The MKHL recoded this *'Gustav'* V.313 — V standing for *vadász* (fighter). Hungarian and Rumanian fighters would meet in battle during Rumania's anti-Axis campaign from September of 1944 to May of 1945. (Punka)

The elite *Grupul 7 vânătoare* suffered casualties to some of their top pilots on 23 June. *Căpitan aviator* Virgil Trandafirescu, commander of the 7th FG, was killed in a dogfight with P-51s, while both *Locotenent aviator* Tudor Greceanu and *Căpitan aviator* Dan Scurtu were wounded. Also killed in action on 23 June were two I.A.R. 80/81 pilots, including the 1st FG commander *Căpitan comandor aviator* (Lt Col) Ion Sandu — the highest-ranking ARR pilot to die in combat. The loss of two of the four fighter group commanders involved in the day's battle was a tremendous blow to the increasingly smaller Rumanian fighter force. The wounding of two experienced Messerschmitt pilots was also a loss ARR could ill afford.

On 3 July, *Subsecretariatul de Stat al Aerului* (SSA; Subsecretariat of State for Air) summarized the previous ten weeks of combat against the USAAF. Fighter availability declined from 115 to 50 machines during the American raids between 4 April and 24 June. ARR lost 33 fighter pilots killed in action. The last I.A.R. 80/81 loss to US fighters was at 0900 hrs on 3 July, when *Adjutant aviator* Grigore Mincu of *Grupul 6 vânătoare* was shot down and wounded by P-51 Mustangs. Citing their inferior performance and the high losses in I.A.R. 80/81-equipped units, ARR Headquarters decided to withdraw the I.A.R. fighters from further operations against the USAAF on 5 July. This left Rumanian home defense to *Grupuri 7 & 9 vânătoare* — both equipped with Bf 109Gs. The latter group was hastily recalled from the Soviet front and replaced with I.A.R. 80/81 units able to compete with less superior V-VS aircraft. Shortly thereafter, the 6th FG began its conversion to the Bf 109G with the 1st FG scheduled to follow.

The 9th FG had one of its most successful engagements with USAAF fighters on 22 July. At 1100 hrs, *Căpitan aviator* Alexandru Serbănescu led his group's Bf 109G-6s from Tecuci air base to intercept a formation of P-38 Lightnings and P-51 Mustangs. This formation was en route to Russia on another 'shuttle mission'. The Bf 109Gs surprised the Americans and claimed eight P-38s without loss. (US 15th Air Force records list only five P-38Js lost over Rumanian territory that day.) The Americans took their revenge four days later, when the shuttle mission returned from the Soviet Union via Rumania. The 9th FG lost seven out of 17 Bf 109G-6s sent to engage the formation which 'The Tiger' reported as 'only 20 bombers with a weak fighter escort.'

Two Luftwaffe Bf 109G-2s and an I.A.R. 81C are parked at Popesti-Leordeni airfield during the summer of 1944. Co-operation between ARR and Luftwaffe fighter units was crucial to the defense of Rumania which had been suffering under the weight of USAAF bombing attacks. German distrust of the obsolescent I.A.R. 80/81, however, meant that co-operation was sought only with the two Bf-109G equipped ARR fighter groups — *Grupuri 7* and *9*. The Luftwaffe employed these Rumanian fighters in a joint 'everybody up' attack formation known as 'Sternflug' (literally, 'Star Flight'). (Bernád)

A group of *vânători* serving with the elite *Grupul 9 vânătoare* gather in front of their ultimate weapon — a Bf 109 'Gheu' (as the Rumanians called the 'Gustav') — at Tecuci airfield in May of 1944. They are, from left: *Adj. av.* G. Scordilă, *Lt. av.* H. Dusescu, *Lt. av.* T. Greceanu, *Cpt. av.* A. Serbănescu, *Of. ech. av.* I. Milu, and *Adj. av.* E. Bălan. Serbănescu and Bălan were killed and Greceanu and Milu were wounded in unequal engagements with USAAF fighters. (Bernád)

Căpitan aviator de rezervă Constantin *'Bâzu'* Cantacuzino — the leading ARR ace — poses with technical officer *Slt. mec.* Marin Bâscă next to the tail of his Bf 109G-6 sometime between 6 and 11 May 1944. Forty white victory bars are painted on the vertical stabilizer with a red star added above each bar. *Cpt. av.* Cantacuzino finished the war with 56 confirmed and 13 probable victories. His nickname *'Bâzu'* (pronounced 'Bue-zoo') was used by everyone in ARR. (Bujor)

Rumanian ground crews feed ammunition belts into an I.A.R. 81C in anticipation of another USAAF raid early on a morning in 1944. Beginning in late July of 1944, Luftwaffe regulations required a thin white spiral on the black propeller spinner. This *Spiralschnauze* marking was used to provide recognition of Axis aircraft from head on. The engine cowling is painted olive green rather than the usual yellow. (Bernád)

The Americans, however, had more bombers than ground control indicated and an escort of over 100 P-38s and P-51s. The ensuing air battle killed three ARR pilots (*Adj. av.* P. Turcanu, E. Bălan, and A. Economu) and wounded three others. Those wounded included two *Grupul 9 vânătoare* veterans, *Adjutant major aviator* Ioan Mucenica and *Adjutant sef aviator* Andrei Rădulescu. The deputy group commander, *Căpitan aviator* Gheorghe Popescu-Ciocănel, was also gravely wounded while leading the Rumanian intercept and died of his wounds ten days later. Popescu-Ciocănel, a 12-victory ace, led the group that day due to Cpt Serbănescu being recalled to Bucharest. 26 July 1944 would be remembered by the Rumanian *vânători* as 'Black Sunday'.

Eleven USAAF aircraft were claimed destroyed by 9th FG pilots on 26 July, however, these results could not make up for the loss of experienced pilots. 15th Air Force loss records indicate only two P-38Js downed that day. Another source, however, lists a total of 20 Lightnings and 10 Mustangs lost over Rumania, Ukraine, and Poland. This second source appears closer to the truth. The Group's heroics were praised in Order of the Day No. 151 issued on 8 August by *General de escadră aviator* (Gen.-Maj.) Emanoil Ionescu, commander of *Corpul 1 Aerian Român*. The order cited the bravery of the *grup*'s pilots in shooting down 11 enemy aircraft. Gen Ionescu's report did not cite the high losses sustained by the unit. *Grupul 9 vânătoare* also lost *Locotenent aviator* Dinu I. Pistol, killed while attacking B-17s and B-24s on 31 July.

Rumanian fighter pilots clashed with the Americans for the last time on 18 August 1944. Thirteen Bf 109G-6s of the 9th FG joined 14 Bf 109G-6s from the 7th FG over Buzău. The Rumanian fighters were joined by 21 Luftwaffe fighters for a total of 48 Bf 109Gs to intercept the Americans. *Sectorul 2 vânătoare* (2nd Fighter Sector) ordered the Rumanian fighters to break off engaging the numerically superior enemy, however, the order came too late.

The Bf 109G-6s clashed with the P-51 Mustangs above the Carpathian Mountains near Brasov. The altitude of the engagement, 24,606 feet (7500 m), was 4823 feet (1470 m) above the G-6's optimum ceiling. The Mustangs enjoyed a two-to-one numerical superiority over their enemy and dived onto the Messerschmitts. Within minutes the Rumanians lost their leader, *Căpitan aviator* Alexandru Serbănescu, to P-51s which had come in from behind. Serbănescu did not hear his colleagues' warning due to an inoperative radio. *Adjutant aviator* Traian Dârjan, flying 328 ft (100 m) to Serbănescu's right, saw his wingman's Bf 109G-6 (No. 1) attacked by a red-nosed Mustang. The out-of-control Messerschmitt dived vertically into the ground with the fatally wounded Serbănescu still on board. *Locotenent aviator* Vasile Gavriliu's aircraft sustained at least 50 bullet holes, forcing him to land his damaged fighter. Two other 7th FG Bf 109Gs were hit and forced to land. The Germans lost at least three Bf 109Gs destroyed and one pilot killed. The Rumanians did not report a single victory, while the Germans only claimed a single P-51 downed by Major Harder of I./JG 53. A USAAF report states P-51s encountered 16 Bf 109Gs in the vicinity of Ploiesti on 18 August. The Americans pilots claimed nine definite (and one probable) victories. 1st Lt Robert J. Goebel of the 308th Fighter Squadron, 31st Fighter Group, claimed three victories that day. The gun camera of Goebel's P-51D, Flying Dutchman, reportedly confirmed all of his kills on 18 August.

The loss of Serbănescu, a veteran of 235 air battles and the leading ace with 55 victories, was the moral defeat of the Rumanian fighter force. ARR Headquarters in Bucharest ordered *Grupuri 7 & 9 vânătoare* to cease engaging the US formations on 19 August. These groups were further directed to move from Buzău to Mamaia on the shore of the Black Sea. *Escadrila 52 vânătoare*, based at Mamaia, was still equipped with older, yet still reliable, Bf 109Es where they defended the coast from Soviet attacks. The Germans were left alone to engage US aircraft until the end of the war in Rumania. Many Rumanian *vânători* regarded the dispersal of *Grupul 9 vânătoare* as an act of cowardice and a retreat in the face of the enemy. *Lt. av.* Ion Dobran noted impulsively in his wartime diary: *"The Group ran away."*

The *Coup*

A powerful Soviet offensive began in the Iasi-Chisinău (Jassy-Kishinev) sector of the front on the morning of 20 August 1944. The Soviet attack was supported by large numbers of V-VS assault and fighter aircraft. By that afternoon, the ill-equipped and outnumbered Rumanian-German defense had collapsed. ARR and Luftwaffe, desperate to halt the Red Army's further advance into Rumanian territory, threw in all available aircraft. These aircraft included level and dive bombers, assault aircraft, and fighters. Despite these efforts, the V-VS fielded two-and-one-half times as many aircraft as the Rumanians and Germans. The total of 1952 Soviet aircraft on the Southern Front included 802 fighters. (The fighter total did not include those assigned to the

German and Rumanian Messerschmitt Bf 109 *'Emils'* undergo maintenance at ASAM at Pipera-Bucharest airfield. ASAM (*Administratia Stabilimentelor Aeronauticii si Marinei*) was a series of Rumanian aircraft repair shops which performed maintenance on both ARR and Luftwaffe aircraft. A Luftwaffe Bf 109 *'Gustav'* and a Bf 108 Taifun await their turn outside the hangar. The Rumanian technicians have removed the cowlings of the Bf 109Es to perform maintenance work on the Daimler-Benz DB 601A engine. (Antoniu)

(Right and Below Right) Two Focke-Wulf Fw 190s seized from the Luftwaffe appear in hastily-painted Rumanian markings during the late summer of 1944. The first machine still wears the pro-Axis 'Michael's Cross' with the former German markings overpainted in white. The second Fw 190 wears the new pro-Allied roundel and white wing tips. Approximately 22 Fw 190s were among the over 200 Luftwaffe aircraft captured in Rumania after the *coup*. Captured Fw 190s were to be handed over to the Red Army, although several were hidden by the Rumanians. (Bernád)

Soviet Black Sea Fleet.) The Axis forces could field some 300 fighters at most, however, less than 200 of these were serviceable.

I.A.R. 80/81s flew alongside the Bf 109Gs of *Grupul 9 vânătoare* in defending the northeastern Rumanian border. As noted earlier, since July, the I.A.R. equipped fighter groups had been prevented from engaging the USAAF due to heavy losses sustained in action with the Americans. Five *Grupul 2 vânătoare* I.A.R. 81Cs, however, were lost to Soviet fighters on 20 and 21 August. Two Bf 109G-6s were shot down by La-5s over Roman, Moldavia on 22 August. Soviet troops temporarily captured one of the downed Rumanian pilots, *Adjutant aviator* Traian Dârjan. Dârjan was repatriated soon after Rumania signed an armistice with the Soviet Union and returned to active duty. Also lost that day were two I.A.R. 81s of *Grupul 4 vânătoare* and another I.A.R. 81 of the 2nd FG.

By 23 August, the King and Rumanian government officials realized that the Soviets could not be held and that the war was lost. That evening the Rumanians ceased hostilities against the Allies and requested an armistice. The surprised German forces in Rumania did not cease fighting. There were some clashes between German and Rumanian aircraft, however, the initial general consensus was to avoid conflict. The situation deteriorated rapidly and ARR fighters joined with the anti-aircraft forces in intercepting Luftwaffe bombers attacking the capital. The Rumanians also attacked German transport aircraft carrying reinforcements to Wehrmacht troops fighting in and around Bucharest. Six Luftwaffe bombers (He 111Hs of I./KG 4 and Ju 87Ds of I./SG 2) were reported downed by Bf 109Gs of *Grupuri 7* and *9 vânătoare* on 25 August. The Rumanians also reported damaging six other German bombers.

The fighting between the former allies around Bucharest peaked on 26 August. Rumanian fighters downed nine Luftwaffe aircraft, including eight by the 9th FG. The eight German aircraft destroyed included two Me 323 Gigants, two Ju 52/3ms, two Bf 109Gs, and two Bf 110Fs. ARR pilots also claimed four probable kills and additional German aircraft destroyed on the ground. *Locotenent aviator* Vasile Gavriliu added to his score by shooting down an He 111H and a Ju 52/3m, as well as destroying three Junkers transports on the ground. His Bf 109G-6 was hit by ground fire, however, and Gavriliu was forced to land. These victories made Gavriliu the most successful pro-Allied ARR ace of WW II.

Rumanian fighter losses during this campaign consisted mainly of aircraft destroyed on the ground or captured by the Germans. Air combat with the Luftwaffe resulted in the deaths of several Rumanian fighter pilots, including *Adjutant stagiar aviator* Constantin Stolică of *Escadrila 58 vânătoare*. His yellow-crossed Bf 109G-6 was shot down by a black-crossed Bf 109G-6 at Căldărusani on 28 August. Another ARR Bf 109G was

downed by friendly anti-aircraft fire and fell into Lake Herăstrău in Bucharest.

The last German troops withdrew from Rumania into Hungarian Transylvania and Bulgaria by the end of August. Others were captured by Rumanian troops and handed over to the Soviets. These German prisoners included wounded Luftwaffe airmen seized in hospitals. One of these airmen was *Oberfeldwebel* Johann Pichler of III./JG 77, an ace with 52 victories. He had been awarded the *Ritterkreuz* (Knight's Cross) only a week

Lt. av. Gheorghe Posteucă (left) meets an unidentified Soviet officer at Turnisor airfield in Transylvania on 7 October 1944. Both officers are standing in front of an I.A.R. 80 while two Soviet U-2 biplanes are lined up nearby. The I.A.R. 80's engine cowling has been repainted olive green, however, the white *Spiralschnauze* — a Luftwaffe recognition marking — has been retained. The Soviet officer is wearing a German white lamb skin flying jacket. (MMN)

Yellow 1, a Bf 109G-6 of *Grupul 9 vânătoare*, taxis for take off in front of two other *'Gustavs'* during the ARR's campaign against Axis forces. These late production Bf 109Gs feature the *'Erla Haube'* canopy, sometimes referred to as the 'Galland Hood'. An I.A.R. 39 observation aircraft is parked at right. (MMN)

earlier and promoted to officer. Pichler was picked up from his hospital bed by Rumanian soldiers and sent to a Soviet POW camp. He returned to Germany after six years of captivity.

SSA summed up the results of the recent fighting at the beginning of September. ARR fighters claimed 22 German aircraft destroyed in the air and another five destroyed on the ground. The Rumanians officially acknowledged losing only four aircraft to the Luftwaffe or their new Allies. (The latter case involved a Ju 52/3m downed by two P-51Bs of the 308th Fighter Squadron on 31 August. The V-VS is also believed to have shot down several Rumanian aircraft.) Thirty additional Rumanian aircraft were destroyed on the ground or captured by German or Soviet troops.

The Transylvanian Campaign

The ARR's Transylvanian campaign began badly when the Luftwaffe raided the flight school at Ghimbav (Vidombák/Weidenbach) on 3 September. The Germans strafed the airfield and destroyed three I.A.R. 80s, five trainers, and two liaison aircraft, along with an airworthy B-24 Liberator. The captured B-24 had been repaired by the Rumanians and was used to train their pilots in air combat techniques. Among the German pilots attacking Ghimbav were two Luftwaffe fighter instructors based there at the time of the 23 August *coup d'état*. The Germans earlier eluded their Rumanian guards and flew to safety in Hungarian territory only to return with a vengeance on 3 September.

The newly reformed *Corpul 1 Aerian Român* (C1AR; 1st Rumanian Air Corps) ordered their aircraft redeployed to airfields in Southern Transylvania on 6 September. These aircraft — freshly painted with the new ARR roundel — were stationed around Bucharest and Wallachia before being moved northwest over the Transylvanian Alps. The C1AR redeployment was in support of a joint Soviet-Rumanian offensive against the Hungarian and German defenders of Northern Transylvania. This air corps included three fighter groups, one being the Bf 109-equipped mixed *Grupul 7/9 vânătoare* (Escadrile 47, 48, & 56) with 27 aircraft. The other two groups, *Grupul 2 vânătoare* (Escadrile 65 & 66) and *Grupul 6 vânătoare* (Escadrile 59, 61, & 62), were equipped with the I.A.R. 80/81 and possessed 57 aircraft. These three groups were augmented by the independent *Escadrila 44 vânătoare*, equipped with nine I.A.R. 80s and six Bf 109Gs. The 44th FS was the first Rumanian fighter unit to arrive at the Transylvanian front on 5 September. The 99 fighters in the nine *escadrile* at the front represented two-thirds of the total combat inventory of the expeditionary air force. (Out of this number more than one-third were German-made aircraft.) V-VS fighter and bomber regiments simultaneously deployed to airfields across Rumanian held Southern Transylvania.

ARR aircraft began operations on the 'Western Front' against German and Hungarian forces on 7 September. The only combat-ready fighter unit at that time was the 44th FS. This squadron was thrown into combat despite its limited number of aircraft and a lack of combat experienced pilots. The unit's pilots were also inadequately trained in formation flying which caused two I.A.R. 80s to collide in mid-air while en route to

the front. Both pilots survived the collision and recuperated in the hospital. Nevertheless, the 44th FS flew four missions on 7 September with a total of 20 aircraft sorties.

Two I.A.R. 80 *patrule* (patrols) carried out the first mission on 7 September. These fighters were tasked with reconnaissance over the front and low-level attacks against enemy columns. Although the Rumanians were instructed to avoid contact with enemy aircraft, there were two clashes between I.A.R. 80/81s and Luftwaffe aircraft. The first encounter involved six I.A.R. 80/81s and eight Focke-Wulf Fw 190s north of Sibiu (Nagyszeben/Hermannstadt). I.A.R. 80 (No. 292), flown by *Adjutant stagiar aviator* Nicolae Zaharia, was shot down in flames over Rumanian-controlled territory. Friendly troops rescued the wounded pilot.

The bulk of C1AR *vânători* arrived at their new frontline base at Turnisor (Kistorony/Neppendorf) during the morning of 8 September. This base was close to Sibiu, the location of C1AR Headquarters. The I.A.R. 81s of the 2nd FG took off on their first combat mission almost immediately after arriving at Turnisor.

The first day of operations saw the death of a Rumanian Messerschmitt pilot, *Adjutant stagiar aviator* Gheorghe Buholtzer of the 9th FG. Buholtzer's Bf 109G-6 (Yellow 8) was shot down while landing at Turnisor by an over-zealous female Soviet anti-aircraft gunner. His aircraft reportedly still carried the old 'Michael's Cross' markings, which the Soviet gunner mistook for an Axis aircraft. This was the first of a series of fatal incidents involving Soviet anti-aircraft gunners erroneously (or deliberately) shooting down German-built aircraft flown by Rumanian pilots. Co-operation between Soviet and Rumanians units was generally tense. Rumanian aircraft, for example, were forbidden to land on Soviet airfields without permission, even in emergencies. (Rumanian aircrews generally did not speak any Russian.) ARR airmen therefore preferred to crash land their aircraft near a 'friendly' airfield rather than risk being suspected of spying — a capital offense punishable by summary execution. The Soviet headquarters also issued an order prohibiting Rumanian airmen from taking any self-defense firearms with them during missions.

The tempo of operations increased in concert with the intensity of the fighting in Transylvania. Airpower became crucial to the Rumanian troops when they faced stiff Axis resistance. This resistance forced the Rumanians to fall back on several occasions. Despite the intensity of the ground fighting, ARR and Luftwaffe fighter pilots still tried to avoid encounters with each other. There were unconfirmed reports of Rumanian and German Messerschmitt pilots — recently comrades-in-arms — meeting in the air and flying side-by-side. These pilots turned off their radios and communicated with hand signals, wishing each other the traditional greeting *'Hals-und Bein bruch!'* ('Break your neck and leg!').

This mutual 'respect' ended with the shooting down of three Rumanian aircraft by Luftwaffe Fw 190s on 14 September. An ARR Junkers Ju 87D of *Grupul 6/3 bombardament în picaj* and two Hs 129Bs of *Grupul 8 asalt* were brought down near Turda (Torda/Thorenburg). Three days later, an I.A.R. 81C and a Heinkel He 111H-6 of *Grupul 5 bombardament* fell victim to a Bf 109G *Rotte* of 6./JG 52. The Bf 109s, led by *Leutnant* Peter Düttmann, shot down the Rumanian aircraft near Kolozsvár (Cluj/Klausenburg), the capital of Transylvania. On 18 September, two I.A.R. 81s of the 2nd FG were hit by anti-aircraft fire north of Nyárádfö (Ungheni) and fell into the Mures

(Maros) River. Both pilots, *Sublocotenent aviator* Nicolae Smeianu and his wingman, *Adjutant stagiar aviator* Dumitru Marinescu, were lost.

Rumanian and German Messerschmitt 109s clashed for the first time over Transylvania on 18 September. Two Luftwaffe Bf 109Gs engaged five similar aircraft of the 9th FG and the Germans prevailed. Red 9 of *Sublocotenent aviator* Andrei Pop was hit in the radiator, forcing him to land on Drâmbari (Dombár) airfield. *Sublocotenent aviator* Stefan 'Kiki' Ciutac had to bail out of his burning Bf 109G near Alba Iulia (Gyulafehérvár/Weissburg). The *grup* had lost a third Messerschmitt when Red 5 crashed on take-off, killing the pilot, *Sublocotenent aviator de rezervă* Prince Gheorghe Brâncoveanu.

Despite their continuing losses, 9th FG pilots performed a unique low-level attack mission on 15 September. Six of the Group's most experienced pilots volunteered to attack Szamosfalva (Someseni) airfield north of Kolozsvár. This attack was one of the few such missions performed by Rumanian fighters on the 'Western Front'. *Locotenent aviator* Vasile Gavriliu , the leading ARR pro-Allied ace, led Bf 109Gs from Turnisor on the flight north to the target. The element made a 180° turn past Kolozsvár and approached Szamosfalva from the north — surprising the anti-aircraft defenses. The six Messerschmitts strafed the airfield in a single low-level pass, with Lt Dobran destroying a Hungarian Reggianne Re-2000 'Héja' fighter, while Lt Gavriliu set a twin-engine Focke-Wulf Fw 58 Weihe on fire. The element also destroyed three German transport gliders (believed to be Gotha Go 242s) and several trucks before all six Rumanian Messerschmitts returned home unscathed.

Escadrila 44 vânătoare was recalled to Rumania on 20 September. Remaining on the 'Western Front' were *Grupul 2 vânătoare* (14 available I.A.R. 80/81s), *Grupul 6 vânătoare* (11 available I.A.R. 80/81s), and *Grupul 9 vânătoare* (17 available Bf 109Gs).

A joint Soviet-Rumanian counter-offensive began in the Turda (Torda/Thorenburg) region on 22 September. Both V-VS and ARR aircraft were to provide air support. The Luftwaffe responded in force to this attack with Bf 109Gs and Fw 190s repeatedly intercepting Rumanian formations. Luftwaffe Fw 190s were unable to close in on

An I.A.R. 80 of *Escadrila 59 vânătoare* is prepared for a sortie during early October of 1944. The fighter was based at Turnisor airfield, near Sibiu, in the Transylvanian Theater of Operations. Ground crewmen applied dark green paint over the entire upper surface and fin of the aircraft, covering the serial number in the process. The white rear fuselage band has started to peel off. A Soviet U-2 biplane (Yellow 8) is parked in the background. (Avram)

ARR Ju 88As due to the escorting Bf 109Gs of the 9th FG. The Germans were more successful in engaging a formation of Hs 129Bs escorted by I.A.R. 81s and shot down one of each. Three engagements involving up to 40 aircraft took place over Turda the following day. Two I.A.R. *patrule* of the 59th FS clashed with six to eight Fw 190s on their second sortie that morning. *Sublocotenent aviator* Petre Mihăilescu was killed when the fuel tank on his I.A.R. 81 was hit and exploded. Additional I.A.R.s of the 6th FG and Bf 109Gs of JG 52 joined the battle. Two other I.A.R. 80s went down with one of the pilots killed and the other wounded. These two aircraft were likely victims of II./JG 52, since *Feldwebel* Willi Maasen of 5./JG 52 reporting shooting down an I.A.R. 80 near Thorenburg that day. A Rumanian Bf 109G (No. 4), flown by *Adjutant aviator* Ion Ioniță, was hit by a Luftwaffe Bf 109G and forced to land in friendly territory near Turda.

Rumanian pilots also enjoyed success over Turda that day. *Locotenent aviator* Dumitru 'Tache' Baciu of the 6th FG and *Adjutant aviator* Stavăr Androne of the 2nd FG each claimed a Bf 109G. *Adjutant aviator* Dumitru Chera of the 6th FG reported downing an Fw 190 on 23 September. (He and Lt 'Tache' Baciu also claimed a further Bf 109G each, however, these kills remained unconfirmed.) These three air victories reported by Rumanian pilots were also mentioned in a rare Soviet assessment of the joint V-VS/ARR air activity in the Cluj area. German documents, however, show only one Fw 190F-8 of I./SG 2 being lost that day. There is no trace in *Verlustmeldungen* (Luftwaffe Loss Reports) of any Bf 109Gs being shot down on the 23rd. These reports do state that *Ofhr.* Gerhard Messner of 5./JG 52 was lost with his Bf 109G-6 (Black 4, W. Nr. 166014) over an unspecified Rumanian loca-

Locotenent aviator **Tudor Greceanu enjoys a cigarette near his Bf 109G-6 (No. 3) which is parked in front of a destroyed hangar at Cluj-Someseni (Kolozsvár-Szamosfalva) airfield on 31 October 1944. Less than six weeks earlier, six ARR fighters strafed this airfield — then still in Hungarian hands — and set several parked aircraft on fire. Some of these aircraft were parked where this 'Gustav' is being serviced.** *Lt. av.* **Greceanu lost this Bf 109G-6 in a landing accident on the muddy Kunmadaras airstrip on 14 December 1944. (Greceanu)**

tion on 24 September. Another unidentified Bf 109G-6 of II./JG 52 was also reported hit in air combat over Rumanian territory the same day. The aircraft's ultimate fate was not recorded by German sources. Both German aircraft could have been downed by Rumanian fighters the day before with their loss reported one day late. These aircraft, however, could also have been shot down by Soviet fighters or anti-aircraft fire. The downing of these three Axis aircraft by the I.A.R. 80 pilots is regarded by Rumanian historians as a unique triumph over the Luftwaffe in the skies over Transylvania.

After a relatively quiet 24 September, aerial combat resumed around Turda on the following day. Eight I.A.R. 80s and 81s of the 2nd FG took off at 1000 hrs to provide escort for Rumanian bomber and assault aircraft and to patrol the region. Additional I.A.R.s of the 6th FG followed the fighters of the 2nd FG. Scores of German aircraft soon bounced the Rumanian fighters. Fifty-five aircraft took part in several overlapping engagements. Such combat had not been seen since the USAAF bombing attacks on Rumania weeks before, however, these now involved former comrades-in-arms fighting each other.

Rumanian documents record four clashes between Rumanian and German aircraft over Turda. These were: six Hs 129Bs of *Grupul 8 asalt* against six Bf 109Gs; eight I.A.R. 80s of *Grupul 2 vânătoare* engaging five Bf 109Gs; eight I.A.R. 80s of the 2nd FG against six Bf 109Gs; and ten I.A.R. 80s of *Grupul 6 vânătoare* engaging six Bf 109Gs. Although the Rumanians enjoyed a numerical superiority in these engagements, the I.A.R. pilots were no match for the experienced German *Jägern*. Six Rumanian fighters were shot down without loss to the Germans. Three pilots, *Locotenent aviator* Ioan Ivanciovici, *Adjutant stagiar aviator* Franz Secicar (an ethnic German from Transylvania), and *Adjutant aviator* Stavăr Androne were killed. Androne had claimed a Luftwaffe Bf 109G only two days earlier. One of the victors on 25 September was *Leutnant* Peter Düttmann of 6./JG 52. Düttmann's three I.A.R. 80 kills in 12 minutes over Thorenburg

Cpt. av. Lucian Toma boards his Bf 109G-6 (White 1) for what would be his last flight on 25 September 1944. He was shot down and killed by the rear gunner of a Luftwaffe Ju 188F high altitude reconnaissance aircraft over Kolozsvár/Cluj a short time later. (Antoniu)

(Turda), noted in his logbook, increased his score to 103 victories. Düttmann added another victory two hours later, when he downed a Soviet La-5 in the same region.

Shortly after noon on 25 September, *Căpitan aviator* Lucian Toma, commander of the elite 9th FG, took off from Turnisor on a free hunt mission. This was Toma's first combat mission on the Western Front. He and his wingman rapidly climbed to 22,591 ft (7800 m) after observing a Ju 188 reconnaissance aircraft. Toma closed in on the German aircraft and opened fire at close range. His machine gun and cannon scored several hits, however, the Junkers' rear gunner hit Toma's Bf 109. Both aircraft dived together at such close distances that they seemed glued together. The Bf 109 and Ju 188 hit the ground together and exploded just south of Kolozsvár/Cluj. *Căpitan aviator* Toma was the last of seven ARR fighter group commanders to be killed in action during WW II. (Among those killed was *Căpitan aviator* Gheorghe Radu, commander of *Grupul 7 vânătoare* attached to III./JG 3 '*Udet*'. Radu, too, had been shot down and killed on his first combat sortie in March of 1943.) A search for the German Ju 188's identity remains inconclusive. 3.(F)/*Aufklärungsgruppe* 121, based at Sárospatak, Hungary, was apparently the sole active Luftwaffe reconnaissance unit equipped with Ju 88/Ju 188s in that area of the Eastern Front.

The following day was rainy and cloudy with visibility reduced to a few feet. An order from Bucharest grounded all I.A.R. 80/81s until ARR Headquarters could assess the situation following the losses of 25 September. The I.A.R. equipped fighter groups had fought ten engagements over the previous four days and had lost 11 aircraft to the Luftwaffe — one-third of their total serviceable aircraft. (On 26 September, C1AR reported the following numbers of serviceable fighters: *Grupul 2 vânătoare*, nine; *Grupul 6 vânătoare*, 11; and *Grupul 9 vânătoare*, 13.) On 26 September ARR Headquarters decided to relegate the I.A.R. 80/81s to close air support, air cover for Soviet ground units, and other secondary duties. The Messerschmitt Bf 109 remained the sole aircraft type assigned to the pure fighter role. An attempt by SSA to re-equip the fighter groups operating I.A.R.s with superior Soviet Lavochkin La-5FNs and Yakovlev Yak-9s did not materialize.

The results of the first month of the 'Western Campaign' were assessed at the end of September. *Grupul 2 vânătoare* reported 60 missions totaling 328 aircraft sorties. *Grupul 6 vânătoare* flew 77 missions with 327 sorties and *Grupul 9 vânătoare* flew 73 missions comprising 314 sorties. ARR fought seventeen engagements against the Luftwaffe and the *Magyar Királyi Honvéd Légierö* (MKHL; Royal Hungarian Air Force) using 105 aircraft. The *vânători* claimed four Luftwaffe aircraft shot down in air combat and four destroyed on the ground at Kolozsvár-Szamosfalva airfield. ARR lost 25 fighters to Axis aircraft and anti-aircraft fire — a one-month record for a single Rumanian campaign.

In Pursuit of the Enemy

Corpul 1 Aerian Român was reorganized between 7 and 10 October 1944. This reorganization also entailed streamlining the chain of command and reducing the size of the Corps' units. *Comandamentul aviatiei de vânătoare* (Fighter Aviation Command), the C1AR department directly responsible for the fighter force, disbanded *Grupul 6 vânătoare* and recalled the surviving personnel to Rumania. This move was prompted by the declining number of available I.A.R. 80/81s. The remaining I.A.R. fighters of the 6th FG were sent to reinforce the decimated *Grupul 2 vânătoare*. That group, however, could only field two squadrons — *Escadrile 65* and *66*. The strength of *Grupul 9 vânătoare* was reduced at the same time to a pair of squadrons, *Escadrile 47* and *48*. The number of fighters available to C1AR had been reduced to about 50 — approximately half the number available at the beginning of the Transylvanian Campaign.

Poor weather and declining morale reduced the number of sorties flown by the *vânători* during October. Most of the missions consisted of providing air cover for both Rumanian bombers and ground troops, along with the occasional strafing attack. Meteorological and tactical reconnaissance missions were also flown. Air combat was almost nonexistent due to the sharp reduction in Axis air activity and bad weather. Three Fw 190s intercepted a lone I.A.R. 39 three-seat reconnaissance aircraft of *Grupul 2 observatie* on 9 October. A pair of ARR Bf 109Gs responded to the I.A.R. 39 crew's desperate call for help, but arrived too late. The Rumanian biplane was shot down in the Cucerdea (Oláhkocsárd) area. A Bf 109G of the 9th FG was also reported missing in action the following day. The pilot, *Adjutant aviator* Ioan Vanca, had apparently defected to the Germans (Vanca reportedly ended up in the USA after WW II).

Both fighter groups moved to the airfield at Cluj-Someseni (Kolozsvár-Szamosfalva) on 23 September. The new base, with its large

Soviet and Rumanian personnel pose for a propaganda photograph in front of a Bf 109G-6. The photo was designed to emphasize the 'camaraderie' between these new allies. The emblem on the fighter's nose is believed to be that of *Grupul 7 vânătoare*, which featured a winged number 7. Despite scenes such as this, relations between the former bitter enemies were often tense. Soviet anti-aircraft gunners on occasion fired on ARR aircraft 'by mistake'. Rumanian aircrews were also prohibited by the Soviets from carrying sidearms, and from landing on Soviet airfields without prior permission — even in emergencies. (Bernád)

size hangars and concrete runway, was a welcome change from the small and muddy airstrips that the groups had used early in the campaign . The hangars and runways at Cluj-Someseni were in ruins, however. Nevertheless, the large airfield could be shared by all ARR single-engine and some twin-engine aircraft: Bf 109Gs, I.A.R. 80/81s, Ju 87Ds, and Hs 129Bs. These were joined by Soviet Il-2s. The ARR *vânători* strength at the date comprised of 26 I.A.R. 80/81s with the 2nd FG and 28 Bf 109Gs with the 9th FG.

Combat operations in Northern Transylvania finally ended on 25 October and the fighting shifted to the present-day territory of Hungary. Fighter activity during October of 1944 was significantly less than the previous month. *Grupul 2 vânătoare* reported 17 missions that month totaling 74 aircraft sorties, while *Grupul 9 vânătoare* flew 21 missions totaling 80 sorties during the same period. Only one engagement was fought (without result) and the sole loss was that of the defecting *Adj.* Vanca.

The weather was unsuitable for flying throughout most of November. Combat sorties were rarely flown due to the muddy conditions prevailing at the new landing ground at Turkeve in central Hungary. Bad weather and accidents while taxiing on the inundated airfields resulted in most of the aircraft losses that month. One such loss occurred on 20 November, when a Bf 109G-6 (W. Nr. 163652) of the 9th FG was damaged at Turkeve with *Adjutant aviator* Pavel Barbu at the controls. (This Bf 109 was specifically mentioned in documents as a captured, ex-Luftwaffe machine.) A Luftwaffe loss report dated 13 November stated that *Uffz.* Uwe Rossen of 2./JG 53 was listed as missing in action. Rossen was reported lost after his Bf 109G-14 (Black 2, W. Nr. 510880) was attacked by an unidentified Bf 109G near Szolnok, Hungary. *Grupul 9 vânătoare*'s log book for the October 1944-January 1945 period, however, has no record of this German loss. The German *Flieger* is believed to have been the victim of a Soviet fighter, however, the possibility this was a captured Bf 109 or one 'loaned' to the Soviets by the Rumanians cannot be excluded.

All ARR units were grounded in early December due to bad weather. Occasional reconnaissance sorties were flown, however, no combat missions were undertaken. C1AR combat records for 4 December do not show any combat missions that day, however, Hungarian documents mention the loss of an Fw 190F of *102. Vadászbombázó-osztály* (102nd Fighter-Bomber Group). Reportedly, the Hungarian fighter was shot down above Börgönd airfield by a Rumanian-marked Bf 109G. (Possibly another example of a captured or 'loaned' Messerschmitt with a Soviet or anti-Nazi German pilot in the cockpit.)

The *vânători* were redeployed to Füzesabony airfield due to the poor conditions at Turkeve air base. Field conditions at Füzesabony were just as adverse, however, which prompted 9th FG to redeploy to Kunmadaras on 11 December. This base, already used by the more robust I.A.R. fighters, had a fairly suitable concrete airstrip. This redeployment, however, was accompanied by several accidents. Three Bf 109Gs turned over during takeoff from Turkeve and another four were damaged while landing at Kunmadaras. More fighters were put out of commission on 12 December, including the Bf 109G of Cpt Cantacuzino, which turned over while landing on the muddy strip at Kunmadaras. The seven unserviceable Messerschmitts represented one-third of the Group's total number of available machines.

Regardless of their losses, Soviet Headquarters insisted that Rumanian fighters be sent over the front-line. These orders were justified by the presence of Axis aircraft and the desperate need for close air support for

the Soviet and Rumanian troops trapped around Eger. Further flying attempts were made, although these inevitably caused more accidents and more losses and resulted in little being achieved. On 13 December, all missions were called off after several futile attempts had been made. Personnel of the 9th FG were commended by a special Order of the Day issued by C1AR Headquarters for their outstanding efforts shown from 12 to 14 December. Compared to what little was accomplished, however, the price of ten damaged aircraft seemed excessively high for a 25-aircraft strong fighter group.

Rumanian historians regard 19 December 1944 as the last day of the

Two Soviet female officers disregard the rain and strike a pose in front of a Messerschmitt fighter. This unlikely picture was taken for the benefit of a Rumanian propaganda photographer. The Soviet armed forces primarily employed women for non-combat support roles during World War Two, however, several Soviet females performed as fighter and night harassment pilots and as anti-aircraft gunners during the conflict with Germany and her allies. (Bernád)

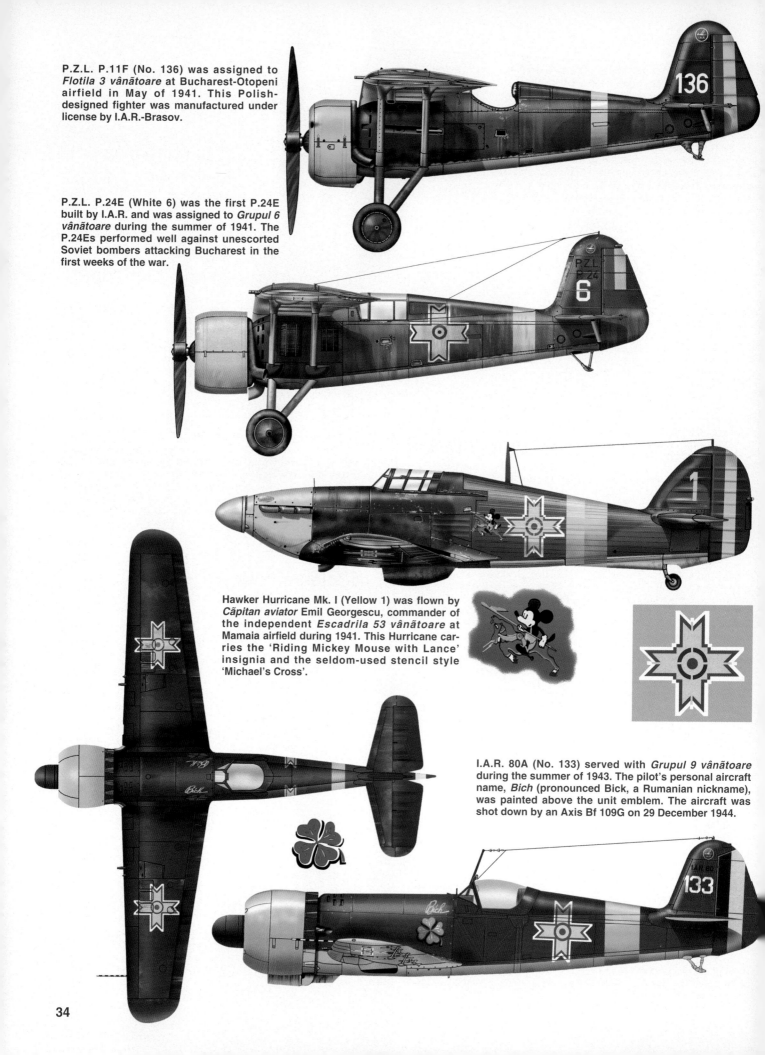

P.Z.L. P.11F (No. 136) was assigned to *Flotila 3 vânâtoare* at Bucharest-Otopeni airfield in May of 1941. This Polish-designed fighter was manufactured under license by I.A.R.-Brasov.

P.Z.L. P.24E (White 6) was the first P.24E built by I.A.R. and was assigned to *Grupul 6 vânâtoare* during the summer of 1941. The P.24Es performed well against unescorted Soviet bombers attacking Bucharest in the first weeks of the war.

Hawker Hurricane Mk. I (Yellow 1) was flown by *Cãpitan aviator* Emil Georgescu, commander of the independent *Escadrila 53 vânâtoare* at Mamaia airfield during 1941. This Hurricane carries the 'Riding Mickey Mouse with Lance' insignia and the seldom-used stencil style 'Michael's Cross'.

I.A.R. 80A (No. 133) served with *Grupul 9 vânâtoare* during the summer of 1943. The pilot's personal aircraft name, *Bich* (pronounced Bick, a Rumanian nickname), was painted above the unit emblem. The aircraft was shot down by an Axis Bf 109G on 29 December 1944.

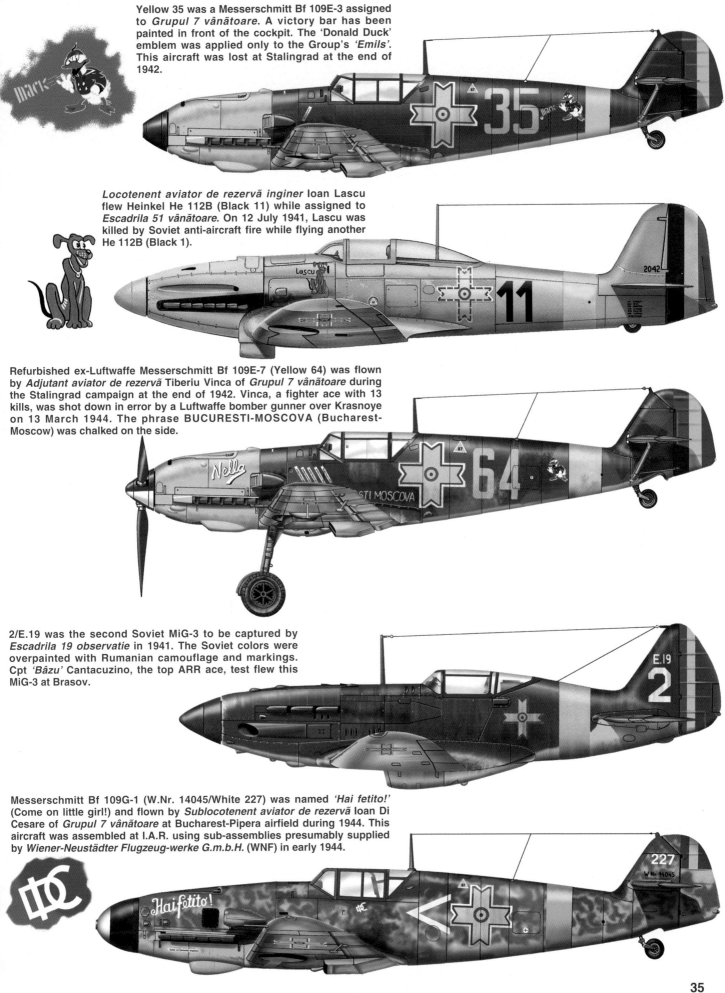

Yellow 35 was a Messerschmitt Bf 109E-3 assigned to *Grupul 7 vânătoare*. A victory bar has been painted in front of the cockpit. The 'Donald Duck' emblem was applied only to the Group's *'Emils'*. This aircraft was lost at Stalingrad at the end of 1942.

Locotenent aviator de rezervă inginer Ioan Lascu flew Heinkel He 112B (Black 11) while assigned to *Escadrila 51 vânătoare*. On 12 July 1941, Lascu was killed by Soviet anti-aircraft fire while flying another He 112B (Black 1).

Refurbished ex-Luftwaffe Messerschmitt Bf 109E-7 (Yellow 64) was flown by *Adjutant aviator de rezervă* Tiberiu Vinca of *Grupul 7 vânătoare* during the Stalingrad campaign at the end of 1942. Vinca, a fighter ace with 13 kills, was shot down in error by a Luftwaffe bomber gunner over Krasnoye on 13 March 1944. The phrase BUCURESTI-MOSCOVA (Bucharest-Moscow) was chalked on the side.

2/E.19 was the second Soviet MiG-3 to be captured by *Escadrila 19 observatie* in 1941. The Soviet colors were overpainted with Rumanian camouflage and markings. Cpt *'Bâzu'* Cantacuzino, the top ARR ace, test flew this MiG-3 at Brasov.

Messerschmitt Bf 109G-1 (W.Nr. 14045/White 227) was named *'Hai fetito!'* (Come on little girl!) and flown by *Sublocotenent aviator de rezervă* Ioan Di Cesare of *Grupul 7 vânătoare* at Bucharest-Pipera airfield during 1944. This aircraft was assembled at I.A.R. using sub-assemblies presumably supplied by *Wiener-Neustädter Flugzeug-werke G.m.b.H.* (WNF) in early 1944.

A Rumanian *vânător* leans on the propeller of a V-VS Yak-1M fighter undergoing repair at a destroyed ex-MKHL airfield somewhere on the vast Hungarian *puszta* (plain) during the fall of 1944. Late production Yakovlevs and Lavochkins were considered superior to the Messerschmitt Bf 109G-6. An I.A.R. 80A (No. 133) of *Grupul 2 vânătoare* is parked in the background. This particular aircraft was shot down by a hostile Bf 109G on 24 December 1944 in northeastern Hungary. The pilot, *Adjutant aviator* Dumitru Niculescu, was reported missing in action. (Bujor)

ARR's Hungarian Campaign, which had officially begun on 26 October. (This period actually covers only the events taking place inside Hungary's present-day borders; the correct timeframe should have been 6 September 1944 to 19 January 1945.) During the 54 days of this campaign, the four fighter squadrons recorded only 25 missions totaling 79 aircraft sorties. No victories were claimed by C1AR pilots. All of the Rumanian losses were caused by landing and takeoff accidents or by anti-aircraft fire.

At the opening of the Czechoslovakian Campaign, *Comandamentul aviatiei de vânătoare* reported the existence of 28 I.A.R. fighters with *Grupul 2 vânătoare* and 27 Bf 109Gs with *Grupul 9 vânătoare* (of which 23 were serviceable). The fighters redeployed from Turkeve to Miskolc during the afternoon of 20 December. That morning the 9th FG had sent all of their airworthy Messerschmitts to provide air cover for 30 twin-engine bombers. The Soviet high command requested the Rumanian effort which involved some 50 aircraft being sent to destroy the railway station and marshaling yards in the northern Hungarian town of Losonc (now Lucenec, Slovakia). The Allies considered the results to be satisfactory. No opposing fighters were encountered.

One day during late December, a pair of Soviet Lavochkin La-7 fighters paid an official visit to the Rumanians and landed at Miskolc. One of the Soviet pilots — reportedly a 'Hero of the Soviet Union' — engaged in a mock dogfight with Cpt Constantin *'Bâzu'* Cantacuzino, the top ace in ARR. The Soviet pilot clearly prevailed in this 'friendly exercise' which demonstrated the superiority of the La-7 over the Group's aging Messerschmitt Bf 109G-6s.

The Luftwaffe and MKHL were still present in northern Hungary at the end of 1944. These forces lacked the ability to conduct extensive operations due primarily to their lack of fuel. Nevertheless, several missions were carried out against Rumanian aircraft over northeastern Hungary despite the fuel shortage. An ARR *patrulă* was engaged on 23 December by a Bf 109 *kette*. The Rumanian fighters were escorting Ju 87D-5 Stukas of *Escadrila 74 picaj* to Poltár. An ARR Bf 109G-6 (White 1), flown by *Adjutant aviator* Ioan Marinciu, was shot down in

the brief clash. The aircraft crashed in friendly territory near Zvolen (Zólyom/Altsohl) and the wounded Marinciu was taken to a local hospital. Two I.A.R. 80As (Nos. 133 and 144) were lost the following day. No. 133 was shot down by Bf 109Gs, while No. 144 was brought down by flak over Vadna, 15.5 miles (25 km) from Miskolc. *Locotenent aviator* Constantin *'Rează'* Rosariu's Bf 109G-6 (Blue 6) was downed by anti-aircraft fire on 24 December. Rosariu, an ace with 27 victories, was able to belly-land his aircraft behind Russian lines. This day marked the last day of major air activity for the following two months due to a lull in operations.

At least one I.A.R. 80 and one Bf 109 shot down during December of 1944 can probably be attributed to one Hungarian unit — the MKHL's *101. 'Puma' Vadászezred* (101st 'Puma' Fighter Wing) based at Veszprém airfield north of Lake Balaton. *Szakaszvezetö* (Sgt) Lajos Krascsenics reportedly shot down a "strangely painted" and hostile acting Bf 109G on 22 December. A radial-engine fighter with a yellow cowling was also reported 'killed' during the same timeframe. (The latter aircraft was probably an I.A.R. 80/81, due to evidence of yellow engine cowlings still being used by some ARR fighters as late as April of 1945.)

During January of 1945, C1AR staff compiled statistics covering the air activity during fall and early winter of 1944. I.A.R. equipped squadrons flew 167 missions consisting of 814 sorties between 7 September and 31 December 1944. The 167 missions consisted of 18 reconnaissance, 36 bomber escort, 103 air cover for Rumanian troops, 9 low-level attack, and 1 free hunting. The Messerschmitt equipped *grup* reported 157 missions comprising 551 sorties during the same period. These missions consisted of 32 reconnaissance, 84 bomber escort, 4 air cover for friendly troops, 30 low-level strafing, and 7 free hunting.

C1AR crews fought 25 engagements with German and Hungarian aircraft. I.A.R. 80/81 pilots claimed three victories while losing 17 aircraft. Nine I.A.R.s were lost in air combat, six to anti-aircraft fire, one force-landed in enemy territory, and one was lost to other causes. The Messerschmitt pilots were credited with one air and five ground victo-

Locotenent comandor aviator (Major) Cornel Adamiu poses by the cockpit of this Bf 110F at Trencín airfield, in Slovakia, during April of 1945. This night fighter was captured from the Germans during August of 1944. It was used by the Rumanians as a fast courier aircraft between Bucharest and the front. The insignia of the Bf 110F's previous operator, NJG 6, is still painted on the nose. The Rumanians successfully hid several captured ex-Luftwaffe aircraft from the Soviets. (Androvic)

Slt. av. Aurelian Barbici (center) engages in an animated discussion with four fellow *Grupul 1 vânătoare* pilots in front of Barbici's Bf 109G-2 at Miskolc airfield, Hungary, in February of 1945. The name *Vally* on the cowl is the nickname of Barbici's wife, Valéria Tóth, a Hungarian woman from Oradea. Barbici defected to the Germans using this Bf 109 on 25 March 1945. He and his wingman, *Adjutant aviator* Virgil Angelescu, flew their aircraft to the Luftwaffe base at Trentschin encouraged by an appeal to defect broadcasted by the German propaganda radio station, *'Donau Funk'*. Barbici returned to Rumania after the war and claimed to have been shot down and taken prisoner by the Germans. (MMN)

ries while losing nine aircraft. Four of the lost Bf 109s were shot down by fighters, two by flak, one force-landed in enemy territory, and two were lost for other reasons. Several fighters were badly damaged in addition to the 26 aircraft officially written off during this period. Damaged aircraft were sent back to the I.A.R.-Brasov plant for general repair. These aircraft were practically removed from service for the remainder of the war.

The Last Year of War

Thick fog and poor weather arrived at the front on New Year's Eve 1944. All of the missions, except for occasional weather reconnaissance sorties, were canceled. The only notable action during the month was the bombing of targets in Budapest on 13 January. Junkers Ju 87Ds and Ju 88As targeted two strategically important bridges over the Danube. A Bf 109G *celulă* of *Grupul 9 vânătoare* and five V-VS Yak-3s provided fighter escort for the Rumanian bombers. The Soviet fighters were reportedly flown by female pilots. The presence of the Soviet aircraft was to frustrate any attempts by the unreliable Rumanians to bomb other targets in the capital of their arch enemies, the Hungarians, or to defect. This raid on Budapest was a rare co-operative effort by V-VS and ARR aircraft, since they normally conducted independent operations. The Danube bridges were not destroyed despite the Rumanians' efforts.

In early February, Rumanian ground troops and technicians arrived at the recently repaired Lucenec (Losonc) airfield, in Slovakia, to prepare the field for new users. The 9th FG redeployed to Lucenec that month and was soon joined by the new *Grupul 1 vânătoare* (*Escadrile 61 & 64*). This latter unit was essentially a scaled-down fighter group previously operating I.A.R. 81s. The 1st FG was re-formed on older Bf 109Gs, along with captured and refurbished ex-Luftwaffe Bf 109s. The new *grup* arrived at the front late, with insufficiently trained pilots and only ten aircraft. The dwindling strength of the 2nd FG (65 & 66 FS) was reinforced by 15 I.A.R. 81Cs at the same time. The inexperienced pilots of the 1st FG began flying combat missions on 20 February in concert with some veteran colleagues. The newcomers' lack of training

or combat experience, however, provided little relief to the exhausted 9th FG. The 1st FG soon found itself assigned to secondary missions, such as air support for ground forces.

General comandant aviator Emanoil Ionescu, the commander of C1AR, met the Soviet 40th Army commander, Gen. Col. F. F. Ymachenko on 21 February. The generals discussed co-operation in the forthcoming joint offensive in the Zvolen (Zólyom/Altsohl) area to drive out strong Hungarian-German defenses. C1AR units were to provide air support for the attacking troops. A record number of aircraft were prepared for the offensive — the last major operation for Rumanian aircrews.

Bf 109Gs took off from Lucenec at 0530 hrs on 25 February to join Savoia bombers coming from Oradea (Nagyvárad/Großwardein) airfield. Junkers Ju 88As based at Miskolc rendezvoused with the Rumanian formation at 0930 hrs, escorted by 9th FG aircraft. C1AR's targets were within the Ocová (Nagyócsa) — Detva (Gyetva) — Zvolenská Slatina (Nagyszalatna) triangle.

Initially, the Luftwaffe's involvement in the battle was limited to a single reconnaissance Bf 109 *Rotte* being spotted before noon. Single-engine German aircraft based at Piest'any (Pöstyén/Pistian) began arriving in the combat zone by 1300 hrs. A *celulă* of 9th FG was alerted to the Germans' arrival and launched from Lucenec around 1400 hrs. *Grupul 9 vânătoare* commander *Căpitan aviator de rezervă* Constantin Cantacuzino and *Adjutant aviator* Traian Dârjan looked for battle. The *celulă* soon spotted two Focke-Wulf Fw 190 *Schwarmen* attacking Soviet troops near Zvolen and engaged the numerically superior Germans. The experienced Cpt Cantacuzino — the ARR's top ace — promptly shot down an Fw 190F-8 (W. Nr. 584057, Yellow 7) of 3./SG 2 near the village of Vigl'as (Végles). The Fw 190's pilot, *Gefr.* Hermann Heim, was killed in the battle. Cantacuzino and his wingman, looking for his fallen victim's crash site to validate the victory claim, failed to see an approaching *Rotte* of Luftwaffe Bf 109Gs. The Germans jumped the unsuspecting and careless Rumanians and shot both fighters down within seconds.

Grupul 9 vânătoare personnel pay their last respects to *Adjutant aviator* Traian Dârjan. Dârjan was killed in air combat with *Hptm.* Helmut Lipfert, *Kommandeur* of I./JG 53, on 25 February 1945. His coffin is draped with the blue-yellow-red Rumanian flag and pine branches and placed in front of one of the Group's Bf 109G-6s. Dârjan's wingman, *Căpitan aviator de rezervă* Constantin Cantacuzino, was also shot down by the Germans that day. Cantacuzino, *Grupul 9*'s commander, survived his last engagement and the war. He went into exile in Spain during the late 1940s. The previous August, Dârjan was shot down and briefly held prisoner by the Soviets until repatriated shortly after Rumania's defection from the Axis on 23 August 1944. (Andrei)

I.A.R. 81 (No. 95) was assigned to *Escadrila 59 vânătoare* and took part in the closing stages of the siege of Odessa during early October of 1941. The I.A.R. 81 was an I.A.R. 80 developed for the dive bomber role.

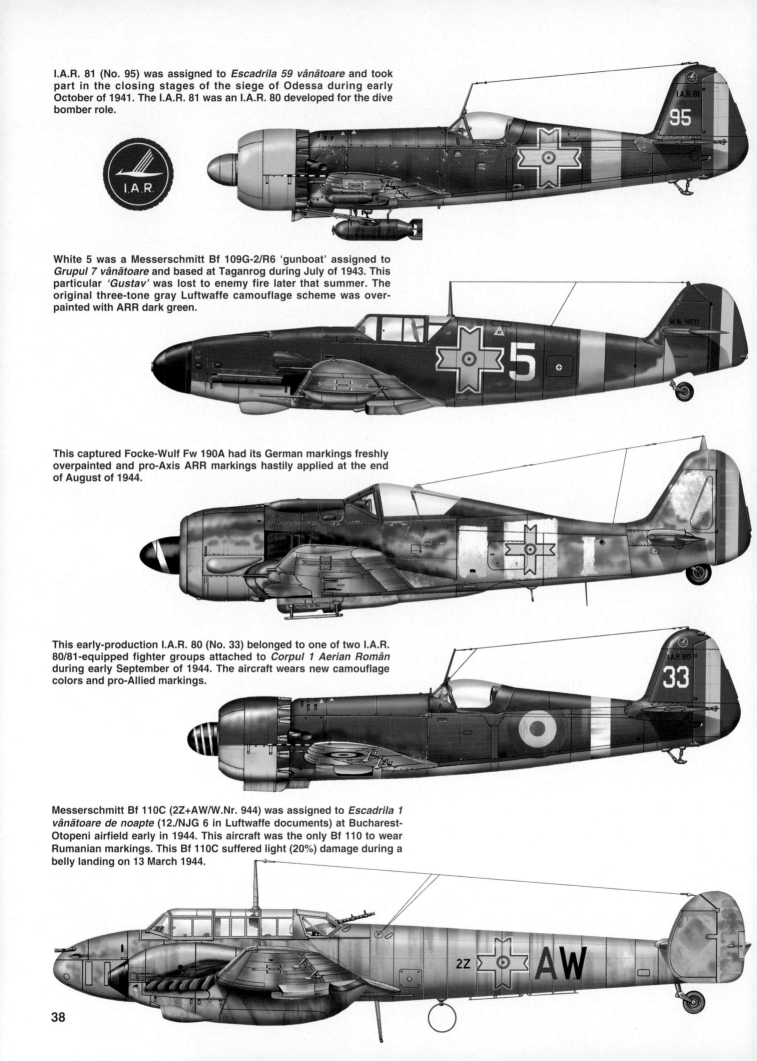

White 5 was a Messerschmitt Bf 109G-2/R6 'gunboat' assigned to *Grupul 7 vânătoare* and based at Taganrog during July of 1943. This particular *'Gustav'* was lost to enemy fire later that summer. The original three-tone gray Luftwaffe camouflage scheme was overpainted with ARR dark green.

This captured Focke-Wulf Fw 190A had its German markings freshly overpainted and pro-Axis ARR markings hastily applied at the end of August of 1944.

This early-production I.A.R. 80 (No. 33) belonged to one of two I.A.R. 80/81-equipped fighter groups attached to *Corpul 1 Aerian Român* during early September of 1944. The aircraft wears new camouflage colors and pro-Allied markings.

Messerschmitt Bf 110C (2Z+AW/W.Nr. 944) was assigned to *Escadrila 1 vânătoare de noapte* (12./NJG 6 in Luftwaffe documents) at Bucharest-Otopeni airfield early in 1944. This aircraft was the only Bf 110 to wear Rumanian markings. This Bf 110C suffered light (20%) damage during a belly landing on 13 March 1944.

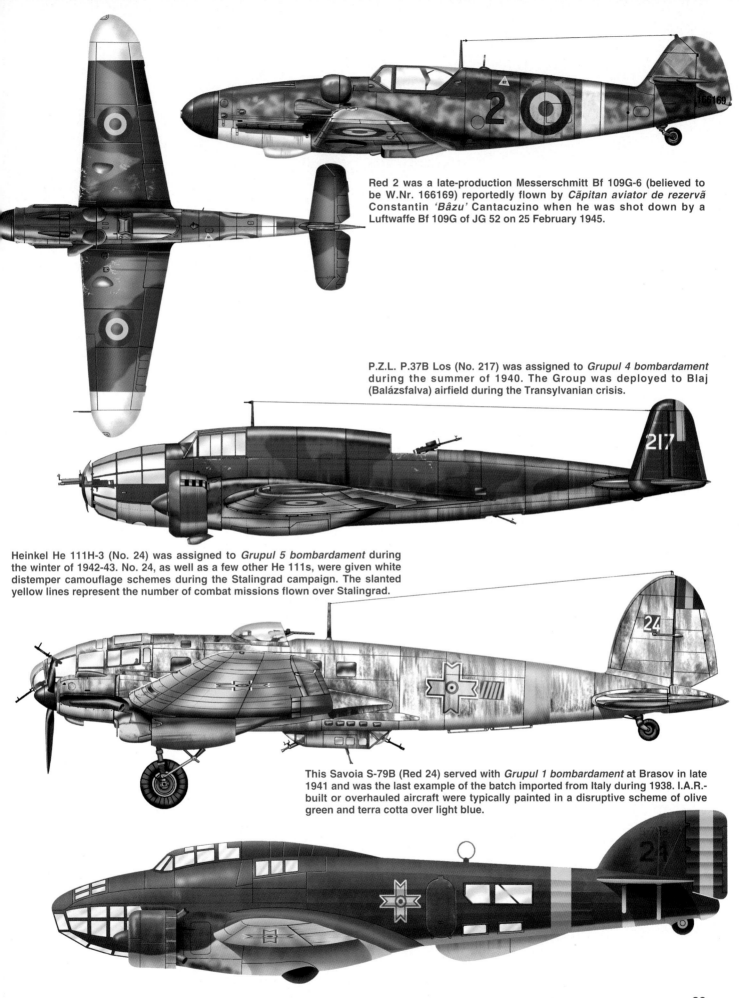

Red 2 was a late-production Messerschmitt Bf 109G-6 (believed to be W.Nr. 166169) reportedly flown by *Căpitan aviator de rezervă* Constantin *'Bâzu'* Cantacuzino when he was shot down by a Luftwaffe Bf 109G of JG 52 on 25 February 1945.

P.Z.L. P.37B Los (No. 217) was assigned to *Grupul 4 bombardament* during the summer of 1940. The Group was deployed to Blaj (Balázsfalva) airfield during the Transylvanian crisis.

Heinkel He 111H-3 (No. 24) was assigned to *Grupul 5 bombardament* during the winter of 1942-43. No. 24, as well as a few other He 111s, were given white distemper camouflage schemes during the Stalingrad campaign. The slanted yellow lines represent the number of combat missions flown over Stalingrad.

This Savoia S-79B (Red 24) served with *Grupul 1 bombardament* at Brasov in late 1941 and was the last example of the batch imported from Italy during 1938. I.A.R.-built or overhauled aircraft were typically painted in a disruptive scheme of olive green and terra cotta over light blue.

I.A.R. 81Cs of *Grupul 2 vânătoare* await their next mission on an airfield in Slovakia during the spring of 1945. The wingtips and rear fuselage band were painted white — the recognition color of the Soviet 5th Air Army. C1AR was subordinated to the 5th Air Army during the ARR's campaign against Germany and Hungary. The I.A.R. 81s were mainly deployed as fighter-bombers during this campaign. (Bernád)

Hauptmann (Capt) Helmut Lipfert, *Kommandeur* of I./JG 53, recalled the event: *"I intercepted one such* [Rumanian] *raid on 24 February* [actually 25 February 1945]. (...) *Two Messerschmitts were coming towards me, so I climbed up into the clouds. Before entering* [into the] *cloud I recognized their Rumanian markings. Perhaps the pilots were two of the Rumanians I had instructed at Tiraspol* [in the spring of 1943]. *A unique situation. I wanted to see what they had learned. Coming out of the clouds, I descended to just above the ground. I saw two machines above and to my right and approached them from behind and below. (...) With my speed I shot past them in the climb and once again noticed their Rumanian markings. When we began turning, I concluded to my relief that these two definitely could not have been at Tiraspol, as they appeared to be very inexperienced* [Hptm. Lipfert was incorrect; both Rumanians converted to the Bf 109F/G at Tiraspol]. *The enemy pilots seemed to be afraid to fly their aircraft to the limit and therefore made rather only gentle turns. Their aircraft also seemed to be rather slow, as I was able to get behind them on my first pass. After the first shots at the trailing Rumanian* [the aircraft of *Adjutant aviator* Traian Dârjan, Cpt Cantacuzino's wingman], *he immediately tried to dive away in the direction of enemy lines. But I sat on his tail, blazing away with my one machine-gun* [the other one, as well as the cannon, had jammed earlier]. *He took no evasive action, seeking safety in flight instead. (...) I didn't want to let this machine get away so easily. The other Rumanian* [Cpt Cantacuzino] *separated from his companion but did not come to his aid* [he actually did not even realize his wingman was pursued and in danger]. *Afterward I maintained an especially close watch behind and continued firing at the 'Me'* [Bf 109G-6, Yellow 9, W.Nr. 166248] *in front of me. It was really smoking heavily and then suddenly it crashed into a hill* [just beyond the Rumanian front line].

There was no fire. [The description is accurate. *Adj. av.* Dârjan actually was already dead when his machine impacted the side of a hill, having been almost decapitated by a .51 in (13mm) bullet]. *I regretted the outcome of this combat a little, because a proper dogfight with a Bf 109, flown by a pilot of equal ability, would have been something."* [Dârjan was not inexperienced at all. He had flown more than 150 combat missions and claimed 12 air victories. Had *Hptm.* Lipfert engaged the more experienced Cpt Cantacuzino, the leader of the enemy pair, the German ace would have probably had the equal fight he was hoping for. Cpt Cantacuzino, the top ARR ace with a total of 69 air victories, was flying one of the best Messerschmitts of his group. Destiny, however, decided otherwise. (All comments are mine, D.B.)]

Seconds after *Adj. av.* Traian Dârjan was killed, Cpt 'Bâzu' Cantacuzino's Bf 109G-6 (Red 2) was also shot down. Another pilot of I./JG 53 or an Fw 190F of SG 2 or SG 10 is believed to have shot down Cantacuzino. [No information, unfortunately, is available on the German pilot's identity.] Cpt Cantacuzino, unlike his wingman, was not wounded and belly landed his stricken fighter just meters from Dârjan's aircraft northwest of Detva. Prince Cantacuzino's last kill, his victory over the Fw 190F, remained unconfirmed due to the death of his sole

Cpt. av. Dan Vizante, commander of *Grupul 1 vânătoare*, is flanked by two colleagues and an unidentified woman at Miskolc airfield during early April of 1945. *Adj. av.* Stefan Florescu, one of the Group's pilots, stands at the far left. Vizante wears the prestigious *'Mihai Viteazul'* ('Michael the Brave') Order, IIIrd Class on his left pocket. Two late-production Bf 109G-6s (White 6 and Yellow 14) are parked in the background. The rearmost *'Gustav'* has had its Luftwaffe markings overpainted in white. The Bf 109G-6 had a top speed of 386 mph (621 kmh) at 22,640 ft (6900 m), and was armed with two 13mm machine guns and one to three 20mm cannons. (MMN)

Lt. av. Ion Galea stands in front of his Bf 109G-6 (Red 1) at Miskolc airfield, Hungary on 31 July 1945. Standing next to Galea is his fiancée, Klára, and her sister Magda — both natives of Miskolc. Squadron commander *Lt. av.* Tudor Greceanu, who shot down some 18 aircraft during the war, sits on the stabilizer of Galea's aircraft. The three pilots standing behind Red 1 are (left-right): *Lt. av.* Constantin 'Reazã' Rosariu, Ion Dobran, and Mihai *'Misu'* Lucaci. A row of I.A.R. 80/81s is parked in the background. The *vânãtori* stopped over at Miskolc on their way back to Rumania. (Galea)

witness. *Hauptmann* Lipfert also lacked witnesses to his kill and this was not credited either. Lipfert finished the war with 203 air victories.

The eventful day of 25 February, however, did not end there. A Bf 109G *patrulã* took off soon after Capt Cantacuzino and his wingman were shot down to engage the increasing number of Luftwaffe aircraft over the battle zone. The four ARR Messerschmitts were bounced from above by four similar Luftwaffe machines just west of Zv. Slatina. Two Rumanian Bf 109Gs were hit during the ensuing dogfight and were forced to break off combat and return to base. *Locotenent aviator* Horia Pop, piloting one of the damaged aircraft, recalled seeing — *"for a fraction of a second"* — a chevron on the fuselage side of a passing German Messerschmitt. The chevron meant that the German pilot was probably a *Staffelkapitän*. The only data on a Luftwaffe fighter pilot claiming a victory that day (apart from *Hptm.* Lipfert) refers to *Oberleutnant* Hans Kornatz from I./JG 53. Kornatz scored his 36th kill over one of the Rumanian Bf 109Gs encountered near Altsohl. This information leads to the question, could Kornatz's *Katchmarek* (wingman), *Fähnrich* Schuhmacher, be the victor over the other ARR Bf 109, flown by *Adj. av.* Laurentiu Manu?

Not all Rumanian Bf 109Gs were taken out of commission that day. *Adjutant aviator* Constantin Nicoarã scored hits on a German Bf 109K which eventually crashed. This rare victory of a Rumanian Messerschmitt Bf 109G over a similar (although superior) German fighter was also the *vânãtori*'s last kill of WW II.

Four engagements took place between ARR and Luftwaffe aircraft on 25 February 1945. Two of those clashes involved fighters. The Rumanians had four Bf 109G-6s shot down and one pilot killed while claiming two air victories. The Museum of the Slovak National Uprising located in Banská Bystrica (Besztercebánya/Neusohl) provided a third information source for this day's events. The museum records three Luftwaffe aircraft had crashed in the area: two Fw 190Fs and a Bf 109K. One destroyed Fw 190F-8 was from 3./SG 2 (mentioned earlier), while the other was from 1./SG 10 (possibly White 10, W. Nr. 584062). The latter Fw 190F was flown by *Uffz.* Günter Breckenfelder and was reported shot down by anti-aircraft fire at Drakove. The downed Bf 109K-4 was flown by an unidentified pilot from I./JG 53.

The Luftwaffe seldom appeared over the Slovak front after 25 February due to the German high command giving this front only secondary importance. Occasional high level, single-aircraft reconnaissance flights were conducted over Rumanian positions. Neither side's fighters, however, met in battle during the closing stage of the conflict.

The Bf 109Gs of *Grupul 9 vânãtoare* were primarily used for air

defense missions during the remaining weeks of the war. Low level attack missions against Axis columns and positions, however, were also common. Most of the ground support missions were flown by the I.A.R. 80/81s of *Grupul 2 vânãtoare*. Few flights were made throughout February and early March due to adverse winter weather. The only losses resulted from technical problems and take off and landing accidents.

The two Messerschmitt-equipped fighter groups flew 105 missions consisting of 328 sorties and 261 flight hours between 25 February and 24 March. *Grupul 1 vânãtoare* sustained one of the few ARR fighter losses during the last year of the war on 26 March. A Bf 109G-2 *celulã* of *Escadrila 63 vânãtoare* disappeared while escorting eight Savoia 79 and three Ju 88 bombers to Kremnica (Körmöcbánya/Kremnitz). The cell, consisting of *Sublocotenent aviator* Aurelian Barbici and *Adjutant aviator* Virgil Angelescu, defected to the Germans. The two Rumanian Bf 109G-2s, after a short tree-top flight, landed at the Luftwaffe base at Trentschin (Trencín/Trencsén). Barbici and Angelescu were guided in to Trentschin by *'Donau Funk'* (Radio Danube), the German propaganda station. The Rumanians expressed their willingness during interrogation to fight against the 'Bolsheviks' on the German side. The pilots believed the Germans were the only force capable of stopping the spread of Communism over their homeland. 2nd Lt Barbici returned to Rumania after World War Two claiming he had been shot down. (This is the first time the truth about Barbici's whereabouts has been revealed.) The fate of *Adj. av.* Angelescu, however, remains uncertain.

The two fighter *grupuri* moved from Lucenec to *'Tri Dvory'* (Badin) airfield, north of Zvolen, on 7 April. This redeployment was necessary to support the upcoming offensive of the Soviet 40th and Rumanian 4th armies. The offensive was aimed at capturing Trencín, a strategically important town in western Slovakia. Luftwaffe fighters rarely appeared, however, the German-Hungarian anti-aircraft defense was consistently effective and took a toll of ARR fighters up to the end of the war. Flak claimed *Locotenent aviator* Gheorghe Mociornitã of the 2nd FG over Vlcnov (north of Nemcice — Nyitranémeti/Niwnitz) on 21 April. Lt Mociornitã was flying his 29th combat mission when his I.A.R. 81C (No. 426) was shot down in flames by the AA defense of an Axis vehicle column. (This aircraft had arrived at the front from I.A.R.-Brasov only three days earlier and curiously retained its 'Axis-yellow' engine cowling. This cowling was recovered and is presently exhibited in the Military Museum in Bucharest.)

C1AR's most active day during the Czechoslovakian Campaign occurred on 26 April. A record 42 missions were flown by the Corps' fighters. *Grupuri 1* and *9 vânãtoare* flew 42 Messerschmitt sorties, while *Grupul 2 vânãtoare* added 68 I.A.R. sorties. C1AR units moved forward after that day to Piest'any (Pöstyén/Pistian) airfield, a former Luftwaffe base.

OPERATION PRAGUE, the final Allied offensive in the European Theater of Operations, began on 6 May. Rumanian troops and aircraft supported this effort with fighters providing air cover, and strafing enemy columns and positions. A cease fire order was issued to ARR airmen on Wednesday, 9 May. Eleven surveillance missions were flown by the fighters to monitor the German surrender. Further surveillance sorties were launched on the next day. C1AR's commander requested four volunteers to escort level and dive bombers sent against the still

Junkers Ju 88A-4 (No. 142) was assigned to *Grupul 5 bombardament* in Southern Ukraine during the fall of 1943. The 'Red E' was a leftover Luftwaffe code.

This P.Z.L. P.23 Karas (No. 17) served with *Escadrila 73 bombardament* during late 1942. The squadron emblem is a Russian-inspired *'Troika'*. *'Lest'* means counterweight.

Potez 63-11 A3s, delivered by pro-Axis Vichy France during 1942, initially retained their *Armée de l'Air* camouflage scheme, French serial numbers, and factory stenciling.

Junkers Ju 87D-3 Stuka (No. 9) was named *'Hai Pusa'* ('Come on Pusha', a Rumanian nickname) and assigned to *Grupul 3 bombardament în picaj* at Bagherovo airfield during August of 1943. On 2 September 1943, this Stuka was hit and exploded in mid-air, killing the pilot *Adjutant aviator* Alfons Auner and the radio operator/gunner *Caporal* Viorel Almăsanu. Stukas of the 3rd DBG did not sport 'Michael's Crosses' on the upper wing.

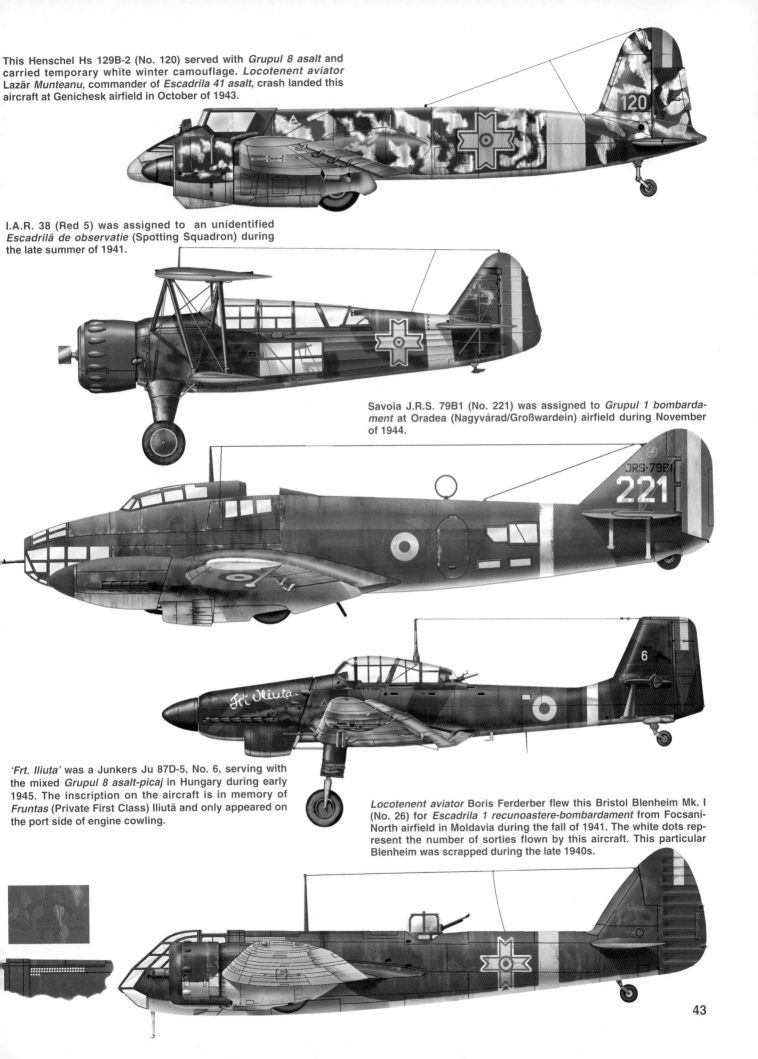

This Henschel Hs 129B-2 (No. 120) served with *Grupul 8 asalt* and carried temporary white winter camouflage. *Locotenent aviator* Lazār *Munteanu,* commander of *Escadrila 41 asalt,* crash landed this aircraft at Genichesk airfield in October of 1943.

I.A.R. 38 (Red 5) was assigned to an unidentified *Escadrilā de observatie* (Spotting Squadron) during the late summer of 1941.

Savoia J.R.S. 79B1 (No. 221) was assigned to *Grupul 1 bombarda-ment* at Oradea (Nagyvárad/Großwardein) airfield during November of 1944.

'Frt. Iliuta' was a Junkers Ju 87D-5, No. 6, serving with the mixed *Grupul 8 asalt-picaj* in Hungary during early 1945. The inscription on the aircraft is in memory of *Fruntas* (Private First Class) Iliutā and only appeared on the port side of engine cowling.

Locotenent aviator Boris Ferderber flew this Bristol Blenheim Mk. I (No. 26) for *Escadrila 1 recunoastere-bombardament* from Focsani-North airfield in Moldavia during the fall of 1941. The white dots represent the number of sorties flown by this aircraft. This particular Blenheim was scrapped during the late 1940s.

Two rows of I.A.R. 80/81s are lined up for a post-World War Two parade. The aircraft parked on the right display various propeller spinner shapes and some have had the lower undercarriage doors removed. An He 111H bomber converted to serve as a transport is parked in the background. (Antoniu)

fighting units of the anti-Communist Russian Vlasov Army on 11 May. This German-raised force of former Russian prisoners of war — commanded by Lt Gen Andrei A. Vlasov — had holed up around Prague and refused to surrender. Four *Adjutanti aviatori* of the 9th FG stepped forward to take on this final task which was regarded as a real mission of 'honor'.

C1AR's 88 fighters flew 423 combat missions during the Czechoslovakian Campaign. The fighters, organized into three groups of two squadrons each, flew 1160 sorties for a total of 975.31 flight hours. At least ten fighters were lost in combat, primarily due to anti-aircraft fire. No air victories were officially acknowledged.

The accomplishments of the *vânători* in the ARR's fifth and final campaign were summarized after the hostilities in Europe ended. Rumania's anti-Axis campaign lasted from 24 August 1944 to 12 May 1945. Twenty-one fighter squadrons with 210 serviceable aircraft were available when Rumania left the Axis in late August. This fighter total represented a 33% decrease from the force level during the spring of 1944 — and prior to the USAAF attacks. (It must be noted that combat losses in German-made *matériel* were partially replaced by the Luftwaffe until 20 August.) Approximately 60 to 80 ex-Luftwaffe fighter aircraft — Messerschmitt Bf 109s and Bf 110s, and Focke-Wulf Fw 190s — could be added to the 210 fighters available during late August of 1944. Forty six additional military aircraft were manufactured or assembled by I.A.R.-Brasov by May of 1945.

The *vânători* flew 701 combat missions from 6 September 1944 until the end of the war. These missions involved 2367 aircraft sorties and approximately the same number of flight hours. This sortie total was approximately one-fourth of C1AR's total sorties for that period.

Rumanian military statistics did not differentiate between claims filed by fighter pilots and anti-aircraft gunners for enemy aircraft shot down. This situation was probably due to the Rumanians avoiding displaying the embarrassing low number of enemy aircraft actually downed in air combat. A total of 101 air victories were awarded, however, only six can be confirmed as air combat kills. ARR fighter losses were also not separated from the overall figure. At least 30 fighters were destroyed by enemy action, while other aircraft were written off in accidents.

"The War is Over. What Now?"

Locotenent aviator Horia Pop of *Grupul 9 vânătoare* wrote this troubling question on the last page of his wartime logbook. The uncertainty of peacetime life in a Rumania now ruled by the Soviets and their Communist affiliates struck not only Lt Pop, but the majority of his colleagues as well.

Several Rumanian pilots reportedly took part in a large Allied-organized air show at Wiener-Neustadt, Austria, on 1 June 1945. These airmen were asked to represent German techniques and equipment, including the Messerschmitt Bf 109G-6, and provide a comparison to the latest US and Soviet aircraft types. *Căpitan aviator* Tudor Greceanu, a squadron commander, was among the ARR fighter pilots sent to Wiener-Neustadt. His personal Messerschmitt (No. 316) was the first Bf 109Ga-6 manufactured at I.A.R.-Brasov. Cpt Greceanu was also given the unique chance to examine an Me 262 jet fighter which was sent to the show for evaluation purposes. Other Messerschmitt pilots present at Wiener-Neustadt were *Ofiter de echipaj clasa a III-a aviator* Ion Milu, the third-highest ARR ace, and squadron commander *Locotenent aviator* Dumitru Baciu. Both airmen were assigned to *Grupul 1 vânătoare*.

Milu and Baciu flew over Hungary after the show while returning to Miskolc airfield. They met several American P-51Ds and waggled their wings as a recognition sign. The Mustangs waved back when the aircraft passed each other. A Soviet Il-2 formation, escorted by Yak-3s, came along a few minutes later. The pair of Messerschmitts again waggled their wings, however, the Soviets did not wave and flew on in the opposite direction. The last two Yaks suddenly broke formation and jumped on the two Bf 109G-6s. Milu already had 51 victories and decided not to engage the aggressors. He put his Bf 109's nose in a dive to shake off the Soviet fighters. 'Tache' Baciu was a competitive person, however, and decided to engage the Soviet pair. Baciu shot down one red-starred aircraft according to the memoirs of an ex-ARR pilot whose story could not be independently confirmed. Baciu's fighter was also hit and he force landed the aircraft, tearing off one wing in the process. He counted 16 cannon and bullet holes in his aircraft. Lt Dumitru Baciu may be the last ARR pilot to score an air victory in combat. Baciu was killed by an armed thug while delivering mail in his Po-2 biplane shortly after the war, thus, he cannot tell his side of the story.

Messerschmitt Bf 109G-6s line up for a review during the late 1940s. The mechanics are turning the engine starting crank while the pilots stand in front of their machines. Several aircraft display the high camouflage demarcation line typical of Bf 109Ga-6s built by I.A.R.-Brasov. The aircraft have had the white wingtips and fuselage band removed. The roundels and rudder stripes were soon to be replaced by red stars enclosing yellow and blue roundels. (Antoniu)

The first batch of Messerschmitt and I.A.R. fighters departed Czechoslovakia on 11/12 July 1945. These aircraft flew southeast to Popesti-Leordeni airfield, near Bucharest, the designated post-war base of *Flotila 1 vânatoare*. The flotilla's former home base of Pipera was occupied in the meantime by the Soviets. Many of these veteran pilots served for four years of war, however, only a few of these were under age 30. When the first veterans landed on the grassy field at Popesti-Leordeni they were alone — not even the officer on duty welcomed them home. Only a few peacefully grazing cattle presented a look of wonderment at the flyers.

Post-war reality for the ARR personnel was harsh. At first, the airmen's efforts were concentrated upon the great military parade held on 23 August 1945. This parade commemorated one year of alliance with the victorious Allies. Veteran ARR personnel were awarded many decorations. The highest military decoration conferred to a low-ranking officer for outstanding activity on the 'Western Front' was the prestigious *'Ordinul Mihai Viteazul cu Spade, Clasa a III-a'* ('Michael the Brave' Order with Swords, 3rd Class). This order was conferred on five *vânatori*, including *Capitan aviator de rezerva* Prince Constantin Cantacuzino, the highest-ranking ARR ace, and *Locotenent aviator* Vasile Gavriliu, the top pro-Allied ARR ace. [By that time — and during the next forty-five years to come — it was not 'politically correct' to talk anymore about the anti-Soviet campaign. Officially, the three-year long 'Eastern Front' was considered not to have existed at all. The decorations were given for events occurring after 23 August 1944.]

The strict resolutions of the Peace Treaty imposed on Rumania began to be implemented once the parades were over and the medals awarded. The number of military aircraft had to be reduced to 150 and personnel cut back to 10,000. ARR had already begun to revert to a smaller peacetime force by June of 1945. The three existing fighter *flotile* (Flotillas) were reorganized into two main units, based on aircraft type. *Flotila 1 vânatoare* consisted of the units equipped with the Messerschmitt Bf 109Gs, while *Flotila 2 vânatoare* brought together the I.A.R. 80/81s. ARR was reorganized again during June of 1946, with the two fighter *flotile* consolidated into a single unit — *Flotila 1 vânatoare*. Obsolete aircraft were withdrawn from service to be either scrapped or relegated to the training role. The Messerschmitt Bf 109G was the sole fighter remaining on active service. Most of these Bf 109Gs were manufactured by I.A.R., however, some of the Messerschmitts were of German origin.

The final reorganization of ARR took place during August of 1947. More aircraft were discarded which reduced the fighter inventory to less than 75 aircraft. Personnel reductions also took place with the first large-scale discharge of officers and NCOs from active duty. All but a few *vânatori* veterans were discharged, particularly those pilots who took part in the anti-Soviet campaign. These discharged veterans were sent without any government support into the civilian population. The government needed to make room for a new generation of pilots with the 'proper' social and political background (i.e., workers and peasants with Communist views). Aircraft of 'fascist' origin were also replaced with inferior Soviet fighters such as the Lavochkin La-9. The story of one of the most powerful Eastern European fighter forces thus came to an inglorious end.

Fighters and Fighter-Bombers

Aircraft Type	Manufacturer	Role	Start of Service	Total Number	Serial Nos.	Notes
P.11f	I.A.R.	F	1937	95	51-145	Polish license
P.24E	P.Z.L.	F	1939	5	1-5	
P.24E	I.A.R.	F	1939	25	6-30	Polish license
He 112B-1/-2	Heinkel	F-B	1939	30	1-30	
P.11c	P.Z.L.	F	1939	28+ [33]	301-311, 313-325*	Ex-Polish A.F., interned in Sept. 1939. *Also original Polish s/n. Originally 50 units ordered
Hurricane Mk I	Hawker	F	1940	12	1-12	
Bf 109E-3/-4/-7	Messerschmitt	F-B	1940	69	1-69	
I.A.R. 80, A/B/C	I.A.R.	F	1940	240	[see at right]	Nos. 1-90, 106-150, 176-230, 241-290
Hurricane Mk I	Zmaj	F	1941	3 [6]	13-15+	Ex-Yugoslav A.F., sold by the Germans. Flown in from Zemun, Yugoslavia
I.A.R. 81, A	I.A.R.	F-B,DB	1941	60	[see at right]	Nos. 91-105, 151-175, 231-240, 291-300
I.A.R. 81C	I.A.R.	F	1943	161	301-450+	Production concluded in July 1944. A few units completed after that date
Bf 109F-2/-4	Messerschmitt	F	1943	5+*	N/A	Some 'Fs used with German numbers & markings. *Including captured Luftwaffe aircraft
Bf 109G-2/-4/-6	Messerschmitt	F	1943	200+	1-43+ (Colors)	
Bf 110C, D, F	Messerschmitt	F	1943	24+* [18]	German Codes	Night fighter role *Includes captured aircraft
Bf 109Ga-4/Ga-6	I.A.R.	F	1945	75	301-375	Deployed to the front only from April 1945. Production concluded post-war

Fighter Trainers

Aircraft Type	Manufacturer	Start of Service	Total Number	Serial Nos.	Notes
I.A.R. 14	I.A.R.	1934	20	1-20	Rarely used
S.E.T. XV	S.E.T.	1934	1	1	Prototype, rarely used
P.11b	P.Z.L.	1934	50	1-50	
P.7a	P.Z.L.	1939	13+ [14]	1-13+Polish s/n	Ex-Polish A.F., interned in September 1939
P.11a	P.Z.L.	1939	10+ [10]	312, 326-328+, Polish s/n	Ex-Polish A.F., interned in September 1939
I-16 type 29	Polikarpov	1941	1+	1	Ex-VVS, captured by *Escadrila 19 observatie* near Dorohoi (Northern Moldavia) on 8 July 1941
MiG-3	Mikoyan-Gurevich	1941	1+	2	Ex-VVS, captured by *Escadrila 19 observatie* at Melitopol airfield (Ukraine) on 3 December 1941
Bf 109G-2	BFW & I.A.R.	1944	48	201-248	Assembled at I.A.R.-Brasov. Not used operationally
Fw 190A, F	Focke-Wulf	1944	22+	N/A	Ex-Luftwaffe, captured at the end of August 1944. Not used operationally. Majority confiscated by the Red Army
Bf 109G-12	Messerschmitt	1944	1	N/A	Ex-Luftwaffe, captured in September 1944 at Arad air field, confiscated by the Red Army

Note: F = Fighter, F-B = Fighter-Bomber, DB = Dive Bomber, [X] = Data from sources of the originating country

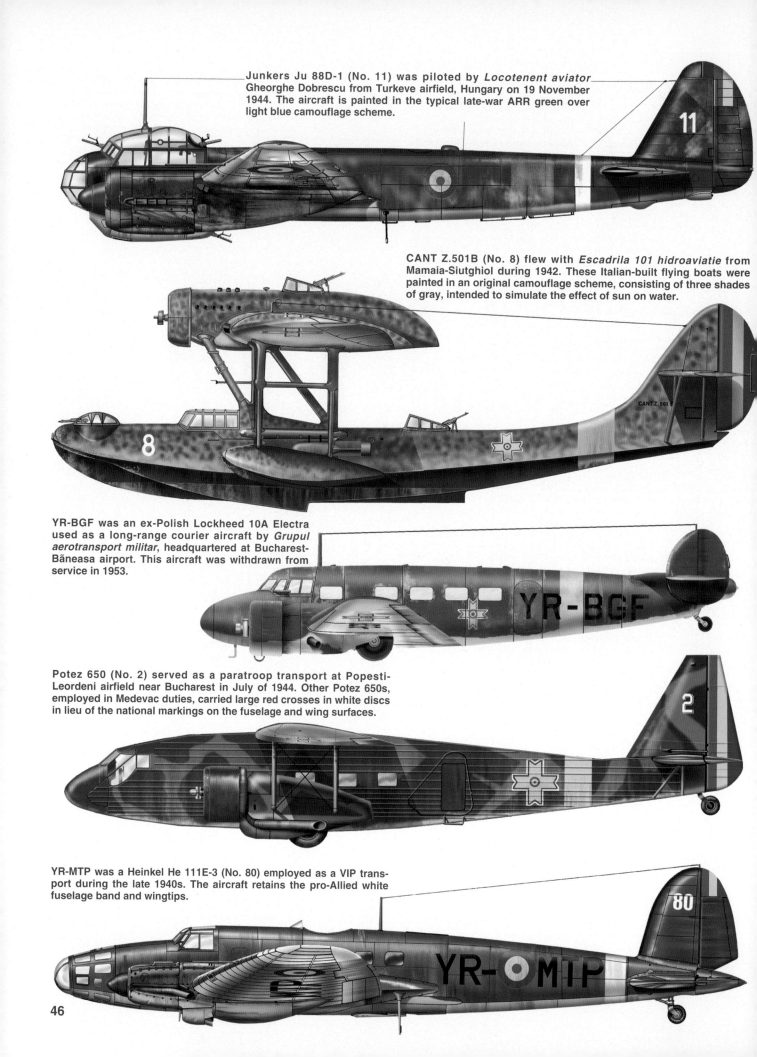

Junkers Ju 88D-1 (No. 11) was piloted by *Locotenent aviator* Gheorghe Dobrescu from Turkeve airfield, Hungary on 19 November 1944. The aircraft is painted in the typical late-war ARR green over light blue camouflage scheme.

CANT Z.501B (No. 8) flew with *Escadrila 101 hidroaviatie* from Mamaia-Siutghiol during 1942. These Italian-built flying boats were painted in an original camouflage scheme, consisting of three shades of gray, intended to simulate the effect of sun on water.

YR-BGF was an ex-Polish Lockheed 10A Electra used as a long-range courier aircraft by *Grupul aerotransport militar*, headquartered at Bucharest-Bāneasa airport. This aircraft was withdrawn from service in 1953.

Potez 650 (No. 2) served as a paratroop transport at Popesti-Leordeni airfield near Bucharest in July of 1944. Other Potez 650s, employed in Medevac duties, carried large red crosses in white discs in lieu of the national markings on the fuselage and wing surfaces.

YR-MTP was a Heinkel He 111E-3 (No. 80) employed as a VIP transport during the late 1940s. The aircraft retains the pro-Allied white fuselage band and wingtips.

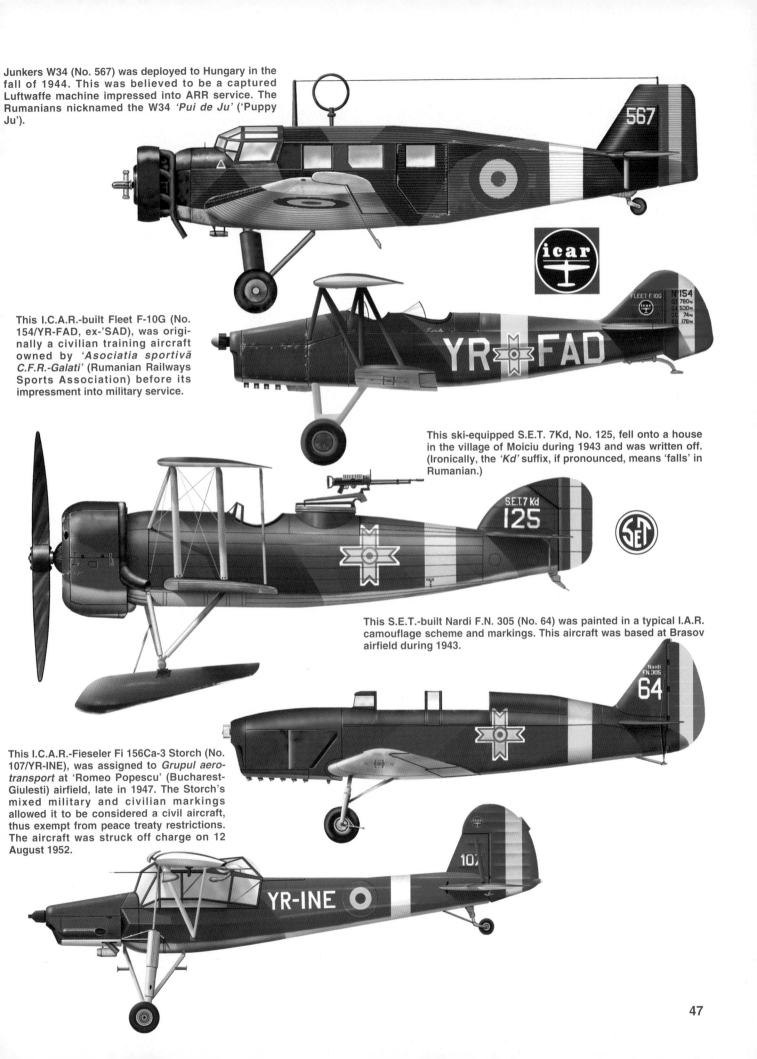

Junkers W34 (No. 567) was deployed to Hungary in the fall of 1944. This was believed to be a captured Luftwaffe machine impressed into ARR service. The Rumanians nicknamed the W34 *'Pui de Ju'* ('Puppy Ju').

This I.C.A.R.-built Fleet F-10G (No. 154/YR-FAD, ex-'SAD), was originally a civilian training aircraft owned by *'Asociatia sportivã C.F.R.-Galati'* (Rumanian Railways Sports Association) before its impressment into military service.

This ski-equipped S.E.T. 7Kd, No. 125, fell onto a house in the village of Moiciu during 1943 and was written off. (Ironically, the *'Kd'* suffix, if pronounced, means 'falls' in Rumanian.)

This S.E.T.-built Nardi F.N. 305 (No. 64) was painted in a typical I.A.R. camouflage scheme and markings. This aircraft was based at Brasov airfield during 1943.

This I.C.A.R.-Fieseler Fi 156Ca-3 Storch (No. 107/YR-INE), was assigned to *Grupul aerotransport* at 'Romeo Popescu' (Bucharest-Giulesti) airfield, late in 1947. The Storch's mixed military and civilian markings allowed it to be considered a civil aircraft, thus exempt from peace treaty restrictions. The aircraft was struck off charge on 12 August 1952.

Bombers

During early 1937, the ARR bomber inventory resembled a giant museum rather than a modern and effective branch of the Air Force. The few existing bomber units consisted of slow and obsolete single and twin-engine aircraft. The ARR's traditional supplier, the French Potez company, had provided the vast majority of bombers in service at that time.

The June 1936 re-equipment plan called for 406 new aircraft to be purchased from foreign sources. Sixty-four bombers were included in the plan. These bombers were to form four new groups of two squadrons each. (At that time, an ARR bomber squadron consisted of eight aircraft). No bombers were to be held in reserve due to the pressing need to re-equip the bomber force. Political debates in Bucharest prevented the first order from being placed until May of 1937. The initial order was placed, not with the traditional French suppliers, but with Italy's Savoia-Marchetti company. Initially, the Italians offered the three-engine S.M. 79 bomber, which was to see combat service in the Spanish Civil War. ARR preferred twin-engine bombers, however, and required their bombers to be powered by Rumanian-built Gnome & Rhône 14K radial engines. Rumania ordered 24 Savoia S-79Bs (ARR designation), which was a twin-engine variant of the tri-motored S.M. 79. Twenty-two S-79Bs arrived in the country by September of 1938. One had crashed in Italy, while the other was lost over Yugoslavia during its delivery flight.

The modern, low-wing bomber became instantly popular with ARR personnel. Accordingly, an order was placed for an additional 36 S-79Bs to be produced under license by the I.A.R. Works even before the last S-79B had been delivered from Italy. The 870 hp K14 II radial engine was initially planned to power the aircraft in either a twin or later three-engine configuration, however, the engine offered insufficient power for ARR requirements. Therefore, the Rumanians decided to use the German-built 1200 hp Jumo 211Da in-line engine in the I.A.R.-built S-79Bs. The airframe redesign required to accept the new powerplant was beyond the I.A.R. Works' design capabilities. Consequently, in early 1940 ARR placed an order with S.I.A.I. for several Jumo-powered Savoias. These aircraft were to be delivered within three months — a deadline that would not be met.

The Rumanian military's powerful French lobby persuaded government officials to balance the Italian purchase with additional orders from French aircraft manufacturers. Immediately after placing the S-79B order, ARR ordered ten MB 210 Bn4s from the Marcel Bloch Company. Additionally, 20 Potez 633 B2 two-seat, twin-engine light bombers were ordered from the Henri Potez Company in March of 1938. The order included 50 Gnome & Rhône 14M radial engines and

an option for ten more aircraft. By the end of the 1930s, ARR had in its inventory all 64 foreign-made bombers that had been requested in the June 1936 modernization plan. Although delayed, the build-up of a potent Rumanian bomber force was underway.

Restructuring

The large number of incoming new bombers forced ARR to both modernize the structure of their bomber units and create new ones. *Flotila 1 bombardament* (1st Bomber Flotilla) was created on 1 April 1937 and based structurally on the existing *Flotila de luptă* (Combat Flotilla). The new unit was based at Brasov (Brassó/Kronstadt) airfield. *Grupul 1 bombardament* (1st Bomber Group) was formed in early 1938 to incorporate the expected 24 Savoia S-79Bs from Italy. The Potez 633 B2s were allocated to *Grupul 2 bombardament* which was formed the following year. By April of 1939, the ARR inventory listed a meager 19 available first-line bombers which represented only 7% of all serviceable aircraft present. These bombers included six Savoia S-79Bs, six Potez 543s, and seven Bloch 210s.

A significant number of light and medium bombers were among the over 250 Polish aircraft that sought refuge in Rumania during mid-September of 1939. Among them, 19 single-engine P.Z.L. P.23 Karas light bombers and 23 twin-engine P.Z.L. P.37 Los medium bombers were recovered and impressed into ARR service. The first batch of 32 modern Heinkel He 111H-3s arrived from Germany during January of 1940. *Flotila 1 bombardament* was split to accommodate the new aircraft in early 1940. The new *Flotila 2 bombardament* was based at Buzău and incorporated the 1st BG (Savoia S-79B) and the 2nd BG (Potez 633 B2). A training squadron equipped with the Focke-Wulf Fw 58 Weihe completed the new flotilla. The recently arrived He 111H-3 'heavy' bombers were assigned to *Grupul 5 bombardament*, 1st BF. *Grupul 4 bombardament* was equipped with the P.Z.L. P.37A and B Los. The flotilla's training squadron included the surviving older multi-engine aircraft.

A third bomber unit, *Flotila 3 bombardament*, was formed on 26 November 1940. This unit was based at Craiova, Wallachia and inherited the remaining bomber aircraft — I.A.R. 37s, Bloch 210s, and Potez 543s. The regiment also took charge of all 35 Bristol Blenheim Mk Is. The Blenheims had been acquired the previous fall for the long-range reconnaissance mission, but also possessed a secondary bombing capability. Additionally, the 3rd BF received the obsolescent P.Z.L. P.23 Karas light bombers which were used to form *Escadrila 73 bombardament*.

ARR bombers saw their first action during the Transylvanian crisis in the summer of 1940. Tensions increased between Rumania and Hungary over the disputed region during August. A *celulă* (cell, a two-aircraft formation) of Heinkel He 111H-3s periodically took off from Brasov during that month in order to monitor, and possibly engage, the long-range reconnaissance aircraft of the *Magyar Királyi Honvéd Légierö* (MKHL; Royal Hungarian Air Force). MKHL Junkers Ju 86Ks and Heinkel He 70Ks regularly penetrated Transylvanian airspace, however, no encounters involving these aircraft were recorded.

War in the East

During early June of 1941, all ARR bomber units were consolidated as part of the build-up for the planned attack on the USSR. The bombers were placed under the command of *Gruparea Aeriană de Luptă* (GAL; Air Combat Grouping), which was the main combat element of the Rumanian air force assembled for the invasion.

The Potez 543 had served with ARR in the bomber role for only two years by the time the Second World War began in September of 1939. The obsolescent aircraft were then relegated to training and transport duties. (Bujor)

GAL bomber units were composed of:
1. *Grupul 1 bombardament* (*Escadrile 71 & 72 bombardament*), equipped with Savoia S-79Bs (part of *Flotila 2 bombardament*);
2. *Grupul 2 bombardament* (*Escadrile 74 & 75 bombardament*), equipped with Potez 633 B2s (part of *Flotila 1 bombardament*);
3. *Grupul 4 bombardament* (*Escadrile 76 & 77 bombardament*), equipped with P.Z.L. P.37A and B (part of *Flotila 1 bombardament*);
4. *Grupul 5 bombardament* (*Escadrile 78, 79 & 80 bombardament*), equipped with Heinkel He 111H-3s (part of *Flotila 1 bombardament*); and
5. *Grupul 6 mixt de bombardament* (*Escadrila 82 bombardament*, equipped with Bloch MB 210s and *Escadrila 18 bombardament*, equipped with I.A.R. 37s; part of *Flotila 2 bombardament*).

GAL inventory listed a total of 80 serviceable and 18 unserviceable bombers on 22 June. This serviceable/unserviceable total was broken down by type: 16/6 Savoia S-79B, 15/2 Potez 633 B2, 12/3 P.Z.L. P.37A and B, 23/4 Heinkel He 111H-3, 8/1 I.A.R. 37, and 6/2 Bloch MB 210. These bombers comprised approximately 41% of GAL inventory and 16% of all ARR aircraft participating in the attack. The Blenheims, although part of *Flotila 3 bombardament*, were used primarily in the long-range reconnaissance role rather than as bombers, while the P.Z.L. P.23 light bombers were not yet operational.

The basic element of a bomber squadron was a *patrulă* (patrol), which consisted of three aircraft flying in a 'V' formation. The bombers' tactical doctrine called for flying below 984.3 feet (300 m) to avoid enemy anti-aircraft fire. These tactics were ill-conceived and caused severe losses. Therefore, the tactics were soon revised.

The first day of the ARR's initial campaign against the Soviet Union was the bombers' busiest day. All 11 squadrons were sent into combat where they were to strike Soviet airfields in Bessarabia. The slow and vulnerable Bloch 210s of *Escadrila 82 bombardament* were sent after dusk to raid the airfield at Akkerman (Cetatea Albă in Rumanian). The bombing raids that day and night produced satisfactory results. Initially, the *bombardieri* (bomber crews) claimed almost 100 V-VS (*Voyenno-vozdushniye sily*; Soviet Air Force) aircraft destroyed on the ground on 22 June. Ten S-79Bs and nine P.37A and Bs claimed to have destroyed at least 36 aircraft on Bulgărica airfield. Bolgad was hit by six S-79Bs and seven Potez 633s which claimed 37 Soviet aircraft destroyed. Eight I.A.R. 37s hit Izmail and claimed to have knocked out several aircraft. Two airfields near Kishinev were attacked by 17 He 111H-3s with 10 to 12 aircraft claimed destroyed. Post-bombing information gathered by

reconnaissance aircraft later resulted in the destroyed aircraft claims being reduced from almost 100 to 37. Nine bombers were lost to Soviet fighters and anti-aircraft fire. This was the heaviest single-day loss during ARR's participation in World War Two. The losses included three Potez 633s, two S-79Bs, two P.37Bs, and two I.A.R. 37s.

A Soviet report for 22 June states that at 1400 hrs 17 aircraft from 96 OIAE ChF (96th Fighter Squadron of the Black Sea Fleet) engaged 14 P.Z.L. P.37s over the Danube in southern Bessarabia. The fighters were led by *Kapitan* Korobichin and included 14 I-152 (I-15bis) and 3 I-153 (I-15ter) biplanes. The Soviet fighters claimed five 'yellow-crossed fascist' aircraft destroyed, including two by I-152s, without reporting any losses. These claims are exaggerated since the two Los bombers were actually destroyed by anti-aircraft fire. This rare Soviet report is valuable, however, in proving the V-VS presence above the Bessarabian battle zone. Soviet fighter pilots claimed at least 20 kills over ARR aircraft on 22 June.

The first Soviet aircraft downed by ARR in the Bessarabian Campaign was by an *Escadrila 72 bombardament* gunner on 22 June 1941. One of the Squadron's Savoia S-79Bs (No. 18) was attacked by six 'Seversky' monoplanes (actually I-16s) above Bulgărica airfield at 0345 hrs. One of the fighters was shot down five minutes later by *Sergent* Iak Peremaus, a radio operator and waist gunner. This victory was probably the first to be claimed by a Rumanian airmen and one of the first of any Axis airman taking part in OPERATION BARBAROSSA. The S-79B was able to return to Pogoanele air base south of Buzău, although it remained under attack by the four remaining V-VS fighters which had followed the bomber back into Rumanian territory. The ground crew counted 26 holes in the S-79B's airframe after the aircraft landed at Pogoanele.

During the first two weeks of the campaign, the primary mission of ARR bombers was to attack various tactical and strategic targets — airfields, bridges, railroad stations, as well as arms, ammunition and fuel depots. This mission changed on the night of 2/3 July, when the joint German-Rumanian ground offensive across the River Prut called for direct air support by the Rumanian bombers.

The week of 7/13 July saw the heaviest fighting in the Bessarabian Campaign. Combat peaked on 12 July around the bridgehead created by units of *Corpul 5 armată* (5th Army Corps) across the Prut at Fălciu. Strong Soviet resistance at Fălciu threatened to push the Rumanians back across the river. GAL flew nine missions totaling 59 bombers between 0850 and 1940 hrs and dropped 40.8 tons (37 metric tons) of bombs. The Rumanian air strikes, according to a prisoner's testimony,

Savoia S-79B (No. 6) bellied in at Dobruja near the Black Sea on 15 May 1941. This aircraft retains the original three-tone Italian camouflage, and has been painted with a narrow yellow fuselage band. This marking was adopted prior to the Axis invasion of Yugoslavia in April of 1941. The 'Michael's Cross' national emblem has not yet been applied to this aircraft. (Crăciunoiu-Modelism)

This P.Z.L. P.23 Karas was one of over 250 Polish aircraft which sought refuge from the combined German and Soviet invasion of Poland. Bombers comprised some 20% of the Polish aircraft which fled to Rumania during September of 1939. By the summer of 1941, the P.23s were already obsolete. Nevertheless, the P.23s were widely employed in the battle for Odessa during 1941 and at Stalingrad during 1942. (Bernád)

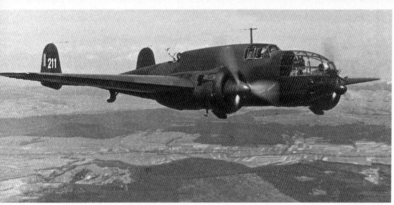

A P.Z.L. P.37 Los (No. 211) cruises over Blaj (Balázsfalva), Southern Transylvania, during the summer of 1940. The aircraft has been repainted in a two-tone ARR camouflage scheme and markings. Although still considered a modern bomber at this time, the P.37 had a tendency to enter a tailspin without warning. This particular Los was lost in an accident at Câmpia Turzii (Aranyosgyéres) airfield shortly after this photograph was taken. (Tulea)

resulted in up to 40% casualties among the Soviet defenders. The intervention of ARR aircraft stopped the Soviet resistance and cancelled the Rumanian withdrawal scheduled for the night of 12/13 July.

Battle for Odessa

GAL Headquarters was able to reorganize some of its units after the battle for Bessarabia peaked in July of 1941. *Grupul 2 bombardament*, one of the hardest hit bomber groups, was included in this reorganization. *Escadrila 75 bombardament*, which had lost its commander on the first combat mission, transferred their surviving Potez 63Bs to *Escadrila 74 bombardament*. The first batch of ten new Jumo engine Savoia J.R.S. 79B bombers was then delivered to the 75th BS. The new squadron leader, *Căpitan aviator* Ion Popescu — nicknamed *'Oita'* ('Little Sheep') — led the new bombers from the I.A.R. Works directly to the

front. These Savoias were originally numbered 1-10, however, these serials were changed to 101-110 in early August to avoid confusion with the older radial-engine S-79Bs. The first of eight Italian-built, Jumo-powered Savoias was delivered to *Grupul 2 bombardament* on 21 August. These bombers were designated J.I.S. 79Bs and were numbered 149-156. All serviceable P.Z.L. P.23 Karas were consolidated into *Escadrila 73 bombardment* on 3 August. This squadron joined the I.A.R 37 equipped *Escadrila 18 bombardament* to re-form *Grupul 6 mixt de bombardament*. *Flotila 1 bombardament* assumed direct command of the Bloch MB 210-equipped *Escadrila 82 bombardament*.

Bessarabia was secured by Rumanian and German troops on 28 July. The end of the campaign prompted additional reorganization within GAL. *Grupuri 2* and *4 bombardament* (Potez 63 & P.37) formed a special unit called *Grupul de bombardament Căpitan comandor aviator Cristescu* (Lt Col Cristescu Bomber Group), named after the unit's commander. On 28 July, the bomber force inventory indicated serviceable/unserviceable aircraft: 18/5 He 111H, 2/5 Bloch 210, 7/6 P.37, 5/1 Potez 63, and 14/4 Savoia 79. Confirmed data on J.R.S. 79Bs, P.23s and I.A.R. 37s is not available, however, it is believed that the serviceable/unserviceable numbers amounted to 8/2 J.R.S. 79B, 9/1 P.23, and 19/2 I.A.R. 37.

Bomber units, along with their restructuring, were deployed forward to new airfields in recently acquired territory on 8 August. This redeployment was immediately followed by a new operation aimed at seizing Odessa, a strategic harbor and communications hub on the northern shore of the Black Sea. The bombers flew tactical missions against such targets as enemy shipping, troops and reserves, communications centers, and railroad stations. The focus of the *bombardieri* switched to destroying military installations in and around Odessa on 2 September. The Soviets were aware, however, of Odessa's importance and amassed one the Southern Front's strongest anti-aircraft defense networks. The Rumanian headquarters was not fully aware of the anti-aircraft threat or possibly did not seriously consider it. The bombers were sent over Odessa at an altitude where the heavy flak was at its most effective. Two Savoias (Nos. 8 and 9) were lost on the first mission on 2 September and a third (No. 111) was downed one week later. A fourth J.R.S. 79B (No. 105) fell to Soviet AA guns on 12 September. Anti-aircraft fire was the primary source of other bomber units' losses. Veteran bomber crews insisted that the effective anti-aircraft defenses — not enemy fighters — were their main threat during the Bessarabian

Heinkel He 111H-3s of *Grupul 5 bombardament* are parked at Zilistea airfield in June of 1941. The propeller spinners of the Heinkel in the foreground are painted 1/4 white according to *Luftflotte 4* regulations. Just beyond the tail of He 111H-3, No. 1, is the tail of an unusually painted (large brown patches over medium green) Luftwaffe He 111 of III./KG 27 or II./KG 4. The He 111H-3 was the ARR's most potent bomber until the arrival of new German aircraft in the spring of 1943. (Bernád)

A row of I.A.R. 37s assigned to *Escadrila 18 bombardament* line up on a Bessarabian airfield during the assault on Odessa during late August of 1941. Various-sized and shaped 'Michael's Cross' markings are painted in front of or behind the yellow Axis fuselage band. A rarely-seen Gotha Go 145A (No. 11) is parked among the I.A.R. 37s. These aircraft are neatly lined up as the threat of a V-VS strafing attack was low at this time. (Bernád)

Campaign. Three-fourths of ARR bomber combat losses during this time were from AA fire.

The 75th BS, the Jumo-powered Savoia-equipped unit, flew one of the 1941 campaign's most outstanding bomber missions. The elite unit was tasked to destroy a large Soviet matériel depot near Tatarka railroad station. The depot was reinforced with protective layers of earth, concrete, and iron and appeared impenetrable by air attack. The Rumanians made several vain attempts to destroy the depot using various bomb loads, including the use of delayed-action bomb fuses to allow deeper penetration. Nine J.R.S. 79Bs flew on one mission against this depot during which anti-aircraft fire hit the starboard engine of Group Commander *Căpitan aviator* Ion 'Oită' Popescu's aircraft. The aircraft entered a tailspin and Popescu immediately ordered his navigator/bombardier to jettison the bombs and starboard fuel tank to lighten the damaged aircraft. The entire 4409 lb (2000 kg) bomb load and the 528 gallon (2000 liter) fuel tank were released from the J.R.S. 79B (No. 4). Popescu was attempting to recover from the tailspin when his Savoia was shaken by a huge explosion. It was later determined that the entire bomb load from Popescu's J.R.S. 79B had penetrated the top of the depot bunker and exploded the ammunition stored inside. Reconnaissance aircraft observed large explosions and thick smoke for days after the attack. The damaged Savoia returned to Tecuci on one engine.

The exhausted and decimated troops of the Rumanian 4th Army finally captured Odessa on 16 October. This ended the ARR's first campaign, during which the 5th BG had lost five out of its 22 existing crews when the war had begun four months earlier. This unit achieved spectacular results in spite of heavy losses. Other bomber units also performed well during the four months of the campaign.

ARR bombers flew 463 combat missions consisting of 3255 sorties during the 1941 campaign and dropped 2519.4 tons (2287 metric tons) of bombs. (Dive bombing missions performed by I.A.R. 81s were detailed in the fighter chapter.) Bomber gunners shot down 35 enemy aircraft — 17 of these were credited to He 111 crews — and 170 Soviet aircraft were destroyed on the ground by ARR bombers. Twenty-nine Rumanian bombers were reported lost. This amounted to 30% of the total number of available bombers at the beginning of hostilities. The losses consisted of seven He 111Hs, seven Potez 633 Bs, six S-79Bs, two J.R.S. 79Bs, three P.37Bs, two I.A.R. 37s, one P.23B, and one Bloch 210. Forty-eight 1st BF crewmen were killed in action during the Bessarabian Campaign. In total, over 70 ARR bomber crewmen killed in action during this campaign.

A Quiet Year

All GAL bomber units returned to their peacetime bases in Rumania by the end of October 1941. Surviving aircraft of *Flotila 2 bombardament* arrived at Tecuci on 21 October. The bombers of *Flotila 1 bombardament* reached Brasov shortly thereafter. New airmen were recruited to replace the personnel losses sustained during the Bessarabian Campaign. The bomber units, however, were of secondary interest since most young flyers sought to enter the fighter arm. New aircraft were also sought to replace combat losses. The first of 15 Heinkel He 111H-6 aircraft arrived from Germany in early 1942. These aircraft were nicknamed 'wide blade' Heinkels by the Rumanians because of their propellers and were equipped with torpedo shackles under the fuselage. The He 111H-6s were used to re-equip *Escadrila 78 bombardament* with the unit being renamed *Escadrila 78 bombardament maritim* (78th Marine Bomber Squadron). The surviving 'narrow blade' He 111H-3s were allocated to *Grupul 5 bombardament*'s other two squadrons, *Escadrile 79* and *80 bombardament*. ARR renewed their attempts to acquire Ju 87B Stukas, however, these attempts were unsuccessful. Eight new I.A.R.-Savoia 'Ds' (J.R.S. 79B powered by Jumo 211Da) and four older S-79Bs were transferred to the 2nd BF on 23 March 1942. These replaced Bloch 210s in *Escadrila 82 bombardament*. All 36 J.R.S. 79Bs were delivered to the newly created *Escadrile 83* and *84 bombardament* by June. When the last of the new Jumo-powered Savoias arrived at front-line units, the older and fatigued S-79Bs were disarmed and assigned to '*Scoala de bimotoare*' (Twin-engine School) for training duties.

At least twelve ex-*Armée de l'Air d'armistice* (i.e., Vichy French) Potez 63.11 A3s arrived during April of 1942 and retained their original French serial numbers. These aircraft were transferred to *Escadrila 3 pilotaj* (3rd Piloting Squadron) at Brasov to help train new crew members for level and dive bomber squadrons. (No trace of delivery of ten Potez 631 C3s has been found, however, five Potez 633s arrived from France, via Germany, on 25 September 1941. Four additional 633s arrived in Rumania the following month.) *Escadrila 81 bombardament* was re-formed during the spring of 1942 and equipped with obsolescent I.A.R. 37 biplanes capable of carrying twelve 26.5 lb. (12 kg) bombs under the wings.

ARR bombers, with few exceptions, were relatively inactive until early September of 1942. These exceptions consisted of occasional sorties flown by the obsolete, yet reliable, I.A.R. biplanes in the Crimea and the Caucasus region in support of the Rumanian 3rd Army. The lull

This early production Savoia J.R.S. 79B (No. 4) has opened its bomb bay doors prior to releasing its bomb load. This particular Savoia was flown against the main Soviet matériel depot near Odessa by *Căpitan aviator* Ion 'Oită' Popescu in late September of 1941. Popescu's crew destroyed the depot by a lucky hit after previous attacks had failed. This J.R.S. 79B was later renumbered 104. (Popescu)

The four-member crew of a faded P.37 Los (No. 202) takes a break between missions at Tarutino airfield in August of 1941. The aircraft was assigned to *Grupul de bombardament Căpitan comandor aviator Cristescu* and took part in strikes on Odessa. (Andrei-Aero Design SRL)

This well-worn Potez 633 B2 wears the rarely-used modified 'Michael's Cross' markings on the fuselage side. A wide yellow Axis band is painted aft of the fuselage cross. The aircraft has been repainted in standard ARR colors (olive green over light blue-gray), however, the latter color was applied French-style halfway up the fuselage sides. The Potez 633 was the ARR's favorite light bomber during the initial stages of the Bessarabian Campaign. (Moisescu)

allowed ARR to integrate its new equipment into the bomber force, train the new crews, and refine its combat tactics.

Over the Don Bend

Stalingrad was the focus of the next major Axis effort in 1942. Rumania participated in this campaign using its 3rd and 4th Armies, other ground units, and an air element. An air expeditionary corps, designated *Comandamentul Aviatiei de Luptă* (CAL: Combat Aviation

Command), was formed to support Rumanian ground operations. Two 'heavy' bomber groups were attached to CAL for this campaign. *Grupul 1 bombardament* of *Flotila 2 bombardament* was equipped with Savoia J.I.S. 79Bs (*Escadrila 71 bombardament*) and J.R.S. 79Bs (*Escadrila 72 bombardament*). *Grupul 5 bombardament* of *Flotila 1 bombardament* was equipped with Heinkel He 111H-3s (*Escadrile 79* and *80 bombardament*). A sole ex-Luftwaffe He 111H-6 was also present in this Group. (This aircraft is believed to be W.Nr. 4690, formerly G1+OP, of KG 55 'Greif'.) These two bomber groups were also joined by a 'light' bomber group. *Grupul 3 bombardament usor* employed a variety of obsolescent aircraft grouped into three squadrons. *Escadrila 73 bombardament* was equipped with P.Z.L. P.23s, *Escadrila 74 bombardament* employed the Potez 633 and Potez 63.11, and *Escadrila 81 bombardament* fielded the I.A.R. 37. (A dive bomber group — *Grupul 6 bombardament în picaj* — equipped with I.A.R 81s was also present at Stalingrad. This unit flew fighter and fighter-bomber missions which were addressed in the fighter chapter.) Some 50 single and twin-engine bombers participated in the Stalingrad campaign, representing approximately 18% of the CAL's total aircraft inventory.

ARR bomber units were deployed to airfields southwest of Stalingrad in mid-September of 1942. In early October, CAL was renamed GAL. By then, one or two bombing missions were being flown daily against tactical and strategic targets in the 155 mile (250 km) wide area between the Rivers Don and Volga and centered on Stalingrad. Few Soviet aircraft were encountered, however, the anti-aircraft fire defending Stalingrad was dense and effective. These defenses took their greatest toll on the 5th BG. He 111 (No. 16) was hit by anti-aircraft fire over Kotluban railroad station and crashed in flames on 14 October. Six days later, flak claimed the He 111 of squadron commander *Căpitan aviator* Mircea Holban south of Stalingrad with all crewmen lost. Another Heinkel (No. 28) piloted by *Adjutant major aviator* Eufimie Zaharcu was lost to engine failure on 23 October. An He 111 flown by *Căpitan aviator* Dumitru Popa fell to ground fire while overflying the Stalingrad 'shooting gallery' on 25 October. Accidents also claimed at least one He 111 in October. A damaged He 111 force-landed on the edge of the snow-covered Tuzov airfield and was rammed shortly thereafter by a Luftwaffe Ju 52/3m.

Despite the painful losses, bomber operations continued until the Red Army's offensive began on 19/20 November. When the Soviet armies broke through the Axis lines, priorities shifted to missions that attempt-

Ground crewmen with a 5 ft (1.5m) bomb pose in front of Savoia J.I.S. 79B (No. 153) in the summer of 1942. This aircraft was one of eight J.I.S. 79Bs imported from Italy during mid-1941. No. 153 was later lost in action. (Bernád)

ed to contain the advancing enemy armor, troops, and supplies. The bombers were also instrumental in flying in provisions for Axis troops cut off by the advancing Soviets. Much of this activity was hindered by bad weather, extremely low temperatures, and thick fog which resulted in few successful missions. Nevertheless, every effort was made by ARR personnel to put aircraft into the air to help their beleaguered comrades. Aircraft of the 2nd BF also parachuted or simply dropped supplies from low level.

The two Savoia squadrons suffered only two combat losses during this period. On 14 November a bomb released from No. 130 was hit by a flak shell the moment it left the bomb bay. The aircraft's entire fabric covering was blown or burned away by the explosion and the structure was heavily damaged. The aircraft remained barely controllable and the pilot was able to land the Savoia in friendly territory. Savoia No. 117 landed next to the damaged aircraft — despite the poor terrain — and picked up the shocked and wounded crew. No. 117 was shot down two weeks later by V-VS fighters over the Perelazovskiy-Petrovka area with its crew bailing out over enemy territory. The heavily engaged Heinkels suffered further losses in November when the He 111 of squadron commander *Căpitan aviator* Dumitru Mihalache was downed by AA fire over Chernicheskaia. V-VS fighters had usually failed to shoot down GAL bombers in the Stalingrad area in numerous attempts, however, they did succeed when several Yak-9s intercepted a He 111H-3 (No. 20) over Stalingrad on 30 November. The damaged Heinkel crashed on the way back to Tatsinskaya airfield.

As the Red Army advanced, Rumanian air units were forced to withdraw from their forward airfields. The Savoia and Potez-equipped squadrons left their endangered base at Morozovskaya and moved back to Tatsinskaya on 18 December. Tatsinskaya itself was evacuated five days later and the air units relocated to Novocherkassk. The hasty retreat left over 70 unserviceable Luftwaffe and ARR aircraft, including a Rumanian He 111H, on these airfields. Novocherkassk was evacuated after Christmas with all personnel and equipment moved to Rostov. The 5th BG was left with less than ten aircraft, of which up to five were usually available for missions. Losses of ARR bombers at Stalingrad were occasionally due to friendly fire. This was the case with Savoia J.R.S. 79B (No. 134) on 29 December. This 72nd BS aircraft was shot down by two Luftwaffe Bf 109Gs between Griasnovskiy and Alexandrovskiy, with the loss of all five crew members.

GAL was reorganized during December of 1942. Units not equipped

with German-built aircraft were transferred back to Rumania. Most of these aircraft suffered poor serviceability rates due to the lack of spare parts and other supplies. Only the Heinkel He 111Hs and Messerschmitt Bf 109Es, which the Luftwaffe could readily service, were retained at the front. These aircraft were combined into an ad hoc fighter-bomber unit, *Grupul mixt Locotenent comandor aviator Iosifescu*. This group was named after Maj Nicolae Iosifescu, the commander of the 5th BG. Only ten Bf 109Es and six He 111Hs were ready for operations on 4 January 1943.

A well-worn Heinkel He 111H-3 (No. 13) is bombed up for a sortie over the Stalingrad front during the winter of 1942-43. The temporary white distemper camouflage scheme has all but disappeared from the aft fuselage section. The Rumanian tricolor flash is painted along the entire rudder surface. Most ARR He 111s had the flash only on the upper portion of the rudder. (Antoniu)

The bombers flew up to four missions per day when the weather permitted. On 22 January, an He 111 under the command of *Locotenent aviator de rezervă* Mihai Oncioiu (observer and on-board commander) became the last ARR bomber lost in combat during the Stalingrad campaign. The Heinkel was being flown by *Adjutant major aviator* Ion Petcu when it was intercepted by P-39 Airacobras over the Don valley. Both engines were knocked out by Soviet fighters which forced Petcu to belly land the aircraft. Fortunately for the crew, the He 111 had crossed the front-line and landed in friendly territory where V-VS fighters usually did not follow their target.

As mentioned earlier, V-VS fighters generally could not inflict serious damage to Axis aircraft due to their light machine gun armament and poor tactics. Another ARR bomber pilot who encountered Soviet fighters over Stalingrad was *Căpitan aviator* Ion Profir. It is believed that Profir, with over 600 missions recorded in his log book, was the ARR's most experienced bomber pilot. During Profir's missions he encountered V-VS fighters about 65 times — roughly once every ten sorties. During these encounters, Soviet fighters seriously damaged his bomber only twice. Profir's gunner, *Sergent mitralior* Ion Gheorghe, achieved two confirmed victories.

ARR bomber units suffered considerable matériel and personnel losses during the Stalingrad campaign — primarily due to ground fire, accidents, or being left on hastily abandoned airfields. GAL lost 79 aircraft between 16 October 1942 and 15 January 1943. From 1 September, nine out of 15 He 111Hs originally dispatched to Stalingrad were written off. The 1st BG lost three Savoia J.R.S./J.I.S. 79Bs. Precise data on the 3rd BG is not available, however, the Group is believed to have lost two P.Z.L. P.23s and two Potez 63s. Rumanian bombers flew 1306 sorties and dropped 2203.2 tons (2000 metric tons) of bombs during the three-month period. The reduction in serviceable aircraft numbers resulted in the last ARR unit at Stalingrad being recalled to Rumania in mid-February 1943. At that point, the combined 'group' was left with a mere three Messerschmitt Bf 109Es and one He 111H — all based at Stalino.

Revitalizing ARR

After the ARR's second campaign, the political decision was made to acquire modern German aircraft — similar to those in Luftwaffe service. These new aircraft would re-equip the newly created *Corpul 1 Aerian Român* (C1AR), the ARR's main combat element deployed to the front. The new aircraft would replace all but a few old Italian, Polish, French, English, and older German aircraft types in service with ARR. As a result, *Grupul 3 bombardament usor* discarded its Potez 633 B2s and 63.11 A3s, P.Z.L. P.23 Karas and I.A.R. 37s. The Group reformed on the Junkers Ju 87D-3 Stuka, still highly effective on the Eastern Front. The 3rd LBG was redesignated *Grupul 3 bombardament usor în picaj* (*Gr. 3 bopi*, 3rd Light Dive Bomber Group). The Group's older aircraft were transferred to various second-line duties. The P.23s were relegated to the training role and sent to *Centrul de instructie al aeronauticii* (ARR's Training Center). The Potez 633 B2s were sent to *Flotila 1 vânătoare* for night fighter training, while the Potez 63.11 A3s were handed over to *Flotila de hidroaviatie* (Hydro Flotilla) for use against naval targets. The accident-prone and unreliable I.A.R. 37s were also relegated to training duties.

Gr. 3 bopi officially came into being on 1 April and consisted of three subordinate squadrons, *Escadrile 73, 81,* and *85 bopi*. The Rumanians initially learned Stuka operations using older Luftwaffe Ju 87Bs at a German school organized at Nikolayev. After a two-week training period, the Group was transferred to the large airfield at Mariupol to begin combat operations on the River Mius front.

The other bomber unit to be re-equipped during this time was *Grupul 6 bombardament*. This unit was officially recreated within *Flotila 3 bombardament* on 3 March 1943 and consisted of three squadrons: *Escadrile 74, 86,* and *87 bombardament*. This group received Junkers Ju 88A-4 level and dive bombers. The 6th BG's personnel arrived for training at the Luftwaffe bomber school (commanded by *Oberst* Weitkuss) at Bolshoy Fontan airfield, near Odessa, on 15 March. The first fatal accident occurred 22 days later, when a Ju 88A (9K+AG) stalled during a slow turn with its flaps and landing gear down. The Ju 88A spun into the ground 1.2 miles (2 km) from the airfield. Additional bombers and crews were also lost during the training period. The unit moved to Kirovograd on 5 May to continue training until the end of the month. Twelve brand new Ju 88A-4s were brought in from Kalinovka on 25 May. These were soon followed by 13 older ex-Luftwaffe Ju 88As. The 6th BG was considered combat ready by early June of 1943.

Grupul 8 vânătoare (8th Fighter Group), the last unit re-equipped at this time, was reassigned with a totally new purpose — assault. This group had been the first fighter unit equipped with the indigenous I.A.R. 80 fighter, but was re-equipped with the twin-engine Henschel Hs 129B. *Grupul 8 vânătoare* was officially renamed *Grupul 8 asalt* (8th Assault Group) and deployed to Kirovograd on 11 May. Conversion training

At least 12 Potez 63.11 A3s, taken from captured French stocks, were delivered by Germany in the spring of 1942. These aircraft retained their French serial numbers while in ARR service. This 'glazed-nose' Potez 63 is equipped with a two-bladed wooden propeller rather than the standard three-bladed metal propeller. (Mattiesen via Petrick)

This Henschel Hs 129B-2 (No. 214) was assigned to *Escadrila 42 asalt* during the winter of 1943-44. This aircraft has received temporary splotches of white paint to improve its camouflage. The white paint allowed the aircraft to blend into the snow covered steppe. Rumanian aircraft were rarely camouflaged with white paint. The Hs 129 spent most of its time at low level, strafing and bombing Soviet troops and armor. The port propeller has apparently been removed from this aircraft. (Bernád)

began on 21 May. Many of the 8th FG's pilots had been unenthusiastic about training for the ground attack mission due to their belief that fighter pilots were superior to bomber and assault crews. Nevertheless, 30 airmen — 12 officers and 18 NCOs — quickly converted to the new assignment and learned to love their steady and highly effective new machines. The 8th AG was redeployed to Mariupol-West on 5 August. *Grupul 8 asalt*, comprised of three squadrons — *Escadrile 41, 42,* and *60 asalt* — arrived at Kramatorskaya on 10 August with 30 serviceable Hs 129B-2s. The Assault Group, two months behind the other bomber groups, was finally ready for combat.

Along with the new (and used) German aircraft, a few new Rumanian types were also delivered to C1AR. The first I.A.R.-Savoia 'F' (a J.R.S. 79B1 equipped with the more powerful Jumo 211F engine) was delivered to *Flotila 2 bombardament* on 12 March 1943. These bombers were numbered from 201 up and assigned to *Escadrile 82* and *83 bombardament* — both new components of the 2nd BG. The J.R.S. 79B1s, however, were not committed to the front. These new aircraft, like the Heinkel He 111H-6s and P.Z.L. P.37s of *Grupul 4 bombardament*, were kept in Rumania for naval or reserve duties.

The ARR's Third Campaign

A large-scale air parade was held at Kirovograd on Saturday, 5 June 1943. The parade was viewed by *Maresal* (Marshal) Ion Antonescu, *Generalfeldmarschall* Wolfram von Richthofen, and other Rumanian and German dignitaries. Antonescu was head of the Rumanian State, while Richthofen was commander of *Luftflotte 4*, the parent German unit of C1AR. *Corpul 1 Aerian Român*, although insufficiently trained, was now considered fit and ready for combat.

Twenty-two Ju 88A-4s of *Grupul 6 bombardament* took off for Zaporozhye on 13 June. This was a large air base, complete with a command post and a concrete runway, which had been built before the war. The next day, the unit commanders took off to reconnoiter the Stalino-Taganrog-Zaporozhye triangle where their crews were to engage the Russians. The first combat sortie took place on 18 June, when each squadron launched a *patrulă*. Additional combat missions, normally two per day, soon followed. The first combat loss was recorded when a Yak-9T's cannon shells hit the cockpit of a Ju 88A-4 (W.Nr. 2559/No. 124) over Petrovskoye on 22 June. The rounds killed the aircraft commander and radio operator. The pilot brought the damaged bomber back to base despite being wounded in the right shoulder. The Group suffered further

Eleven pilots of *Grupul 3 bombardament în picaj* (3rd Dive Bomber Group) pose next to one of their unarmed Ju 87D-3s (No. 26/W.Nr. 110617) while it is serviced by a ground crew. This Stuka was lost in a landing accident at Bagherovo airfield on 30 September 1943. The accident killed both the pilot, *Adjutant aviator* Stefan Gherman, and the rear gunner, *Caporal* Constantin Stancu. (Moisescu)

losses in the following days.

The statistics compiled after the 6th BG's first month of combat were gloomy. Only seven out of the 25 bombers initially equipping the group were available. Eight Ju 88As were lost in combat, while three others belly landed due to seized engines. These three Ju 88s were recovered for later service. The fuselages of four machines twisted during extreme maneuvers, another turned over during landing, and the remainder were under repair. Approximately 20% of the Group's personnel were also

Ju 88A-4 (No. 132/W.Nr. 6651) taxies on the dusty runway of a Ukrainian airfield during the late summer of 1943. No. 132 had the yellow fuselage identification band painted immediately behind the wing and in front of the fuselage insignia. This location was unusual — most ARR followed the standard practice of painting the band just in front of the horizontal stabilizers. This Junkers received a general overhaul at the Luftwaffe *Fliegertechnische Gruppe* repair shop at Zaporozhye-East during June and July of 1943. (Bernád)

BOILER MAKER II was a B-24D Liberator (41-23782/Red E) assigned to the 415th Bombardment Squadron, 98th Bombardment Group. The bomber was shot down during OPERATION TIDAL WAVE — the low level strike on the Ploiesti oil complexes — on 1 August 1943. The Liberator is equipped with non-standard twin waist guns. ARR Headquarters decided to restore this aircraft to flight status and appealed to the Germans for assistance. *Hptm. Dipl.-Eng.* Hans-Werner Lerche, a Luftwaffe test pilot with previous experience flying the B-24 and other captured Allied aircraft, was sent to Rumania. Contrary to Rumanian sources, Lerche flew the Liberator — still in its USAAF livery — assisted by I.A.R. chief test pilot *Dipl.-Eng.* Alexandru 'Dudu' Frim. The 23-minute flight took place from Ploiesti to Zilistea on 3 December 1943. (Bujor)

lost. The 6th BG's heavy toll continued into the following month.

Locotenent comandor aviator Alexandru Zaharescu assessed the desperate situation within his Group in a report issued in early August of 1943. He indicated that the 6th BG had carried out 351 sorties during seven weeks of action and its gunners had shot down five enemy fighters. Thirteen aircraft (50% of the group's original inventory) had been destroyed and 23% of the crewmen killed in action. Zaharescu reported that of the 22 surviving pilots, nine were considered excellent, five good, and eight mediocre. C1AR responded to this report by ordering the decimated group to cease activity and re-deploy to Nikolayev. *Grupul 6 bombardament* transferred the surviving Ju 88As to *Grupul 5 bombardament* and started to re-equip with the increasingly available Ju 87D Stuka. The latter unit had been equipped with He 111Hs and was converting to the Ju 88 at that time. The 5th BG had more skilled pilots with extensive combat experience, two factors that made this unit more suitable for the fast and effective Ju 88. The best Ju 88 crewmen from the 6th BG also transferred to the 5th BG, which resulted in *Grupul 5 bombardament* becoming the ARR's elite bomber group.

Members of the 5th BG began transitioning to the Ju 88 bomber on 3 May 1943. The majority of the pilots and aircraft commanders possessed at least three years experience in twin-engine bombers and had dozens of combat missions logged. This resulted in an easier transition for the Group's personnel. Despite the apparent quality of the crews, accidents occurred. The first training casualties were sustained during a bad landing by a Ju 88A-14 (VH+GH) on 21 June. All aboard the Ju 88 were killed in the crash, including Luftwaffe instructor *Obergefreiter* Neumann. Conversion training ended on 10 August and the Group's three squadrons (*Escadrile 77, 79, & 80 bombardament*) were deployed to Zaporozhye-East air base. The newly trained crews joined the selected members of the 6th BG at the new base.

Between 11 and 14 August, the crews of *Grupuri 5 & 6 bombardament* flew a number of training and reconnaissance flights designed to familiarize them with the area of operations. The first combat missions were flown by the 5th BG against targets in the Izyhum-Stalino-Taganrog area and the Kuban region on 15 August. The Group suffered its first casualty five days later, when an AA round hit the port engine of Ju 88A-4 (No. 115, possibly W.Nr. 5692) over Bogoroditnoye. The

shell set the engine on fire and gravely wounded the pilot, *Sublocotenent aviator* Florin Vasiloschi. The crippled bomber was successfully belly landed in friendly territory, however, Vasiloschi died in his comrades' arms minutes after landing. He had recently celebrated his 24th birthday. The Group shook off this loss and flew additional combat missions to relieve the hard-hit Wehrmacht troops trapped in the mid-Donetsk area. The effects of the Rumanian bombings were officially acknowledged by, among others, General von Mackensen of the German 1st Panzer Army.

The crew of pilot *Adjutant stagiar aviator* Alexandru Istok-Suba achieved a double victory by downing two P-39 Airacobras over Bolshoy Tokmak on 20 September. The Ju 88, however, was hit by the Soviet fighters and force-landed north of Melitopol without injuries to the crew. The 5th BG paid the toll to V-VS fighters the next day. An extended *patrulă* was sent to attack Bolshoy Tokmak on the Group's third mission of the day. The Ju 88s, like the previous missions that day, flew without fighter escort. The five Rumanian bombers were suddenly faced with up to 14 P-39s and Yak-9Ts descending from the clouds and surrounding the bombers. The Soviets engaged the Rumanian formation *en masse* with concentrated cannon fire. A Ju 88A-4 (No. 115A) was flying on the right flank of the formation when it was hit by the fighters on the first pass. The bomber's fuel tanks were punctured and instantly exploded. A second Junkers (No. 135) was hit minutes later and severely damaged. The pilot, *Adjutant sef aviator* Eufimie Zaharcu, force landed the aircraft near Gavrilovka. Another Ju 88 (No. 119A) also fell victim to the Soviet onslaught and crashed near Dunyevka, killing all on board, including Cpt Ion Gheorghe, the commander of *Escadrila 80 bombardament*. The two surviving Ju 88As managed to return to base despite receiving hits by cannon and machine gun rounds. One of the victors was probably Aleksandr I. Pokryshkin, the second-leading V-VS ace. Pokryshkin claimed three Ju 88s while flying a P-39 Airacobra on the same day and location. Only one Soviet fighter was reported shot down by the bombers — an Airacobra shared by the gunners of No. 137 and 105. The victory over the Soviet fighter was cold comfort for the gunners due to the tremendous loss of the two crews sacrificed over Bolshoy Tokmak.

The Red Army's continuous advance prompted the 5th BG to evacu-

BOILER MAKER II was repainted in full ARR markings at Zilistea and ferried from Zilistea to Brasov, then to nearby Ghimbav airfield by I.A.R. chief test pilot *Dipl.-Eng.* Alexandru 'Dudu' Frim. The Liberator was set on fire at Ghimbav by marauding Luftwaffe Bf 109Gs on 26 August 1944. ARR personnel repaired and flew at least two more B-24s during World War Two. Captured and flyable aircraft such as BOILER MAKER II were primarily used to train fighter pilots in interception techniques. (Bujor)

A Junkers Ju 88A *patrulă* (including Nos. 127A and 105A) fly through Moldavian skies in a futile attempt to halt the Red Army's offensive during the early summer of 1944. These aircraft were assigned to *Grupul 5 bombardament*. The much-photographed No. 105A was written off after a hard belly landing at Ivesti on 21 August 1944. The letter A (and in other cases B, C, or D) after the aircraft's serial (tail) number indicates a replacement aircraft sharing the same number as one previously lost. This system was used on German-built aircraft of *Corpul 1 Aerian Român* (C1AR). (Bujor)

ate Zaporozhye and move to Nikolayev-East on 15 September. The 5th BG would stay there until the end of the year. The Group, weather permitting, usually carried out two to four missions per day. The Rumanians' victories and defeats reflected the fortunes of the war. The 80th BS lost its second commander, *Căpitan aviator* Demetriu Benedict *'Dem Ben'* Cârâc on 1 November. Cârâc was replaced by Cpt Wilhelm Schmaltz, an ethnic German from Transylvania. The last loss of 1943 occurred on 28 November, when eight V-VS fighters bounced a Ju 88 (No. 128/W.Nr. 8559) flown by *Adjutant aviator* Gheorghe Varjoghie. The severely damaged Ju 88 force landed near Rubanovka and burned out after landing. The bomber's gunners claimed two Yaks shot down before the forced landing. Both ARR and Luftwaffe officials rewarded the continuous efforts of 5th BG with several decorations.

The Group's 23 available Ju 88As transferred from Nikolayev to Tatarka airfield (near Odessa) on 8 February 1944. Tatarka, however, was found to be unsuitable for heavily loaded bombers. The group was forced to suspend operations for two weeks until nearby Dalnik airfield became available. The 5th BG's stay at Dalnik was also short-lived due to the Soviet breakthrough north of Nikolayev in mid-March. All 22 remaining Ju 88As were ordered to redeploy to Tecuci, a well-equipped peace time base in Moldavia (northeastern Rumania) in early April 1944. The move to Tecuci meant that the veteran crew members of *Grupul 5 bombardament* were back where they had started the war three years earlier.

Enter the Stuka...

The Ju 87Ds of *Grupul 3 bombardament usor în picaj (bopi)* deployed to the River Mius, north of the Sea of Azov, in early June of 1943. The Stukas were sent to participate in the Kuban Campaign and — like the twin-engine bombers — support the 1943 Axis summer offensive in the area. This offensive was launched by the German 17th Army, the German 1st Panzer Army, and the Rumanian 3rd Army.

Grupul 3 bopi had moved to Mariupol on 15 April after hastily painting Rumanian insignia on their recently arrived Stukas. The Group's air and ground crews continued advanced training with the Ju 87 *'Dora'*. The first fatal accident occurred on 22 May, when *Adjutant aviator* Marin Dumitrescu's aircraft failed to recover from a dive and crashed

into a house used as a target at Nikolayev. Both the inexperienced pilot and his rear gunner were killed.

The first combat mission was launched from Mariupol West under German command on 17 June. Ten Stukas struck targets in the villages of Lissagorska and Krinitshiy. These targets usually consisted of artillery and anti-aircraft artillery positions, troop and vehicle concentrations, ammunition and fuel depots, railroad stations, and trains. The 3rd DBG recorded its first combat loss on its second day of combat, when the Stuka of *Cpt. av.* Mihai Mântuță was damaged by flak over the Politotdelskoye area. Despite being wounded, Mântuță crash landed the aircraft at Mariupol. This marked the Group's only loss during June of 1943.

The 3rd DBG moved to Bagherovo, on the Kerch Peninsula, on 5 July. The Group's first personnel loss in action came the next day, when aircraft No. 29 was shot down by ground fire 0.6 mi (1 km) south of Proletarskiy. The pilot, *Sublocotenent aviator* Ovidiu Cercel, escaped, however, rear gunner *Sergent* Emil Dumitrescu was killed. Ju 87D-3 (No. 8/W.Nr. 100455) of *Adjutant aviator* Mihai Anghel stalled during take off from Bagherovo for the day's third mission on 18 July. This aircraft crashed into another Stuka (No. 27/W.Nr. 100338) which was preparing for take off. No. 8 burst into flames, killing both Anghel and his rear gunner, while No. 27, flown by *Adjutant aviator de rezervă* Teodor Negulici, sustained only minor damage. The *grup* lost two Stukas (Nos. 31 and 37) to flak on 7 August, however, both crews escaped unhurt. The unit's second crew loss came to the crew of Ju 87D-3 (No. 9, nicknamed *Hai Pusa*) on 2 September. A direct anti-aircraft hit destroyed the Stuka — instantly killing the pilot, *Adjutant aviator* Alfons Auner and his rear gunner, *Caporal* Viorel Almăsanu. Despite their losses, several important successes were achieved by *Grupul 3 bopi*. Three strikes annihilated Soviet troops and armored vehicles preparing to attack at Sapovakova on 12 August. Despite poor weather, the Stukas also set a large fuel depot ablaze 0.6 mi (1 km) southwest of Chankov on 16 September.

The 3rd DBG had carried out 119 combat missions and lost nine Stukas by 1 October 1943. That same day, the Group moved from Bagerovo to Rykovo Partizan, north of the Perekop Isthmus, to participate in the fighting raging south of Melitopol. The *'stukisti'*, as the

A pristine Savoia S-79B warms up its G&R K14 engines at Buzău-Zilistea airfield during July of 1942. The radial-engined 'Old Lady' was relegated to the training role by this time and all armament has been removed. A pair of Focke-Wulf Fw 58B Weihe trainers are parked in the background. (Bernád)

A *Grupul 8 asalt* Henschel Hs 129 B-2 (believed to be No. 122A) warms up its Gnome & Rhône 14M radials prior to take off from Kherson in November of 1943. *Adjutant aviator* Constantin Boghian, a pilot assigned to *Escadrila 41 asalt*, slides into the cramped cockpit of the Hs 129. Shortly after this photograph was taken, this Hs 129A was damaged by AA fire and destroyed in a hard landing. (Avram)

Rumanians nicknamed Stuka crews, flew 48 missions on this front. Three Stukas were lost in combat by the end of October, including No. 29 (W.Nr. 1145) which was downed by Soviet fighters on 8 October. The first upgraded Ju 87D-5s were reported in *Grupul 3*'s inventory during this period.

The Stuka *grup* officially ended their campaign in the Kuban Peninsula on 10 October, when it was fully integrated into *Corpul 1 Aerian Român*. The 3rd DBG was used to support the evacuation of Perekop during the retreat from the Kuban area. Their attacks were aimed at slowing the advance of Soviet armor closing in on the trapped German and Rumanian troops. The unit experienced a particularly bad day on 8 December, when two Ju 87D-3s were lost in action and a third damaged. The Stukas (Nos. 6 and 7) were downed by P-39 Airacobras and AA fire respectively despite escort by the usually effective Croatian flown Bf 109Gs of JG 52's *'Kroat. Staffel'*. Three days later, a Ju 87D (No. 20) flown by *Adjutant aviator* Paul Lăzăroiu suffered an engine failure and ditched into the sea. The crew was able to swim to shore.

Throughout the winter of 1943 and 1944, sporadic missions were flown on the front as the Russians moved south on the Kerch Peninsula. ARR Stuka crews reported flying only 62 missions by mid-April 1944, when the Kerch Peninsula was finally evacuated. The personnel of *Grupul 3 bopi* were withdrawn to Rumania after a year of continuous service at the front. The Group had flown 320 combat missions during that time. The Germans repossessed the 13 remaining Stukas on 10 April. Most of them were blown up on Khersones airfield, although No. 5A, for example, escaped full destruction and was captured by Red Army troops. During early May, some 25 new Ju 87D-5s were received by the Group at Malacky airfield near Bratislava (Pressburg/Pozsony), the capital of Slovakia. The crews flew the Ju 87D-5s to Tecuci air base on the Moldavian front to put the *grup* back into operations — just in time for the hot campaign of the summer of 1944.

...and the Henschel

The 'latecomer' *Grupul 8 asalt* equipped with Hs 129B-2s flew its first combat mission during the early hours of 15 August 1943. Twelve Hs 129B-2s bombed the village of Kotovka. Twelve Il-2 Shturmoviks, escorted by 16 fighters, struck Kramatorskaya airfield at 1820 hrs that evening. The Soviets destroyed one Henschel Hs 129 (No. 114/W.Nr.

140741) and lightly damaged two others. During the morning of 17 August, 46 assault aircraft carried out six bombing and strafing missions. The 8th AG flew these missions against Soviet troop and vehicle concentrations 0.6 mile (1 km) north of Sinskiy and east of Dolgenskoye. This attack created havoc among the Red Army units prepared to assault the German lines. The Germans intercepted a Soviet radio message at 1130 hrs which reported the impossibility of achieving any progress due to the repeated air attacks by Rumanian assault aircraft. The Henschel Hs 129 proved to be a successful and effective weapon in Rumanian hands.

The 8th AG suffered its first combat loss on 19 August. Hs 129B-2 (No. 317/W.Nr. 140738) was hit by a Red Army column's AA defenses during a low-level attack. Despite being wounded, *Adjutant stagiar aviator* Petre Sârbu attempted to fly his damaged aircraft back to Kramatorskaya. Sârbu crashed and died on the edge of the airfield.

Heavy fighting between the Rivers Don and Mius continued throughout the summer of 1943. The 8th AG was fully involved in the fighting and flew three to four missions daily when the weather permitted. The Soviet offensive in early September broke through the German lines south of Kiev and forced the 8th AG to fall back to Staryy Bliznetzy. One week later, the Group moved to Dnepropetrovsk where they stayed until 19 September. The 8th AG assisted in the fighting around Melitopol by moving first to Genichesk, then to Kherson. The Group moved to Tchaplinka on 29 October. The *'asaltisti'*, as the Rumanian Henschel pilots were frequently called, flew hundreds of sorties during those hard days — more than any other C1AR combat unit. There were days when the assault pilots flew up to 16 sorties from dawn to dusk, often with just a single meal and almost no sleep. The maintenance personnel provided excellent service which made the high sortie rates possible. The Hs 129 pilots were also helped by the short distance to the front — less than ten flying minutes from their base. The high mission rate also meant a high loss rate. At least ten Hs 129B-2s were written off and one pilot killed between 23 October and 2 November. Four Hs 129s were lost on 2 November. As with other C1AR units, effective anti-aircraft fire was the principal cause of these losses.

Several times during these missions a Henschel pilot would often land in 'no-man's-land', sometimes even in enemy territory, to retrieve a pilot shot down by AA fire. The pilot of the downed aircraft was put

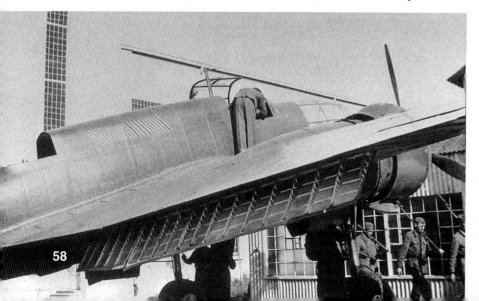

P.Z.L. P.37B Los (No. 220) is serviced at Brasov airfield in 1943. The aircraft displays 23 oblique yellow stripes representing combat missions flown on the Eastern Front. This P.37B was one of dozens of ARR aircraft destroyed on the ground by Luftwaffe fighters during the first week of September 1944. These obsolescent aircraft were parked on secondary airfields in Southern Transylvania when they were attacked. The lowered split flaps reveal their interior structure. (Bernád)

A Heinkel He 111H-6 (White 48) of *Escadrila 78 bombardament maritim* is parked at Călărasi airfield during the spring of 1944. On 7 May 1944, this aircraft was shot down by five Soviet fighters over northeastern Moldavia. The crew bailed out although the He 111's navigator/on-board commander, *Locotenent aviator de rezervă* Mihai Oncioiu, was already wounded when he evacuated the bomber. Oncioiu was reportedly shot at and killed by the fighters while descending in his parachute. The pilot, *Lt. av. rez.* Sorin Tulea, hit the fin while bailing out and was crippled for the rest of his life. (Tulea)

into the cockpit or the small radio compartment of the Hs 129. These unselfish acts of camaraderie strengthened the already close bonds among assault pilots — Rumanians and Germans, officers and NCOs.

The 8th AG moved to Lepetika on 7 January 1944 and then to Nikolayev on 7 February. The Red Army's seemingly unstoppable offensive prompted the Group to retreat to Tecuci airfield, in Rumania, by early April. This redeployment practically ended the eight-month-long Ukrainian campaign for *Grupul 8 asalt*. A new and more difficult phase for the assault group had begun with the fate of Rumania now at stake.

In Defense of the Homeland

World War Two reached Rumania's northeastern frontiers during the spring of 1944 — a situation many Rumanians believed would never happen. This alarming situation prompted the ARR Headquarters to concentrate all available resources to engage the rapidly advancing Red Army. The reserve bombers were formed into *Corpul 2 Aerian Român* (C2AR) and thrown into the fighting. *Grupul 4 bombardament* was re-formed to complete the elite bomber groups of C1AR. One of the two squadrons attached to this group, *Escadrila 78 bombardament*, consisted of 12 He 111H-6s transferred from maritime patrol duties. Another squadron, *Escadrile 76 bombardament*, flew obsolete and fatigued P.Z.L. P.37 Los bombers. These two squadrons deployed to Ianca, Moldavia, at the end of April of 1944. The two Savoia J.I.S./J.R.S. 79B/B1-equipped groups of *Flotila 2 bombardament* were also activated and arrived at Tãndãrei airfield on 7 April. These groups were *Grupul 1 bombardament* (*Escadrile 71 & 72 bombardament*) and *Grupul 2 bombardament* (*Escadrile 82 & 83 bombardament*).

Following a lengthy transition to the Ju 87D at Krosno in occupied Poland, the hard-hit *Grupul 6 bombardament* was ready to re-enter combat by mid-May of 1944. The Group was renamed *Grupul 6 bombardament în picaj* (6th Dive Bomber Group) and consisted of three squadrons — *Escadrile 74, 86, & 87 picaj*. The Group was assembled at Husi, Moldavia, where they joined the famous SG 2 *'Immelmann'*. (The top Stuka ace, *Oberst* Hans-Ulrich Rudel, was assigned to this Luftwaffe unit.) *Grupul 7 bombardament usor* (*Escadrile 17 & 18 bombardament*) was hastily assembled and equipped with obsolescent I.A.R. 37 biplanes armed with light bombs. Outdated Polish aircraft and Nardi

F.N. 305 advanced trainers fitted to carry grenades were assembled into a special, unnumbered group, called *Grupul grenadier* (Grenade Group). The Polish machines in this unit included P.Z.L. P.11c, P.23 Karas, and P.W.S. 26 aircraft. The slow and antiquated aircraft of this ad hoc group were intended for use as night bombers, however, no record of their actual combat use has surfaced.

ARR had assembled a significant, if somewhat obsolescent, bomber force in Moldavia by mid-April 1944. The force consisted of 12 squadrons (100 aircraft) in C1AR and ten squadrons (75 aircraft) in C2AR. The Rumanian airmen faced increased numbers of new generation V-VS fighters and pilots, in addition to the effective anti-aircraft defenses moving forward with Soviet troops. AA fire hit a Ju 88A (No. 112) over Motca on 2 May and downed a P.37 Los (No. 210) over Orhei the next day. V-VS fighters shot down an He 111H-6 (No. 48) on 7 May forcing the crew to bail out. *Sublocotenent aviator de rezervă* Mihai Oncioiu, the He 111 commander, was reportedly killed in his parachute by Soviet fighters. Oncioiu had been a recent recipient of the highest award for ARR officers, *'Mihai Viteazul clasa a III-a'*.

ARR experienced an unusually black day, particularly for the Savoia units, on 30 May. Three J.R.S. 79Bs and their five-man crews of the 1st BG (Nos. 101, 102, and 129) were lost to Soviet fighters while on their second mission of the day. Two other Savoias (Nos. 109 and 121) were so heavily damaged that they were written off after returning to their home field. Five Stukas and an I.A.R. 81 were shot down on 30 May, while two Stukas and a Bf 109G were damaged in combat over the Iasi sector. Three Ju 87Ds of the 6th DBG and five I.A.R. 81s were written off the next day. Several V-VS fighter pilots enjoyed great success over the Rumanians, including Cpt Ivan N. Kozhedub — the top scoring Allied ace. Kozhedub downed eight 'German' aircraft with his La-5FN over northeastern Rumania in one week during the summer of 1944. ARR bombers were sometimes able to turn the tables against Soviet bombers. Orders of the Day No. 96 and 101 of 3 July 1944 confirm victories by *Adjutant sef aviator* Stefan Pucas and *Adjutant aviator* Victor Dumbravã of the Hs 129B-equipped 8th AG.

Marauding USAAF P-38s and P-51s began to appear in Rumanian skies during early April and destroyed ARR aircraft both in the air and on the ground. One such case was an unarmed Ju 88A-4 (No. 133) flown from Ivesti on a technical check flight by *Escadrila 77 bombar-*

The pilot of an I.A.R. manufactured Savoia J.R.S. 79B warms up the engines prior to take off. The Rumanian version of the Savoia bomber featured a 'cut-off' nose section in order to improve the field of fire for the .312 in (7.92 mm) caliber Browning PWU machine gun. (Bujor)

Mât, a Junkers Ju 87D-5 assigned to *Grupul 6 bombardament*, prepares for a mission at Husi airfield on 14 August 1944. The Stuka is armed with a 551 lb (250 kg) bomb under the fuselage and four anti-personnel bombs with extended fuses mounted under the wings. The extended fuses were designed to detonate the bomb above ground level and maximize the blast and shrapnel effects against ground troops. This aircraft was sent into action against Soviet armor and troops advancing in northeast Moldavia. The name *Mât* painted on the cowling loosely translates to 'pussy cat'. (Bujor)

dament's commander, *Căpitan aviator* Gheorghe Stroici on 26 July. The bomber was shot down by a P-38J flown by Maj W.F. Gardner of the 95th FS, 82nd FG. (Gardner officially claimed an He 111 over Mănesti, however, the twin-engine Junkers could have been easily confused with the twin-engine Heinkel bomber.) Cpt Stroici had logged over 130 combat missions at the time of his death and was the recipient of both high Rumanian medals and the German Iron Cross, 1st and 2nd Classes. Reportedly, Stroici's father was visiting Ivesti that day and witnessed his son's death. In mid June, ARR Headquarters grounded this elite Ju 88A equipped unit for 'higher reasons'. This unusual order could not be fully explained.

'*Re-equipment of Aeronautica Regală Română*' (the air force's official title) was a prospective plan compiled by the headquarters at Titu on 8 August 1944. This plan called for all twin-engine bombers to be replaced by the Focke-Wulf Fw 190, the Ju 87D by the 'tank-buster' Ju 87G, and the Hs 129B-2 by a 'new variant' of this aircraft — believed to be the Hs 129B-3 which was equipped with a large caliber underbelly cannon. A Luftwaffe-assisted familiarization course on the Fw 190A/F began during mid-August 1944 at Lugoj (Lugos/Lugosch) airfield in Southern Transylvania. Due to political events this familiarization course did not progress beyond its initial stage. New bomber groups were to be created in line with the new equipment. The first of three planned squadrons of the new *Grupul 11 asalt* was formed in Craiova, Wallachia, using refurbished Hs 129B-2s arriving directly from *Henschel Flugzeugwerke A.G.* Other re-equipment plans existed only on paper.

The Red Army launched OPERATION JASSY-KISHINEV during the morning of 20 August. This operation ended three stagnant months on the front lines. Supporting the Soviet attack were 320 day bombers and 726 Il-2 Shturmoviks of the 5th and 17th Air Armies. (These totals do not include participating aircraft of the Black Sea Fleet.) The Soviets enjoyed an overwhelming four-to-one numerical superiority in aircraft over the Axis. The German-Rumanian front had collapsed by the early afternoon, and Soviet armored units penetrated the line at several points. Rumania's available bomber strength dwindled to the Ju 88As of the 5th BG, Ju 87D Stukas of the 3rd and 6th DBGs, and the Hs 129Bs of the 8th AG. These ARR aircraft flew alongside Luftwaffe Stukas,

Henschels, and Fw 190s in opposing the Soviet offensive. Rumanian and German aircraft knocked out dozens of Soviet armored fighting vehicles and scores of Red Army troops, however, these efforts were to no avail. The Soviet tide simply could not be stopped. ARR paid a heavy toll, losing at least two Ju 88As, five Ju 87Ds, and seven Hs 129Bs between 20/23 August.

The Turning Point

The Royal Proclamation announcing Rumania's exit from the war aired during the evening of 23 August. This proclamation took virtually everyone — Rumanians, Germans, and Soviets alike — by surprise. A tacit non-aggression policy was initially established between German and Rumanian airmen, however, the situation rapidly began to deteriorate by 25 August. Luftwaffe units began confiscating German-built aircraft loaned to their former ally for front-line use only. Some of these aircraft were later employed by the Germans in bombing the 'treacherous' Rumanian government's headquarters and other strategic sites in Bucharest. These confiscated aircraft included Ju 87Ds of *Grupul 6 picaj* which retained their ARR markings when used by the Germans.

Rumanian bomber crews quickly regrouped at *Flotila 3 bombardament*'s base in Craiova to avoid losing aircraft they considered their own. The majority of these crews succeeded in escaping from the Germans except for the aforementioned Stukas and six Ju 88As seized by the Luftwaffe. Other ARR aircraft were captured by still hostile Soviet troops.

Some of the Craiova-based ARR bombers struck Axis convoys retreating west on the Danube River during the final days of August. These bombers included He 111H-6s, Ju 87D-5s, and Hs 129B-2s.

The reorganized *Corpul 1 Aerian Român* (Rumanian 1st Air Corps), the ARR's expeditionary force, redeployed to airfields in Southern Transylvania on 7 September. These aircraft were to participate in the so-called 'Western Front' against Germany and Hungary. The C1AR bomber element consisted of three groups comprising six squadrons. One group was the Ju-87D-equipped *Grupul 3/6 picaj* (*Escadrile 74* and *81 picaj*) with 15 aircraft. The second was the Hs 129B-equipped *Grupul 8 asalt* (*Escadrile 41* and *42 asalt*) with 32 aircraft. The third group was the mixed *Grupul 5 bombardament* consisting of *Escadrila*

Two Savoia bombers, a J.R.S. 79B1 (No. 216), and a J.I.S. 79B (No. 154), of *Grupul 1 bombardament* head for Slovakian targets in April of 1945. These aircraft display broad wingtips and narrow fuselage bands — all painted white, the recognition color of the Soviet 5th Air Army. (Bujor)

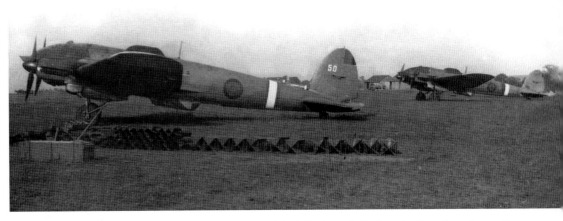

Two Heinkel He 111H-6s of *Escadrila 78 bombardament* are parked on Balomir airfield, southern Transylvania, early in the ARR's Western Campaign. The overall Rumanian green (approximately olive green) upper surfaces are well faded on this aircraft. This aircraft displays the new markings adopted by ARR on 3 September 1944. Individual codes, unit markings, and miscellaneous symbols remained unchanged. The bomber's cockpit glazing has been covered and a row of light bombs lay in the foreground. (Moisescu)

77 bombardament with Ju 88A-4s and *Escadrila 78 bombardament* with He 111H-6s. The 5th BG comprised a total of 18 aircraft. A joint command designated *Comandamentul aviatiei de bombardament* (Bomber Aviation Command) was formed to control the 65 level and dive bombers. The bombers were assigned to the base at Balomir, near Sibiu (Nagyszeben/Hermannstadt). Balomir was also the home of Soviet A-20 Boston bombers and Il-2 Shturmovik assault aircraft. The primary mission of these Soviet and Rumanian bombers was to support the ground operations of the 2nd Ukrainian Front. This front was composed of the Soviet 27th Army, the 4th and 6th Armored Armies, as well as the Rumanian 1st and 4th Armies.

The *bombardieri*'s involvement in the battle was limited at first, primarily due to the lack of ground support and poor supply conditions. (Only 26% of C1AR's bombers were combat ready when the fighting began on 8 September. The available aircraft consisted of five Ju 87Ds, five Hs 129Bs, as well as seven He 111Hs and Ju 88As.) The dive bombers and assault aircraft flew most of their combat missions against the Wehrmacht and *Honvédség* (Hungarian Army). The first bomber loss occurred on 9 September when Hungarian flak hit Ju 87D (No. 14) near Marosvásárhely (Târgu Mures/Neumarkt). No. 13 was damaged the next day near Timisoara (Temesvár/Temeschwar). No. 18 was hit by 'friendly' Soviet AA fire, while No. 18 was fired on by Luftwaffe Bf 109Gs. The 8th AG experienced its first loss in the brutal Transylvanian campaign on 14 September. Four Hs 129B-2s were shot down — two by Luftwaffe fighters and two by Soviet AA fire — and two pilots were killed.

The battles around Kolozsvár (Cluj/Klausenburg) were also harsh. This was due to the experienced twin-engine bomber crews of the 5th BG facing the German Luftwaffe for the first time. A Heinkel He 111H-6 (No. 57) fell victim to Luftwaffe Bf 109Gs near Csernakeresztúr (Cristur) on 15 September. The Ju 88A squadron lost No. 108 the following morning. Another He 111H-6 (No. 60) was shot down south of Kolozsvár by *Hauptmann* Peter Düttmann of 6./JG 52 on 17 September. C1AR's bomber losses continued to rise.

The Hs 129B-equipped *Escadrila 60 asalt* and the Ju 87D-equipped *Escadrila 85 picaj* were deployed to the front on 20 September in order to reinforce C1AR units and counter their heavy attrition rates.

Bucharest grounded C1AR aircraft during the last four days of September to avoid further losses. During the 12 days of operations in the 'Western Campaign' the *bombardieri* dropped 300.5 tons (272.8 metric tons) of bombs on Axis targets. This intense portion of the campaign saw C1AR bombers flying 67 missions comprising 520 aircraft sorties, while losing at least 15 single and twin-engine bombers.

On 5 October C1AR was directed to support the right flank of the 2nd Ukrainian Front in OPERATION DEBRECEN, an offensive aimed at capturing the important Hungarian town of Debrecen. Between 7 and 10 October the ARR's expeditionary force was restructured for this assignment. This restructuring resulted in the disbanding of the 5th BG and the transfer of the 77th BS's five Ju 88A-4s to the existing Ju 88D-1 squadron. This new mixed reconnaissance-bomber unit was designated *Escadrila mixtă de recunoastere-bombardament*. The three remaining He 111H-6s of the 78th BS were returned to Popesti-Leordeni base, outside Bucharest. The surviving aircraft of the hard-hit assault and dive bomber groups were consolidated into a single squadron of each type. *Escadrila 41 asalt* and *Escadrila 74 picaj* were combined to form the mixed *Grupul 8 asalt/picaj*. C1AR reported 13 serviceable Hs 129Bs, nine Ju 87Ds, and five Ju 88As on 11 October.

On 14 October 1944, *Grupul 1 bombardament* was deployed to Balomir to reinforce the greatly reduced C1AR bomber strength. This group was composed of two squadrons, *Escadrila 72 bombardament* (eight J.R.S./J.I.S. 79Bs) and *Escadrila 82 bombardament* (four J.R.S. 79B1s). The number of available Savoias, however, was gradually increased to the prescribed nine aircraft per squadron. The 1st BG's first combat mission over the Western Front was not flown until 22 November. Thirteen Savoias of the 82nd BS took off from the muddy airfield of Oradea (Nagyvárad/Großwardein) to bomb the railroad station at Székesfehérvár (Stuhlweißenburg). The 72nd BS simultaneously bombed the nearby Seregélyes airfield, while the Ju 88As of the mixed bomber-reconnaissance squadron struck targets in Perkáta.

Rumanian historians consider 19 December 1944 to be the first day of C1AR's Czechoslovakian Campaign. C1AR mounted its largest 'Western Front' combat mission early the next day, when 30 bombers departed Oradea at 0700 hrs. The aircraft were sent northwest to strike the railroad station and marshaling yards of Losonc, a strategic town in

Căpitan aviator Ioan Mogâldea stands by his Ju 88A-4 (No. 116B) at Lucenec airfield, Slovakia, on 8 April 1945. Mogâldea was the commander/navigator of this aircraft assigned to *Sectia bombardament* of the Ju 88-equipped *Escadrila mixtă recunoastere-bombardament*. This aircraft has a white 728 painted on its nose — the last three digits of its original *Werknummer*. (MMN)

61

A decommissioned I.A.R.-made Savoia J.R.S. 79B1 sits on a secondary airfield outside Bucharest on 3 September 1948. The old bomber was used for fire fighter training by for local fire fighters and was set on fire minutes after this photograph was taken. The terms of the post-war treaties did not allow a Rumanian bomber force. Consequently, the bombers were either scrapped or stripped of their armament and relegated to transport duties. Eventually, these aircraft were used for maintenance and fire-fighting training before they were scrapped. Unfortunately, no bombers were preserved for posterity. (MMN)

northern Hungary. (Losonc today is the Slovakian city of Lucenec.) The bomber force included two aging P.37B Los and several He 111Hs. The bombers were unable to knock out Losonc despite repeated attacks. The town held out until evacuated by the Hungarians in mid-January of 1945.

C1AR activity on the Western Front was summarized at the end of 1944. The *bombardieri* dropped 507.7 tons (460.9 metric tons) of bombs between 7 September and 31 December. 'Heavy' bombers flew 35 missions totaling 217 aircraft sorties, while the 'light' bombers flew 88 missions totaling 604 sorties. C1AR acknowledged 25 combat losses, although actual losses were slightly higher. The acknowledged losses included one Savoia, two Ju 88As, three He 111Hs, six Ju 87Ds, and 13 Hs 129Bs.

The Last War Effort

Another highlight of C1AR's anti-Axis campaign was the mission aimed at destroying the bridges of Budapest. These bridges spanned the Danube River and were the last links connecting Buda and Pest, the two main districts of the Hungarian capital. The Soviet High Command, probably irritated at earlier — and futile — attempts by V-VS units to destroy the bridges, ordered C1AR to fly this mission on 13 January 1945. Four Ju 88As targeted bridge No. 2, known as *'Erzsébet'* (Elisabeth), while seven Ju 87Ds headed for Twin Bridge No. 3, nicknamed *'Margit'* (Margaret). The bridges were not put out of commission despite the bomber crews' reports and later Rumanian historians' claims. A reconnaissance mission flown over Budapest by a lone ARR Ju 88D-1 that afternoon concluded, *"the bridges did not break"*. There were no losses on the high-risk mission.

The assault squadron reported that two Hs 129B-2s had disappeared while striking targets in the Felvidék (Upper Hungary; today, Southern Slovakia) region on 13 January. These targets were in Losonctamási (Tomásovce) and Lónyabánya (Lovinobana). It is believed, however, that the Rumanian Hs 129 pilots defected to the Germans, which was a rather desperate decision at this point in the war. Another Henschel 129 (No. 105) was written off in an accident near Miskolc airfield on 14 January. The crash killed the pilot, *Adjutant stagiar aviator* Vasile Scripcaru, who was also the Rumanian aviators' beloved cartoonist. The recently repaired Hs 129B was destroyed in the crash which was blamed on pilot error.

The C1AR's next effort concentrated on the entrenched Axis troops around Zvolen (Zólyom/Altsohl). The Soviet-Rumanian ground offensive began during the early morning hours of 25 February with C1AR bomber units assisting at full strength. Rumanian bombers dropped 79,034 lbs (35,850 kg) of bombs against various Axis targets. This day also marked the last time ARR bombers were lost to enemy fighters. A Ju 88A (No. 101) was repeatedly hit by a Luftwaffe *Schwarm* led by *Hauptmann* Helmut Lipfert, commander of I./JG 53. The damaged bomber was able to reach Lucenec, where it belly landed on the icy airfield. Two Savoias and a Henschel were also damaged in forced landings that day. This was the last large-scale, one-day operation flown by ARR during WW II.

Bombing missions became routine for the experienced *bombardieri* crews during the spring of 1945. By March of 1945 their task was made easier due to the lack of Luftwaffe fighters in Slovakian skies. Axis anti-

aircraft fire, however, remained as dangerous as ever and caused losses until the last days of the war. Several C1AR bombers fell victim to this effective ground fire. These losses included Hs 129B-2 (No. 313A) on 16 April, Savoia J.R.S. 79B (No. 114) on 21 April, and a Ju 88A-4trop. (W.Nr. 2425/No. 116A) on 27 April. The latter bomber was brought down by German flak while returning from a rare mission over Austy, in northeastern Austria. The Ju 88 crashed northwest of Nové Mesto nad Váhom (Vágújhely/Waagneustadt) killing all aboard. Among those killed was the 21-year old commander/navigator, *Sublocotenent aviator* Aurel Alexandroaia (Alexandru). This Ju 88 crew, however, was not the last ARR bomber crew victim of the war. A Ju 87D flown by *Adjutant major aviator* Paul Lãzãroiu was hit by flak over Dobikovice, Bohemia, on 29 April. The Stuka crashed behind enemy lines after Lãzãroiu bailed out. Lãzãroiu became a prisoner. His gunner, *Sergent mitralior* Gheorghe Popescu, was killed in the crash. A Savoia bomber, according to the memoirs of an ex-ARR airmen, was reportedly shot down on 11 May by the AA defenses of the 'Vlasov Army' — two days after WW II officially ended in Europe. This account cannot be confirmed by original documents.

ARR Headquarters assessed the activities of C1AR bombers after the end of hostilities. The 'heavy' bomber groups took part in 77 missions comprising 806 aircraft sorties during the eight months of action against the Axis forces on the 'Western Front'. These bombers flew a total of 1475.4 hours. Dive bomber units flew 160 missions comprising 722 sorties and 794 flight hours during this period. Assault units flew 457 missions totaling 1526 sorties and 1467 flight hours. Henschel 129s flew the most missions, 66 percent, of all of the bomber/attack aircraft during this period and suffered the heaviest losses as well. Less than 30 single and twin-engine bombers were left in the C1AR inventory by early May of 1945. These aircraft were grouped into four and one-half squadrons.

The first wave of ARR aircraft, which included dive bombers and assault aircraft, left Czechoslovakia to return home on 11 and 12 July. The withdrawal ended on 29 July, when the 'heavy' bombers departed Trencín and headed towards Rumania. This element included eight Ju 88As & Ds of *Escadrila (2) mixtã recunoastere-bombardament* and 12 Savoia '79s of *Grupul 1 bombardament*.

The ARR strength was reduced in accordance with the restrictive provisions of the post war peace treaty. This treaty, at least on paper, actually stripped the Rumanian air force of its entire bomber force. Most of the German-origin level and dive bombers and assault aircraft were withdrawn and gradually scrapped by the end of the 1940s. The only such aircraft that were retained were several Heinkel He 111Hs converted into transport aircraft and some late production Savoia J.R.S. 79B1s kept as trainers. These aircraft were assembled into two units, *Flotila 3 mixtã* ('light' bombers and assault aircraft) and *Flotila 4 bombardament* ('heavy' bombers) during June of 1946. One year later, these two flotillas were consolidated into a single unit, *Flotila 3 asalt si bombardament*, and based at Brasov with only a handful of serviceable aircraft remaining. The elderly bombers were soon replaced by Soviet aircraft — the Ilyushin Il-10 assault aircraft and the Tupolev Tu-2 bomber. Not one single Second World War bomber survived the post-war years to remind us of the glorious days of the ARR *bombardieri*.

This B-17G-55-DL (44-6606) landed near Miskolc airfield in northern Hungary after being damaged by flak over Vienna on 21 January 1945. The aircraft was assigned to the 20th BS, 2nd BG, 15th AF. A group of ARR technicians led by *Maistru mecanic clasa a III-a* (Technical NCO 3rd Class) Nicolae Cujbă replaced several damaged items. An Hs 129B main wheel was used to replace the damaged B-17's tail wheel. The B-17 returned safely to its Italian base despite grazing a truck with the port wing tip during take off. (Bernád)

Bomber and Assault Aircraft

Aircraft Type	Manufacturer	Role	Start of Service	Total Number	Serial Nos.	Notes
Potez 25**	I.A.R.	LB	1929	217* (250***)	1-217	Still in use as bomber/trainer in the early 1940s. (*+12 original French production aircraft) **Potez 25.14 B2 was the bomber version (***Delivery of 43 additional aircraft of the last batch unconfirmed)
Potez 543	Potez	HB	1935	10*	1-10	Still in use as bomber trainer and transport in the early 1940s (*+ Potez 541 prototype)
MB 210 Bn4	Bloch	HB	1937	10+	1-10	
S-79B	SIAI	HB	1938	24*	1-24	*Only 22 arrived in Rumania
I.A.R. 37*	I.A.R.	LB	1939	50	1-50	*No. 5 modified and tested as dive bomber (I.A.R. 371), later reverted to original form
Potez 633 B2	Potez	LB	1939	29* [21]	1-20+	Originally 40 ordered, the last 20 requisitioned by *l'Armée de l'Air* in 1939. *The final nine delivered in Sept. and Oct. 1941.
P.23A, B Karas	P.Z.L.	LB	1939	19 [31*]	1-19	*Only 11 were armed
P.37A, B Los	P.Z.L.	HB	1939	22 [27*]	201-222	*Only 19 were armed
He 111H-3	Heinkel	HB	1940	32 [32]	1-32	
J.I.S. 79B	SIAI	HB	1941	8 [24]	149-156*	Aircraft type given by Italian sources as S.M. 79JR. *Originally numbered 49-56
J.R.S. 79B	I.A.R.	HB	1941	36	101-136*	*Initially, the first ten aircraft were numbered 1-10 (210 Jumo 211 engines ordered in February 1940 for J.R.S. 79Bs)
Potez 631 C3*	Potez	LB	N/A	10	N/A	Originally a three-seat day fighter type, ordered 27 Aug. 1939. *Delivery unconfirmed
He 111H-6	Heinkel	HB	1942	15 [15]	47-60*	*Confirmed serial numbers only (German sources give a total of 57 'He 111s' - including old E models, trainers - exported to Rumania)
Potez 63.11 A3	Potez	LB	1942	12+ [53*]	French s/n	Originally a tactical reconnaissance and army co-operation type, used as light bomber/trainer. *The rest delivered to Italy & Hungary
J.R.S. 79B1	I.A.R.	HB	1943	36	201-236	Production concluded post-war
B-24 Liberator	Consolidated	HB	1943	3+	N/A	Rebuilt from crashed aircraft, used as trainer only
Hs 129B-2	Henschel	A	1943	200+	101-132+, 211-238+, 311-338+	Nos. 111 & up (*Escadrila 41 asalt*), Nos. 211 & up (*Escadrila 42 asalt*), Nos. 311 & up (*Escadrila 60 asalt*); Nos. 101-110 against the Axis only. (German sources give 54 aircraft exported to Rumania proper)
Ju 87D-3/-5 Stuka	Junkers	DB	1943	160+	1-45**, 178-205*, 860-872*	**Grupul 3 picaj. (Nos. 37-45 given lower numbers on arrival) *Grupul 6 picaj (German sources give 104 aircraft exported to Rumania)
Ju 88A-4/-14	Junkers	HB,DB	1943	80+	101-145+, & 300	(German sources give a total of 97 'Ju 88s' — A and D models — exported to Rumania)

Note: LB = Light Bomber, HB = Heavy Bomber, A = Assault, DB = Dive Bomber, [X] = data from sources of the originating countries

Reconnaissance and Army Co-operation Aircraft

The so-called 'Greater Rumania' created in the turbulent aftermath of World War One was surrounded by countries who sought to re-acquire their lost territories. This situation made aerial reconnaissance an absolute necessity for Rumanian Army Headquarters. Aviation was the primary tool of surveillance and the reconnaissance aircraft arm was the primary operator of such aircraft. Reconnaissance efforts consisted of the surveillance of the borders and obtaining information on troop strengths and front-line dispositions of potential enemies.

The primary mission of ARR was supporting the army. Initially, the reconnaissance mission was given to the 'observation' or spotter/army co-operation aircraft. These aircraft primarily flew short-range reconnaissance missions, directed artillery fire, carried messages and messengers, and performed other secondary tasks. The aircraft were also capable of attacking soft enemy targets with small bombs and guns.

The Potez XXV (Potez 25) was the primary reconnaissance aircraft used during the inter-war period. This sturdy, two-place biplane was manufactured in substantial numbers at the I.A.R.-Brasov Works. The I.A.R. engineers used the Potez XXV design as the basis for their own model — the I.A.R. 37. This biplane proved to have some design shortcomings, most notably in the powerplant. Despite these problems, and before the prototype's first flight, ARR ordered 50 I.A.R. 37s during November of 1936. The I.A.R.-built Gnome & Rhône 14K II engine was to be fitted to the I.A.R. 37, however, there were insufficient numbers of the engine to meet the demand. The engine was also to be used by S.I.A.I.-built S-79B bombers which had priority. Supply would not meet demand until 1938, which meant that the I.A.R. 37s would not be delivered until early 1939 — two years after the planned introduction date. The first examples were delivered to *flotile de gardă* (Guards Flotillas), which were later renamed *flotile de informatie* ('Information Gathering' or Intelligence Flotillas). The I.A.R. 37 was assigned to the light bomber role early in the war. The aircraft was not well liked by Rumanian airmen due to its lack of power, erratic maneuvering, and its propensity for take off and landing accidents. The I.A.R. 37 nevertheless represented the basis for more successful biplane observation aircraft types.

The German BMW 132A radial engine was chosen as an interim powerplant for the I.A.R. 37 until large numbers of Rumanian-built G&R engines were available. The 725 hp engine was fitted to the second batch of 75 I.A.R. 37s produced at Brasov. These aircraft, redesignated I.A.R. 38, featured a bulged cowling to accommodate the larger diameter BMW engine. They were also fitted with a 15.75 in (400 mm) larger diameter two-blade wooden propeller. The first I.A.R. 38 flew in early 1937, although it was fitted with a 640 hp I.A.R. K9 radial. The lower-powered engine meant that this aircraft failed its acceptance tests during March of 1937. A BMW 132A arrived in April and was promptly installed in the second I.A.R. 38. This aircraft demonstrated acceptable performance and I.A.R. ordered 85 of these engines from *BMW Flugmotorenbau G.m.b.H.* during January of 1939. Deliveries of BMW 132As began the following April, only weeks after the first I.A.R. 37 was delivered to ARR.

The I.A.R. 39 was the final version of this biplane series. The aircraft incorporated further airframe refinements and a more aerodynamic cowling. Ninety five I.A.R. 39s were powered by an 870 hp I.A.R. G&R

14K II engine before the long awaited 960 hp 14K IV engine became available (I.A.R. 39A). The first 95 I.A.R. 39s were produced at Brasov during 1940 before manufacturing was shifted to the S.E.T. plant in Bucharest. A further 160 aircraft were produced by S.E.T. by late 1944.

The ARR's order of battle at the end of 1939 — with World War Two already raging for four months — included 82 reconnaissance and observation aircraft. These consisted entirely of I.A.R. 37s and I.A.R. 38s. The *'Ipoteza* (Hypothesis) *32'* plan, dated 12 June 1940 and reflecting current and projected deliveries, listed 20 observation squadrons with ten aircraft each. This plan included 44 I.A.R. 37s, 75 I.A.R. 38s, and 50 I.A.R. 39s in service with an additional 45 I.A.R. 39s on order. There were only a few I.A.R. 39s that had actually been delivered up to that time. Only 12 *escadrile de observatie* (spotting and army co-operation squadrons) — Nos. 11 through 22 — would eventually be raised during the war.

During wartime, an I.A.R. 38/39 squadron was usually attached to each army corps or armored division to provide tactical intelligence and photographic reconnaissance. Missions were often flown up to 12.4 miles (20 km) deep into enemy territory. These aircraft were also used to observe and correct artillery fire and transport important couriers or messengers. I.A.R. 38/39s were occasionally employed as light bombers during police and anti-partisan duties behind the front line. Although slow and obsolete, the I.A.R. biplane family performed well in these roles. These aircraft, nicknamed *'Mos Neată'* (The Geezer) by ARR airmen, remained in active service until the end of the war in Europe.

Another aircraft that appeared in the *Ipoteza 32* plan was the British-built Bristol Blenheim Mk. I. Blenheims equipped five long-range reconnaissance squadrons, each with a theoretical strength of eight aircraft. The Blenheims had been acquired for reconnaissance duty, however, they also possessed a limited bombing capability. Only 35 of the original 40 Blenheims remained in service by 1941. This resulted in only four *escadrile de recunoastere-bombardament* (reconnaissance-bomber squadrons) — Nos. 1 through 4 — being fielded. These four squadrons were assigned to the three existing *flotile de informatie*, each covering one of the three major provinces of the pre-war Rumanian Kingdom. *Escadrile 2* and *4* of *Flotila 1 informatie* were based in Iasi, Moldavia, while *Escadrila 1* of *Flotila 2 informatie* was based at Cluj, Transylvania. *Escadrila 3* was assigned to *Flotila 3 informatie* at Galati to cover Wallachia and Dobruja.

The Blenheims were put to good use during the summer of 1940 when Rumania had to cede large geographical areas to her neighbors. These aircraft clandestinely observed Soviet, Hungarian, and Bulgarian lines and troops prior to and during the territorial hand-off. The Blenheims fed vital information on these troop movements to Rumanian Army Headquarters. The first operational loss of a long-range reconnaissance aircraft occurred on one of these secret missions. In early September of 1940 a reconnaissance *patrulă* (patrol) of three Blenheims had returned to Northern Transylvania after previously flying over this region days before. One Blenheim became lost in bad weather and crashed in the Carpathian Mountains. Only the aircraft's pilot, *Locotenent comandor aviator* Traian Muresanu, was able to bail out before the aircraft hit a mountain peak. *Escadrila 2 recunoastere-bombardament* was dissolved in early 1941 and its Blenheims were redistributed among the three remaining reconnaissance-bomber squadrons. This allowed each of the remaining squadrons to reach their theoretical strength of ten aircraft.

The ARR's inventory included 28 Blenheims (plus three unserviceable), 46 I.A.R. 38s (plus six unserviceable) and 77 I.A.R. 39s (plus 13 unserviceable) on 22 June 1941. The start of the Eastern Front fighting

I.A.R. 38 (Red 56) wears a rare four-color camouflage scheme that was employed early in 1941. The I.A.R. 37/38/39 family was inspired by the French Potez 25 and represented the backbone of the ARR's observation squadrons. The sturdy biplane was built in large numbers until late in 1944. The aircraft's top speed was limited to 208 mph (335 kmh), however, the I.A.R. 37/38/39 performed combat missions until the end of World War Two. (Bernád)

The pilot of I.A.R. 39A (No. 144/S) warms up the aircraft's engine on the snowy Morozovskaya airfield near Stalingrad in October of 1942. A ground crew member wearing a black 'căciulă', the traditional Rumanian lambswool hat, assists the navigator/commander with his parachute. This I.A.R. 39A wears the rarely applied white distemper paint over the original upper camouflage color. The rear gunner operated a .312 in (7.92 mm) Rheinmetall machine gun. (Antoniu)

that day saw *Flotila 2 gardă* (2nd Guards Flotilla) being assigned to *Gruparea Aeriană de Luptă* (GAL), the ARR's main combat element. The flotila's *Grupul 1 gardă* consisted of the I.A.R. 38-equipped *Escadrile 11 & 12 observatie. Grupul 2 gardă* was also assigned to *Flotila 2* and included *Escadrile 13* (equipped with I.A.R. 38s) & *14 observatie* (with I.A.R. 39s). *Escadrila 1 recunoastere-bombardament*, equipped with Blenheims, reported directly to GAL headquarters. The 2nd GF remained under GAL command until 30 June 1941, when it was transferred to the control of *Aero Armata 4 Română* (Air Element of the Rumanian 4th Army). *Aero Armata 4 Română* also controlled the Blenheim-equipped *Escadrila 3 recunoastere-bombardament* and the I.A.R. 39s of *Escadrile 17* and *22 observatie. Aero Armata 3 Română* included *Escadrila 4 recunoastere-bombardament*'s Blenheims and the I.A.R. 39-equipped *Escadrile 19, 20,* and *21 observatie. Escadrila 15 observatie*, flying I.A.R. 39s, was assigned to *Divizia 1 blindată* (1st Armored Division). *Comandamentul Aero Dobrogea* (Air Command of Dobruja), was tasked with defending the Black Sea coastline and was assigned the I.A.R. 39s of *Escadrila 16 observatie*. The 'missing' *Escadrila 18* — the only I.A.R. 37-equipped squadron — was relegated to a light bomber role.

Several missions were conducted on the opening day of the war against the USSR, and heavy losses were sustained by reconnaissance units. Four Blenheims took off at 0350 hrs to fly reconnaissance missions over V-VS airfields in Southern Bessarabia. These missions were flown at altitudes below 984 ft (300 m). The Rumanian aircraft observed Soviet strengths and activities and dropped light bombs on enemy positions. A Blenheim of the 1st RBS was the ARR's first combat loss of the war. The aircraft, flown by 40-year old *Locotenent comandor aviator* Corneliu Bătăcui, was shot down by Soviet fighters near Cetatea Albă (Byelgorod/Akkerman). Bătăcui and his crew were officially considered the ARR's first casualties of the war. Three other Blenheims were lost on 22 June, mainly due to erroneous orders regarding the mission altitudes. The Blenheims were directed to fly at an altitude which put them within the effective range of small- and medium-caliber AA guns. Major V. N. Orlov, commander of the Soviet 4 IAP, reportedly shot down a Blenheim (Red 38) of the 3rd RBS.

I.A.R. 38s/39s of the eleven army co-operation squadrons carried out

Potez 633 B2 (No. 11) is prepared for takeoff from an airfield near Stalingrad in late 1942. Two crewmen carry the camera that is to be fitted onto the aircraft. Potez 633s were sent to Stalingrad as reconnaissance-bomber aircraft following major losses sustained in 1941. These solid nosed Potez 633 B2s were augmented by several glazed-nosed Potez 63.11s. *Cirip* (Chirp) is painted under the windshield. (Moisescu)

several short-range reconnaissance and observation sorties on 22 June 1941. These aircraft also flew a number of low-level bombing and strafing missions. One I.A.R. 39 (No. 84) assigned to the 22nd OS was shot down by Russian fighters. Other aircraft barely returned to base after being riddled with bullet or shrapnel holes. This was the case for one I.A.R. 38 (No. 2) of 12th OS. The crew counted 64 holes in their airframe after making an emergency landing at Iasi airfield.

ARR had lost 40 reconnaissance and observation aircraft by the end of their first campaign. The losses included two I.A.R. 37s, nine I.A.R. 38s, 19 I.A.R. 39s and ten Blenheims. The number of serviceable Blenheims gradually dwindled due to the lack of spare parts from Great Britain. An effort to obtain ex-Yugoslav Blenheims and spare parts from Germany was of only limited success. ARR was down to 27 operational Blenheims by the end of August of 1942. The air force, requiring additional long-range reconnaissance aircraft, ordered ten Dornier Do 17Ms

The Bristol Blenheim Mk Is were the mainstay of the ARR's long-range reconnaissance arm up through the Stalingrad Campaign. The Blenheims also possessed a limited bombing capability. These aircraft were regarded as front-line equipment until 1943, although the last surviving Blenheim remained in combat service until early September of 1944. (Matthiesen)

Ten second-hand Dornier Do 17Ms were delivered to *Escadrila 2 recunoastere* in May of 1942. These aircraft boosted the ARR's long-range reconnaissance capability, however, the obsolescent Do 17M was not considered a long-term solution by the Rumanians. Nevertheless, the Do 17Ms performance in the Stalingrad campaign was satisfactory. (Bujor)

from Germany on 22 April 1942. These aircraft, delivered the following month, were previously operated by Luftwaffe *Flugzeugführerschulen*. *Escadrila 2 recunoastere îndepãrtatã* (2nd Long-Range Reconnaissance Squadron) was reactivated during the early summer of 1942 and equipped with the Do 17Ms. This unit participated in the ARR's second campaign alongside the 1st LRRS, which was equipped with six serviceable Blenheims. These two squadrons were augmented by a weak third *escadrilã* which possessed four Potez 63s. The parent unit, *Grupul 1 recunoastere îndepãrtatã* (1st Long-Range Reconnaissance Group), arrived in the Stalingrad area in September of 1942. Equipment losses were high due to attrition, combat, and the hasty retreats from airfield to airfield. The latter came about when the Red Army's constant pressure on the German and Rumanian forces caused a significant amount of matériel to be abandoned. Eventually, only a few aircraft remained operational in each squadron on the doomed Stalingrad front. The Potez 63 and Do 17-equipped squadrons were withdrawn to Rumania in early December, followed at month's end by the last Blenheim squadron. ARR losses at Stalingrad included one Do 17, three Blenheims, four I.A.R. 38s, and nine I.A.R. 39s between 1 September 1942 and 15 January 1943. There is no data available on Potez 63 losses.

Corpul 1 Aerian Român (C1AR), the ARR's combat element on the Eastern Front, was re-equipped with modern German aircraft in mid-1943. New aircraft included top-of-the-line Junkers Ju 88D long-range reconnaissance aircraft. The Ju 88D was equipped with two high altitude cameras (Rb 50/30 and Rb 75/30) and extra fuel tanks. Twelve Ju 88Ds (Nos. 1-12) were delivered to Rumania and assigned to the reformed *Escadrila 2 recunoastere* (2nd Reconnaissance Squadron). The 2nd RS was manned by the most experienced personnel. The Germans supplied further replacement aircraft to allow the squadron to sustain operations throughout the ARR's war on the Eastern Front. The 2nd RS moved to Mariupol and began operations in early June of 1943. Missions were flown over the area west of Stalingrad between the rivers Donets and Mius. The Ju 88Ds usually flew without fighter escort and relied on high altitude and speed for protection. The Ju 88D could climb up to 27,887 ft (8500 m), which was well above the maximum Soviet fighter ceiling of approximately 21,325 ft (6500 m). The Russians, nevertheless, did catch up with a solitary Ju 88D on occasion and shot down a number of the aircraft. The first loss occurred on 23 June, when a Ju

88D-1 (No. 4) was intercepted and shot down by V-VS fighters over the Sea of Azov, south of Rostov. The Rumanian aircraft was piloted by *Sublocotenent aviator* Constantin Constantinescu. Six Ju 88Ds had been lost by the end of 1943, including No. 1, W.Nr. 430650, piloted by *Sergent T. R. aviator* Nicolae Teodoru, on 22 July. This aircraft was flown alone without maps from Mariupol to Limassol, Cyprus, allowing Sgt Teodoru to defect to the Allies. (This aircraft has been preserved at the USAF Museum at Wright-Patterson AFB, Dayton, Ohio. The Ju 88D is exhibited wearing its original ARR markings, however, with an erroneous tail number.)

Escadrila 1 recunoastere, the other long-range reconnaissance squadron, was based in Rumania while the Junkers-equipped squadron operated on the Eastern Front. The 1st RS flew the last serviceable Blenheims and covered the northern and western areas of the Black Sea. The now fatigued and mechanically unreliable Blenheims were kept close to the coast on their overwater flights.

On 1 April 1943, the ARR inventory included 54 I.A.R. 38s and 107 I.A.R. 39s. The I.A.R. 39-equipped squadrons flew short-range reconnaissance and army co-operation missions at the front. These units also performed coastal reconnaissance and convoy escort in the Constanta-Odessa-Sevastopol triangle. The observation squadrons were not part of the restructuring involving C1AR combat units in the spring of 1943.

By the spring of 1944, C1AR units had retreated to airfields in Rumania while under constant pressure from the advancing Red Army. The 2nd RS returned to Tecuci, Moldavia, in mid-April to reconnoiter southern and western Ukraine, Bessarabia, Bukovina, and eastern Poland. The squadron ranged as far as Lemberg (Lwów), located over 310.7 miles (500 km) from Tecuci. The 2nd RS later moved to Ivesti airfield where they remained until the armistice of 23 August 1944. Only six Ju 88Ds had been lost in combat, while two others were written off in accidents. Another eight Ju 88Ds were damaged and returned to the Germans. Four serviceable Ju 88s were listed with the squadron on 23 August. Six Blenheims were reported with the 1st RS the same day at Ciocârlia airfield. Following the royal coup, one Blenheim inadvertently penetrated the air defense zone around Ploiesti on 26 August and was promptly shot down by friendly anti-aircraft fire. That same day another Blenheim was captured by Soviet troops at Ciocârlia. The observation units also experienced substantial losses to their I.A.R.

The first S.E.T.-built I.A.R. 39 (No. 96/S) flies past an Axis patrol boat cruising in the northwestern section of the Black Sea. The aircraft wears a two-tone green upper surface camouflage while the upper surface wingtips are painted yellow — an unusual marking for ARR aircraft. Beginning in 1942, I.A.R. 39s assigned to *Escadrile 20 & 22 observatie* flew coastal reconnaissance and convoy escort missions over the Constanta-Sevastopol-Odessa section of the Black Sea. The 'S' following the serial number indicated an I.A.R. 39 manufactured by S.E.T. in Bucharest. (Petrick)

Ju 88D-1 (No. 2A), was parked on an ARR airfield in the summer of 1943. Standing in front of the long-range reconnaissance Ju 88 are (from left): *Sublocotenent aviator* Gheorghe Dobrescu, pilot; *Căpitan observator* Ilie Teodorescu, commander/navigator; and *Maistru RTFF-mitralior* (radio operator-gunner) Stefan Bran. Twelve Ju 88Ds were provided by Germany in the summer of 1943. Eight additional Ju 88Ds were received as attrition replacements during the following months. The aircraft parked behind the Ju 88 is believed to be the sole S.E.T. XV fighter prototype. (Bernád)

biplanes during this time. Their losses, however, were replaced by the constant delivery of new aircraft from the I.A.R. and S.E.T. Works.

The once-again reformed *Corpul 1 Aerian Român* was sent to the new anti-Axis Western Front in early September of 1944. Although subordinate to the Soviet 5th Air Army, C1AR retained its own reconnaissance element. *Escadrila 1/2 recunoastere* initially fielded four Ju 88Ds and three Blenheims, however, the unreliable Blenheims were soon withdrawn from the front and relegated to transport duties. Only the Ju 88Ds remained on duty to carry out long-range reconnaissance missions.

The reliable I.A.R. 39s were retained for short-range reconnaissance duties. Two observation squadrons, the 11 & 12 OS, arrived in Southern Transylvania on 7 September 1944. Each squadron was equipped with 12 I.A.R. 39s. These aircraft joined another squadron of *Flotila 2 informatie* already on duty for several days. An I.A.R. 39 from this flotilla was the first combat loss of the ARR's fifth and last campaign. The aircraft, based at Blaj (Balázsfalva) airfield, was shot down by Hungarian anti-aircraft fire over Sepsiszentgyörgy (Sfântu Gheorghe), Northern Transylvania, on 1 September 1944. C1AR was reorganized and streamlined on 7 October after an intense month of fighting. The four existing Ju 88Ds joined the surviving Ju 88A bombers in a mixed reconnaissance-bomber squadron, designated *Escadrila mixtă recunoastere-bombardament*. This unit continued to be called *Escadrila 2* in some documents. Two new observation squadrons, the 15 & 16 OS, were sent from Rumania to the Transylvanian front and joined the two existing squadrons. These four squadrons created two groups within C1AR, *Grupuri 1 & 2 observatie*.

C1AR units had advanced deep into Hungary by the end of 1944. Ten I.A.R. 39s were lost in combat by that time — three were shot down by Axis fighters, two by flak, four destroyed on the ground, and one landed in enemy territory due to technical problems. Only one Ju 88D was written off, however, this represented a 25% loss to the ARR's long-range reconnaissance fleet. The four observation squadrons had flown 306 combat sorties on the 'Western Front' by the end of 1944. The reconnaissance section of *Escadrila mixtă* flew 49 missions behind the front lines and ranged as far as Austria and southern Poland.

On 20 December, Soviet Headquarters redirected the Rumanian air corps' principal effort towards Slovakia. The increased mission pace contrasted sharply with the virtual disappearance of Luftwaffe fighters, a factor which contributed to the successful completion of these missions. Nevertheless, some I.A.R. spotter aircraft did fall prey to enemy fighters. On 22 December an I.A.R. 39A (No. 133) was reported missing after taking off from Turkeve to Miskolc. It is believed that this aircraft was downed by *Föhadnagy* (1st Lt) Sándor Halasi of *101 'Puma' Vadászezred* (Fighter Wing), MKHL (Royal Hungarian Air Force). He reported shooting down an enemy biplane, later identified as an I.A.R. 38, near Bicske on 25 December.

German and Hungarian anti-aircraft fire remained effective right to the end of the war in Europe. This fire claimed an I.A.R. 39 near Voderady, in Eastern Moravia, on 8 May — the final day of the war. This was the last ARR combat loss during its nearly four-year long participation in World War Two. The unknown lieutenant pilot, whose charred body was buried in the local cemetery, was also the last Rumanian airman confirmed to have lost his life in the conflagration that had engulfed Europe.

The reconnaissance section and the observation units did not cease their activities in the final days of the war. These units included the recently arrived *Escadrila 13 observatie*, which joined the 12 & 16 OS of *Grupul 2* and the 11 & 15 OS of *Grupul 1*. These units performed 29 missions on behalf of the Soviet 40th Army and the Rumanian 1st and 4th Armies between 1 and 9 May. The aircraft flew reconnaissance and leaflet-dropping missions until the last renegade units of the Wehrmacht and the Vlasov Army, holed up around Prague, surrendered on 12 May. The 54 observation and reconnaissance aircraft had performed a record number of 475 sorties consisting of 591.3 flight hours. During the eight-month long anti-Axis campaign I.A.R. 39s and Ju 88Ds flew 814 sorties totaling 1052.5 hours. At least 15 I.A.R. biplanes and two Ju 88Ds were lost to enemy action.

The first C1AR unit left Slovakia and headed southwest towards Rumania on 11 July 1945. The Ju 88s were followed by the I.A.R. 39s on 26 and 27 July. The following day these biplanes landed at their peacetime base of Blaj.

The reconnaissance Ju 88s were soon discarded following drastic cutbacks within ARR. The last survivors of the I.A.R. 37/38/39 family, some of which were given civilian markings, remained in service until the early 1960s. This family of aircraft was one of the few biplane types to perform combat missions right up to the end of World War Two. Not one I.A.R. 37/38/39, however, has been preserved for posterity.

Short and Long-Range Reconnaissance/Army Co-operation Aircraft

Aircraft Type	Manufacturer	Start of Service	Total Number	Serial Nos	Notes
I.A.R. 38	I.A.R.	1939	75	1-75	
I.A.R. 39, A	I.A.R./S.E.T.*	1940	95/160	1-255**	*Marked by '/S' after the s/n.
					**Nos. 244-255 glider tug version, 1944
Blenheim Mk I	Bristol	1940	40*	1-40**	*Only 37 reached Rumania in late 1939
					**Documents also mention unnumbered aircraft
Blenheim Mk I	Ikarus	1941	3 [6]	41-43	Ex-Yugoslav, delivered by Germans in late 1941. Delivery of 3 additional aircraft in 1942 unconfirmed.
Do 17M	Dornier	1942	10	1-10	Ex-Luftwaffe, used aircraft
Fw 189A	Focke-Wulf	1943	2+ & 1* [7]	1-2+	Photo-mapping and cartographic purposes *Ex-Luftwaffe, captured
Ju 88D-1	Junkers	1943	20	1-12+	
Do 17P	Dornier	1944	3	11-13(?)	Ex-Luftwaffe, used aircraft for schooling purposes only

Note: [x] Data from German sources

Seaplanes

Rumania's position along the western shore of the Black Sea put the nation next to other Eastern European nations which shared the strategically important sea. These neighbors included the unfriendly USSR and Bulgaria as well as neutral Turkey. This state of affairs made the existence of a strong Rumanian seaplane fleet essential.

ARR created *Escadrila de hidroaviatie* (Hydroaviation Squadron-HS) during July of 1920. The squadron's first aircraft were several Hansa-Brandenburg W.12s and U.C. Is captured from Hungary during the 1918-19 campaign. *Escadrila de hidroaviatie* was based at Mamaia, north of Constanta harbor, on the southern shores of Lake Siutghiol.

Rumania attempted to indigenously produce the R.A.S. 1 Getta seaplane in 1925, however, this aircraft was a failure. Therefore, ARR turned to Italy and its vast experience in seaplanes. This resulted in the Savoia-Marchetti (later SIAI) company gaining a monopoly over the Rumanian seaplane fleet in the next decade. Twelve obsolescent S. 59bis flying boats arrived in 1928. This order was followed by 14 modern S.62bis aircraft in 1930. (This type was similar to the 58 examples produced simultaneously for the Soviet Union.) Six small S.56s, suitable for training, were delivered in 1932 to complete the fleet.

The existing *Grupul de hidroaviatie* (Hydroaviation Group) was enlarged into *Flotila de hidroaviatie* (Hydroaviation Flotilla-HF) on 17 July 1930. Extensive and improper use of the seven surviving S.59s prompted their replacement by seven Savoia-Marchetti S.55 torpedo bombers in 1933. These large, twin-engine aircraft featured a twin-hull design. (The Soviets ordered five civilian versions of the S.55 that same year.) The HF fielded 19 combat-ready flying boats by the end of 1933.

The ARR's combat-ready seaplane fleet had been reduced to 18 aircraft when World War Two began on 1 September 1939. These aircraft included seven S.55s and 11 S.62bis. [Three S.62s had been lost in accidents during *Marina Regală Română* (Royal Rumanian Navy) maneuvers in Southern Moldavia in October of 1938. Ten S.62 crewmen were also lost in these accidents, including *Flotila de hidroaviatie*'s commander, *Căpitan comandor aviator* (Lt Col) Constantin Negru.] ARR ordered 12 fully equipped CANT Z.501 Gabbiano flying boats and six spare engines from the CRDA company of Monfalcone, Trieste, in May of 1939. These high-winged monoplanes were armed with three .312 inch caliber (7.92 mm) machine guns and carried up to 1764 lbs (800 kg) of bombs. Z.501 No. 5 was lost on 11 July 1940 during its delivery flight to Rumania, while No. 6 crashed six days later. Among the crewmen killed in these accidents was *Comandor aviator* (Col) Hermann Wester, the new commander of the HF. (Wester had replaced *Căpitan comandor aviator* Negru who had died under similar circumstances less than two years earlier.)

Comandamentul Aero Dobrogea (CAD; Air Command Dobruja) was formed on 1 January 1941 to co-ordinate air operations along the Black Sea coastline. This mixed unit of three squadrons was composed of both seaplanes and land-based aircraft. The command incorporated *Flotila de hidroaviatie*, which consisted of *Escadrila 101 hidro-patrulare* (101st Hydro Patrolling Squadron), equipped with CANT Z.501s, and *Escadrila 102 hidro-informatie si bombardament* (102nd Hydro Reconnaissance and Bomber Squadron), equipped with the surviving Savoia-Marchetti S.55s and S.62bis. *Escadrila 53 vânătoare* (53rd

The last of seven Savoia-Marchetti S.55As delivered to ARR flies in formation with another S.55. These large, twin-hull seaplanes were capable of carrying torpedoes, however, the S.55s did not fly any actual torpedo-launching combat missions. (Crăciunoiu-Modelism)

Fighter Squadron), equipped with ten Hawker Hurricane Mk. I fighters, was temporarily attached to CAD in order to provide a measure of coastal air defense. CAD also worked with the Heinkel He 59C-equipped Luftwaffe seaplane unit (*8. Seenotstaffel*) which had arrived on Lake Siutghiol in early April of 1941.

By the outbreak of the war in the east, the Rumanian seaplane unit was equipped with ten CANT Z. 501s, seven S.62bis, and four S.55s. The CANTs were the only modern machines fit for combat due to the S.62's increasing obsolescence, while the S.55's mechanical unreliability did not allow it to fly more than 25 nautical miles (46 km) beyond the coast. The HF included on its unit roster 48 officers, 52 NCOs, and 64 mechanics and other ground crewmen.

ARR seaplanes flew their first combat sorties during the early morning of 22 June 1941. Their primary missions included:
1. Short-range coastal reconnaissance to detect small vessels and commandos that could land behind the front line. (These missions were mainly performed at dawn and dusk, and occasionally during day time. The task of these aircraft included destruction of targets with

A CANT Z.501 of *Escadrila 101 hidroaviatie* lifts off from the calm waters of Lake Siutghiol during the early 1940s. These modern seaplanes were camouflaged in a three-tone gray scheme intended to imitate the reflection of sunlight off the water. (Antoniu)

An I.C.A.R./I.A.R.-manufactured S.62bis (No. 18) assigned to *Escadrila 101 hidroaviatie* cruises over the *Hidroscalā* (seaplane base) of Mamaia-Siutghiol in 1942. ARR seaplanes flew reconnaissance and patrol missions over the Black Sea, monitoring, and occasionally attacking, Soviet naval and merchant vessels. A Luftwaffe Do 24 is moored on the water below. (Petrick)

bombs and on-board weapons.)

2. Long-range reconnaissance — extending to the Crimean and Turkish coasts — where they reported the movements of larger allied, enemy, or neutral ships and other vessels.
3. Air cover for Axis convoys to protect them from enemy submarines or surface ships.
4. Surveillance of existing mine fields.
5. Search and rescue for sunken ships or downed aircraft, both friendly and enemy.
6. Resupply of food and ammunition to the garrison on Serpent Island and other difficult-to-reach outposts along the seacoast.

The flotilla's first bombing mission took place on 26 July, when four S.55s carrying 17 110 lb (50 kg) splinter bombs struck Soviet troops attempting to cross the Danube River into Rumanian territory at Chilia (Kiliya). The same day, a CANT crew claimed the first air victory, when one of two MBR-2s encountered was shot down 120 nautical miles (222 km) east of Constanta. Both the Rumanian Navy and *Flotila de hidroaviatie* were placed under German command and subordinated to the German Naval Mission for the Black Sea on 6 July 1941.

The two Rumanian hydro *escadrile* carried out 586 sorties totaling 1711 flight hours during 1941. These totals increased to 905 sorties totaling 2218 hours in 1942. ARR seaplanes dropped over 5.5 tons (5 metric tons) and expended 1984 lbs (900 kg) of ammunition on enemy targets. The Rumanian squadrons sank one 2000-ton ship and damaged two other vessels and four submarines during 1941. The HF lost one S.62 and four CANT Z. 501s during the first year of the war. The S.62 and one of the Z.501s were shot down in combat, while the other three CANTs were destroyed in accidents. Five worn-out S.62bis and two S.56s were withdrawn from active duty and written off during 1941.

Comandamentul Aero Dobrogea was restructured on 26 March 1942 and designated *Comandamentul Aero Marinā* (Aero Marine Command). The command comprised *Escadrile 101* and *102 hidro, Grupul 7 bombardament usor, Escadrila 22 observatie,* and *Escadrila 1 recunoastere.* By this date, the seaplane force had been reduced to seven CANT Z.501s, four S.62bis, three S.55s, and one S.56.

Seaplane attrition during 1942 included the loss of two more CANT Z.501s, two S.55s and the last S.56. That year also marked the delivery of ten new Heinkel He 114B floatplanes from Germany. These aircraft were assigned to the 102 HS, while the serviceable Italian seaplanes were concentrated into the 101 HS. At least six more He 114s, including the He 114C version, arrived in 1943. Three older Heinkel He 42s also arrived to replace the obsolete S.56 trainer aircraft. In 1943, the last surviving Italian aircraft were withdrawn from service and replaced by higher-quality German aircraft. The survivors included five S.55s, four S.62bis, and four CANT Z.501s. Both 'hydro' squadrons (101 & 102 HS) were fully equipped with He 114s by late 1943. The Rumanian aircrews liked the twin-float He 114 which had a top speed of over 199 mph (320 kmh) and a range of 475 nautical miles (880 km). This performance was found to be more than adequate for the types of missions flown by the He 114. Additionally, the Rumanians appreciated the Heinkel's powerful armament. The first operational mission of ARR He 114s took place on 3 March 1942. Only one He 114 was lost during 1942 when a storm sank aircraft No. 10.

The difficulties of defending the Rumanian seacoast, and Constanta harbor in particular, increased following the Axis defeats at Stalingrad and the Don Bend. Sixteen land-based aircraft were deployed to Mamaia and Odessa during early 1943 in order to increase maritime surveillance capabilities. Six of these aircraft were Bristol Blenheim Mk. I long-range reconnaissance aircraft assigned to *Escadrila 3 recunoastere* (3rd Reconnaissance Squadron). The remaining ten aircraft were I.A.R. 39 biplanes from *Escadrila 20 observatie* (20th Spotting Squadron). Two fighter squadrons, equipped with obsolete P.Z.L. P.11Fs, were redeployed to bases close to the Bessarabian coastline. The ARR's maritime strike capability was increased when *Escadrila 78 bombardament maritim* (78th Marine Bomber Squadron) was deployed to Ciocârlia/Carol I airfield, near Constanta. This squadron was equipped with He 111H-6 bombers. Additional land-based aircraft were later concentrated along the Black Sea coast.

The 101 HS flew only 91 sorties totaling 288 flight hours during 1943, while the 102 HS flew a record 884 sorties and amassed 2223 flight hours. The latter squadron had become operational on the He 114s prior

This obsolescent S.55 carries the pro-Axis 'Michael's Cross' markings in this poor, but rare photograph. Beginning in 1942, the original white Italian scheme was replaced by the standard ARR maritime scheme of green over blue-gray. (Crāciunoiu-Modelism)

A *Marina Regală Română* (Royal Rumanian Navy) motor boat guides an He 114B (No. 9) of *Escadrila 102 hidroaviatie* to the wooden debarking platform of *Hidroscală* Mamaia. The He 114 could deliver two 110 lb (50 kg) bombs or other ordnance in both level and dive bombing attacks. ARR markings and the yellow Axis fuselage band have been painted over the original German crosses. (Petrick)

(Above) The unmarked S.E.T. 4H/7H prototype is equipped with floats for trials. A limited number of these aircraft, powered by 360 hp Jaguar 3 radial engines, was manufactured in 1936. The S.E.T. 4H/7H was primarily equipped with wheeled undercarriages and used as training and courier aircraft beginning in 1938. Seven S.E.T. 4H/7H aircraft were still in use on 2 February 1944. (Bernád)

to the 101st. Two He 114s were lost due to accidents. None were lost in combat.

ARR Headquarters ordered 13 additional He 114s and 50 Arado Ar 196s to both replace their earlier losses and increase the seaplane fleet. The Rumanians also notified the *Reichsluftfahrtministerium* (RLM - the Reich Air Ministry) of their interest in purchasing larger torpedo-capable seaplanes. These aircraft included He 115s and ex-French *Aéronavale* Latécoère 298s. The Latécoère 298s had been withdrawn from Luftwaffe use and were available in some numbers. Some sources suggest ARR also purchased nine pre-production Fieseler Fi 167A carrier-based biplanes, however, this information cannot be confirmed by Rumanian documents. (These aircraft actually went to Croatia.) The order for He 114s was filled by the mid-summer of 1944 and the first batch of Ar 196s was reportedly delivered by that time. The Rumanian request for larger aircraft, however, was denied by the Germans.

The Red Army reached Rumania's northeastern frontier during the spring of 1944. The Soviet advance dramatically increased the danger of Soviet troops landing on the seacoast. The number of coastal ARR units and the time they spent over the Black Sea increased in

(Below) He 42 (No. 2) was one of three older He 42s imported from Germany for training in 1943. A Luftwaffe BV 138, nicknamed the 'Flying Clog', is visible to the left of the port wing struts of the He 42. (Bujor)

He 114C (No. 16) is anchored to the wooden debarking platform at Siutghiol in September of 1943. *Locotenent aviator de rezervă* (1st Lt Res) Vasile Buzban holds a little girl, while *Sublocotenent aviator* (2nd Lt) Sorin Tulbas watches from the port float of the aircraft. The port in the top of the engine cowling is for one of the He 114C's two fixed 20mm cannons. (Bernád)

response to this threat. The fully equipped *Escadrila 101 hidroaviatie* had flown 283 sorties totaling 670.2 flight hours by 23 August. During the same period *Escadrila 102 hidroaviatie* flew 254 sorties totaling 635 flight hours. Four He 114s were reported destroyed in accidents during the first eight months of 1944.

The Ar 196s ordered from Germany arrived too late to take part in the final stage of the anti-Soviet war. All but two of these aircraft were reportedly still in their crates when the Red Army occupied the Siutghiol hangars on 8 September 1944. The Soviets seized the new aircraft and shipped them to the USSR without issuing any official documents. The *Flotila de hidroaviatie*'s archives and equipment, except for the He 114s, were also confiscated by the Soviets. The seaplanes were immediately ordered to leave Siutghiol and move to tiny Lake Snagov. The flotilla, unlike other ARR units preparing for the anti-Axis campaign, practically ceased to exist. The commander of the HF handed the unit's battle flag to the *Flotila de aerostatie* (Balloon Flotilla) in mid-December of 1944. The unit's 20 He 114s were first dispatched to Ovidiu Island in September and then to Lake Snagov in November. One He 114 was left abandoned near the village of Urziceni, while nine new Heinkels were left unassembled in their crates. No trace of the Ar 196s was ever found. Two surviving He 42s were left behind in the Siutghiol hangars occupied by Soviet troops. A third example was shot down in late August by an 'allied' V-VS fighter. The last He 114s were withdrawn from service and scrapped during May of 1960, when *patrula de hidroaviatie* was finally disbanded.

An I.C.A.R./I.A.R.-built Savoia-Marchetti S.62 bis (No. XVIII) rests on its beaching gear at Mamaia-Siutghiol *hidroscală* (seaplane base) early in World War Two. A CANT Z.501 *Gabbiano* (Seagull) is being refueled while anchored at the water's edge. Two Luftwaffe seaplanes — believed to be Heinkel He 59s — are anchored among the marsh vegetation in the background. The tracks leading to the water's edge guided the beaching gear used to haul seaplanes from the water to the hardstands and hangars on land. (Bujor)

Seaplanes

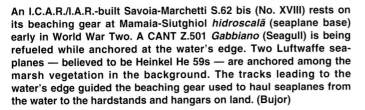

Aircraft Type	Manufacturer	Start of Service	Total Number	Serial Nos.	Notes
S.56	Savoia-Marchetti (SM), SIAI	1932	6	I-VI	School seaplane
S.55A	SM, SIAI	1933	7	I-VII	Torpedo bomber
S.62bis	SM, SIAI	1932	14	I-XIV	
S.62bis	SM/I.C.A.R./ I.A.R.	1938	5	XV-XIX	
S.E.T. 4Ha/7H	S.E.T.	1938	8	51-58	Often used with wheel undercarriage
CANT Z.501 Gabbiano	C.R.D.A.	1940	12	1-12	
He 114B, C	Heinkel	1942	38+ {43}	1-29+*	* At least 9 aircraft of the last batch received in 1944 were not assembled; these were left in crates unnumbered
He 42	Heinkel	1943	3	1-3	School seaplane
Ar 196*	Arado	1944	24	N/A	* Two aircraft were reportedly assembled, the rest remained in containers and were captured by Soviet troops

Note: {X} = maximum number of He 114s

Transports

ARR did not possess a purpose-designed military transport aircraft when World War Two began on 1 September 1939. Most transport missions were flown by obsolete French bombers, such as the Bloch MB 210, Potez 543, and Potez 651. VIPs (Very Important Persons) — such as government ministers and generals — were flown to their destinations on airliners operated by L.A.R.E.S. (*Liniile Aeriene Române Exploatate cu Statul*; Rumanian Airlines Operated with the State). L.A.R.E.S. was formed on 20 July 1937 when the older, state-owned L.A.R.E.S. was merged with privately owned S.A.R.T.A. (*Societatea Anonimã Românã de Transporturi Aeriene* - Rumanian Air Transport Society Ltd.). The new L.A.R.E.S. was quickly expanded with the addition of advanced Lockheed 10A Electra and Douglas DC-3 transports. These new airliners joined the existing fleet of Junkers F13, Potez 560/561, de Havilland D.H. 89 Dragon Rapide, and D.H. 90 Dragonfly aircraft. L.A.R.E.S. purchased four Savoia-Marchetti S.M. 83s from Italy during 1938, however, these were found unsuitable for Rumanian needs and returned to Italy in 1943. The Lockheed 14 Super Electra was also purchased by the airline during 1938. Fourteen PLL LOT (Polish National Airline) aircraft sought refuge in Rumania during September of 1939. These aircraft were immediately added to L.A.R.E.S. Many single-engine light transports, primarily Polish-built R.W.D. 13 aircraft, were also impressed into Rumanian civil service.

L.A.R.E.S. was placed under the direct control of *Subsecretariatul de Stat al Aerului* (SSA - State Undersecretariat of Air) and was militarized on 16 October 1940. As a result, L.A.R.E.S. aircraft began to carry both ARR and civil registration markings. The airliners' original silver dope finishes were initially retained, however, military camouflage schemes were applied to these aircraft in 1941. The transports also wore the mandatory yellow rear fuselage band carried by all Axis aircraft operating in Eastern Europe. SSA also inducted L.A.R.E.S. personnel into ARR service, including the future top ARR ace, Constantin Cantacuzino. Inducted personnel and aircraft were formed into the squadron-size *Grupul aerotransport militar* (Military Air Transport Group) and based at Bucharest-Bãneasa International Airport. This airport was also the home of *Escadrila sanitarã* (Medevac Squadron), which was formed on 25 June 1940.

Several Junkers Ju 52/3m three-engine transports were imported from Germany during November of 1941 in order to increase the Group's inventory and transport capacity. The Junkers aircraft were assigned to the newly formed *Escadrila 105 transport greu* (105th Heavy Transport Squadron). The ex-L.A.R.E.S. and other older aircraft were assigned to *Escadrila 106 transport* (also known as *Escadrila L.A.R.E.S.*). *Escadrila 107 transport greu* was formed when additional Ju 52/3ms became available. This unit flew all Ju 52/3ms transports with odd serial numbers, while Ju 52/3ms with even serial numbers were retained by the 105 HTS.

L.A.R.E.S. Squadron, using the conscripted Lockheed airliners, provided transport for the ARR's expeditionary force on the eve of the Bessarabian Campaign. The Medevac Squadron evacuated wounded troops to rear-area hospitals. MS crews were primarily women with the rank of *Ofiter echipaj clasa a III-a* (Deputy 2nd Lieutenant). Both L.A.R.E.S. Squ. and *Escadrila sanitarã* were directly subordinate to *Statul Major al Aerului* (Air Force Headquarters). The transports were primarily tasked with flying supplies and mail to the front, evacuating wounded personnel, courier, and other general duties. No transport aircraft were lost in combat during the ARR's first campaign.

The next major task for Rumanian transports occurred at Stalingrad during late 1942. By the start of the ARR's second campaign, sufficient Ju 52/3ms were available to send the 105 HTS to the front. This unit was accompanied by the newly created *Escadrila sanitarã 108 transport usor* (108th Medevac Light Transport Squadron), a female-piloted unit equipped with ex-Polish R.W.D. 13s. These two squadrons were formed into *Grupul aerotransport* (Air Transport Group), which was placed under the direct command of *Comandamentul Aviatiei de Luptã* (CAL; Combat Aviation Command).

ARR transports performed some of their most daring missions during the Stalingrad Campaign — the supply and personnel evacuation of the encircled *Grupul 7 vânãtoare* and the armored division of General Nicolae Mazarini. Additional supply missions were also flown to Rumanian troops at Mineralnyye Vody, in the Northern Caucasus Mountains. Three Ju 52s landed at Pitomik airfield near Stalingrad on 4 December. The aircraft brought in badly needed supplies despite severe weather conditions and temperatures down to -4° F (-20° C). Another trio of Junkers transports flew the same mission to Pitomik on 7 December, however, on the return flight V-VS fighters shot down the Ju 52 piloted by Aurel Ifrim. The last Rumanian transport aircraft to land in the isolated Stalingrad pocket came on 15 January 1943. That Ju 52 evacuated Gen Lãzãroiu and his staff leaving the remaining troops of *Divizia 20 infanterie* (20th Infantry Division) to face the advancing Soviets. Soviet troops captured Pitomik, the last remaining Axis airfield in the Stalingrad area, on 16 January.

Three Ju 52s and two civilian registered R.W.D. 13s were lost at Stalingrad. The Ju 52 piloted by Victor Ghitã was lost in

This L.A.R.E.S. Potez 561 (c/n 4387/YR-AFK) suffered a collapsed port landing gear following a hard landing. Beginning in 1941, most L.A.R.E.S. airliners were given camouflage paint schemes instead of all-white or silver finishes. The Potez 561 also carries the yellow Axis aft fuselage band and undersurface wingtips. (Moisescu)

L.A.R.E.S. DC-3-227 (c/n 1986/YR-PAF) is parked at Budapest-Budaörs International Airport, Hungary, during the summer of 1941. The 'Michael's Cross' markings have been added next to the civil registration, however, the yellow Axis identification band has not yet been applied to the rear fuselage. This DC-3's sister ship (c/n 1985/YR-PIF) was lost in a fatal accident on 23 August 1940. (Bernád)

An R.W.D. 13S (No. 3) assigned to *Escadrila sanitară 108 transport usor* awaits its next mission at Salz airfield, Trans-Dnestra in the late summer of 1941. National markings, except for the blue-yellow-red stripes on the upper rudder and wingtips, were not carried. This squadron, known as *Escadrila albă* (The White Squadron) due to the overall white finish of its aircraft, was used for medevac duties. The red crosses are painted in all six positions. One of the squadron's female pilots stands beside the aircraft. An olive green R.W.D. 13 courier aircraft is parked in the background. (Greceanu)

a collision with another Ju 52 over Melitopol airfield during the spring of 1943. Everyone on board Ghitã's aircraft was killed, however, the other Ju 52 was able to land safely.

The next major assignment for the ARR's transports came during the evacuation of the Crimean Peninsula in early 1944. A combined German-Rumanian sea-air operation, code named OPERATION 60,000 after the estimated number of people to be rescued, was launched on 14 April 1944. All available ARR Ju 52/3ms were flown between Rumania and the Crimea to bring in food, ammunition, and other supplies and then evacuate wounded personnel. Obsolete transport aircraft were also pressed into service for this operation. Germany halted the flights on 28 April citing 'higher interests', however, the operation restarted on 11 May and lasted for three more days. The Soviets overran the last available airfield in the Crimea on 14 May. A total of 42,190 Rumanians were evacuated to Rumania by that date, including 3056 personnel who were flown out — a 90% success rate. A Ju 52/3m flown by L.A.R.E.S. pilot Radu Gligorz disappeared over the Black Sea early in the operation and was believed to have been shot down by Soviet fighters.

Transport aircraft flew few sizable missions once the air war came to Rumania during the summer of 1944. The proximity of the war not only reduced the supply lines, but also subjected Rumanian transports and airfields to repeated Allied air attacks. Protecting the transports was a

A Potez 543 (No. 3) is serviced at Brasov during 1942. Uncommonly, the aircraft serial number is painted in black on the upper wing, however, the number has not been applied to the fin in white — a standard practice within ARR. The Potez 543 and other obsolete French bombers were also used for transport duties. (Bujor)

Rumanian paratroopers board a Potez 650 prior to an exercise held during the war. Five Potez 650/651s were purchased for paratroop and medevac transport duties in 1938. The paratroopers are wearing the Irvin-type parachute which was manufactured in Rumania under a US license and used throughout the 1950s. The only combat seen by Rumanian paratroopers took place against German troops in and around Bucharest during the 24/28 August 1944 period. (Bujor)

A Rumanian Lockheed 14H Super Electra (c/n 1464/YR-LID) taxis out to the runway at Zagreb (Agram), the capital of Croatia, during the late summer of 1941. Although impressed into military service, the L.A.R.E.S. fleet continued to fly regular international passenger flights to friendly countries. Four Super Electras delivered to L.A.R.E.S. in 1938 were joined the next year by four ex-PLL LOT Lockheed 14s which fled the German advance into Poland. (Bernád)

great concern for ARR, however, this protection was not always successful due to USAAF fighters engaging any Axis aircraft they could find. The transport units suffered particularly heavy losses on 10 June 1944, when P-38 Lightnings struck Boteni airfield outside Bucharest. The P-38s destroyed four Ju 52s, one Savoia S-79B, and one Lockheed 10A of ATG — all on the ground.

Germany continued to supply Rumania, their most important Balkan ally, with a significant amount of obsolete aircraft during 1944. These aircraft were only suitable for training and transport. Aircraft deliveries during the summer of 1944 included ten Junkers W34his, ten He 111E-3s, and 12 Ju 86E-5s.

Escadrila 109 transport cu planoare (109th Glider Transport Squadron) was the last unit to be assigned to *Grupul aerotransport*. The

The crew of He 111E (No. 77) stands in front of their aircraft at Balomir, Southern Transylvania, during September of 1944. This aircraft displays the pro-Allied roundel and the white rear fuselage band and wingtips associated with the Soviet 5th Air Army. Both ARR and Soviet V-VS aircraft used Balomir airfield during the campaign against the Axis. This obsolescent He 111E was delivered to Rumania, along with Junkers W34s and Ju 86Es, in the summer of 1944. These older aircraft, no longer suitable for combat operations, were used primarily for training and transport duties. (Bujor)

squadron was created on 11 November 1943 and equipped with 15 DFS 230 military transport gliders that had been delivered the year before. The gliders were towed by modified I.A.R. 38s and later by I.A.R. 39s. Germany supplied another 12 DFS 230s during 1944, although a planned order for Gotha Go 242s remained unfilled. Rumania also imported the DFS-Kranich, JS-Weihe, and Schneider Grunau Baby IIB gliders from Germany during World War Two. The glider unit moved from Băneasa to Spătaru, Moldavia, on 1 April 1944, however, the unit performed only a limited number of supply missions. The majority of the DFS 230s, including some still in their shipping crates, were lost when the Red Army overran Spătaru on 27 August. Luftwaffe fighters, after turning hostile towards ARR on 24 August, destroyed several transport aircraft at Boteni on 25 August. *Lt.* Hans-Werner Renzow, *Staffelkapitän* of 10./JG 27 and his wingman, *Ofhr.* Peter Esser, destroyed a Lockheed Electra and a Douglas along with some single-engine trainer aircraft at 1240 hrs.

The ARR's transport fleet was deployed to the Western Front after the *coup d'état* of 23 August 1944. *Escadrila mixtă aerotransport* was deployed to Turnisor (Kistorony) airfield, in Southern Transylvania, when the anti-Axis campaign officially began on 7 September. The Squadron's 17 aircraft included the reliable Ju 52/3m, He 111E, Fw 58B, Ju 86E, Junkers W34, and single-engine aircraft. A captured Luftwaffe He 111H-20, No. 1001, was quickly overpainted with Rumanian markings to avoid confiscation by the Soviet occupation forces. The Heinkel was assigned for VIP transport.

Due to the uneasy alliance between Rumania and the Allies, transport crews often had to watch for both friend and foe. One such case involved three Ju 86s carrying a Rumanian and Soviet delegation to Arad in September. Soviet anti-aircraft gunners in the valley of the River Mures (Maros) fired on the slow-moving aircraft and hit all three Ju 86s. The Junkers flown by *Adjutant major aviator* Ionită was destroyed in the air, while the other two damaged aircraft force-landed near Ilia (Marosillye). Several high ranking Rumanian and (ironically) Soviet officers were killed or wounded in this incident. Luftwaffe fighters also proved dangerous to the slow-flying transports. A Ju 52/3m (No. 25) was lost to a Bf 109G near Fil'akovo (Fülek), Slovakia, on 20 February 1945, while another Junkers barely escaped destruction. *Escadrila mixtă aerotransport*, equipped with 12 serviceable aircraft, was located as Piest'any (Pöstyén) airfield at the end of the war. The DFS 230-equipped 109 GTS joined C1AR (*Corpul 1 Aerian Român*; 1st Rumanian Air Corps) early in 1945. The transports flew 258 missions totaling 360 flying hours during the Czechoslovakian Campaign.

All single and twin-engine aircraft were consolidated into a single unit

A Ju 52/3mg4e (No. 6) is parked at an airfield in southeastern Europe during Rumania's war against the USSR. The Junkers Ju 52/3m was the mainstay of the ARR's transport fleet and performed well throughout World War Two — from Stalingrad in 1942 to Czechoslovakia in 1945. The last Ju 52 was withdrawn from Rumanian service during the early 1960s. (Bernád)

Escadrila 109 transport cu planoare personnel gather near one of their DFS 230 (No. 7) transport gliders in 1945. The squadron's commander, *Locotenent aviator* Mircea Găbureanu, holds his cap in the center of this group. All of the pilots in this squadron were Non-Commissioned Officers (NCOs). (Bernád)

after C1AR's return to Rumania. This unit, *Flotila 7 aerotransport-legătură* (7th Air Transport-Liaison Flotilla), was based at Romeo Popescu airfield at Giulesti, on the outskirts of Bucharest. The regiment was reduced to group size in 1946. Several bombers were converted to transports to avoid their being scrapped by the Allied Commission. The Commission also supervised the reduction of the Rumanian armed forces in accordance with post-war treaties. The surviving W34s, Ju 52/3ms, He 111s, Savoia S-79Bs, and other types served in the transport role until the end of the 1950s.

Transports

Aircraft Type	Manufacturer	Start of Service	Total Number	Serial Nos.	Notes
F13	Junkers	1931	5	Civilian	Initially in service with L.A.R.E.S., still used in 1941
Potez 560	Potez	1936	6 & 1*	Civilian	Initially in service with L.A.R.E.S. *Private aircraft of Prince G.V. Bibescu (head of F.A.I.)
D.H. 89 Dragon Rapide	de Havilland	1936	4	Civilian	Initially in service with L.A.R.E.S.
D.H. 90A Dragonfly	de Havilland	1937	3	Civilian	Initially in service with L.A.R.E.S.
Potez 561	Potez	1937	9	Civilian	Initially in service with L.A.R.E.S.
Potez 566T*	Potez	1937	2	N/A	*Delivery unconfirmed
Model 10A Electra	Lockheed	1937	7 & 5*	Civilian	Initially in service with L.A.R.E.S. *Ex-PLL LOT aircraft
Potez 62	Potez	1938	1+	Military, Civilian	For medevac duties. One registered civilian in 1944
Potez 650/651	Potez	1938	5+	N/A	For paratroop transport/casevac duties
DC-3	Douglas	1938	2	Civilian	Initially in service with L.A.R.E.S.
S.M. 83*	SIAI	1938	4 & 1**	Civilian	Initially in service with L.A.R.E.S. *Returned to Italy in 1943 **Private aircraft of Prince Bibescu
Ju 52/3m	Junkers	1938	33 & 1* & 11**	1-32+ & Civilian	1st Ju 52/3m (CV-FAI) for Prince Bibescu in 1932; *Ex-PLL LOT aircraft; **Ex-Luftwaffe, captured. Two from Trans-Dnestra Government, impressed into ARR
Model 14H Super Electra	Lockheed	1938	4 & 4*	Civilian	*Ex-PLL LOT aircraft
ST-25 Universal/Jubilee/ Ambulance	GA/Monospar	1939	3+	1-2+ Civilian	Medevac purposes, initially painted in white
DC-2	Douglas	1939	1	Civilian	Ex-PLL LOT aircraft
R.W.D. 13S*, '13ST**	D.W.L.	1939	[3* & 2]	*1-3 & Civilian	*Medevac duties. Initially painted in white **Other 23 aircraft used as courier a/c (see chapter)
F-VIIB/3m	Lublin-Fokker	1939	[3* & 1]	Civilian	Rarely used *Ex-PLL LOT aircraft
DFS 230	DFS	1943	29 [38]*	1-29	Transport glider. *Last aircraft remained in crates unassembled and were captured by Soviet troops
DFS Kranich	DFS	1944	14	N/A	Paratrooper commando transport glider
W34hi	Junkers	1944	10 & 6*	51-60 & Lw s/n	*Ex-Luftwaffe, captured
He 111E-3	Heinkel	1944	10	71-80	
Ju 86E-5	Junkers	1944	12	I-XII	
Go 242	Gotha	1944	[5]	N/A	Transport glider. Ordered in July 1944, delivery unconfirmed
He 111H-20	Heinkel	1944	1	1001	Ex-Luftwaffe, captured. Used as VIP transport

Note: [X] = data from Polish and German sources

Training and Liaison Aircraft

Rumanian aviation students followed a three-step process to become fully qualified military pilots. The first phase of training introduced the students to the basics of flight using slow, yet well-proven biplanes. The second stage strengthened and expanded the students' skills and knowledge using a variety of faster and more demanding monoplanes. The final stage of training directed the student toward the air force arm best suited to his abilities (fighters, bombers, transports, etc.), and later, towards the specialized combat training centers within each combat *flotilă*. Training flights in the latter units were performed using older and obsolete single or twin-engine aircraft withdrawn from front-line service, yet specific to that particular branch of the air force.

ARR established six *escadrile de pilotaj* (Piloting Squadrons) in various parts of Rumania during the inter-war period. These squadrons were controlled by a branch of the Ministry of Air and Navy known as *Comandamentul scolilor si centrelor de instructie ale aeronauticii* (Headquarters of Schools and Training Centers of ARR). Civilian flight schools were also active in pilot training in concert with the specialized military units. Large numbers of civilian graduates were recruited into the Air Force prior to and during WW II.

Two license-manufactured aircraft were employed in initial pilot training by ARR. One was the US-designed Fleet F-10G which was manufactured in all three major Rumanian aircraft plants. The other trainer was the French Potez 25, built under license at the I.A.R. Works. The second and intermediate phase initially employed the docile I.A.R. 27, but was later followed by the more demanding Italian Nardi F.N. 305 monoplane. ARR employed both Italian-made and license-produced Nardi F.N. 305s. Other intermediate training aircraft included (although in smaller numbers) the S.E.T. 31/4/7, Miles Hawk, and Gotha Go 145A. Similar aircraft were employed by civilian flight schools, although other aircraft were also used. These aircraft included the I.C.A.R. Universal; the ex-Polish P.W.S. 26, Lublin R.XIII, R.W.D.-8 and 14; as well as the German Bücker Bü 131 and Klemm Kl 25/35.

By 1 March 1940, the aircrew rosters listed only 243 fighter pilots trained out of a planned 504, 219 bomber pilots out of a planned 435, and 992 reconnaissance pilots trained of a planned 1317. Out of 1159 planned civilian reserve pilots, 838 were trained, while 267 navigators (of 395 planned), 218 radio operators (of 260 planned), and 239 air gunners (of 379 planned) were trained. These represented a total of 3341 trained personnel existing compared to a required 4124 personnel. The statistics indicated a shortfall of 473 pilots and 128 navigators. New military and civilian flight schools were established to increase the number of airmen. Airmen were also recruited from other organizations, such as the national airline, L.A.R.E.S. Despite these measures, the total number of ARR crewmembers available on 22 June 1941 was only 1947. Pilots made up 1066 of the total crewmembers, including 355 fighter, 164 bomber, 523 short and long-range reconnaissance, and 24 navy pilots. The 1947 crewmembers also included 385 navigators and on-board commanders (career officers only), 129 radio operators, 83 on-board mechanics, and 284 air gunners.

Fighter pilots were trained in Rumania by experienced Luftwaffe personnel under the command of *Oberstleutnant* Gotthardt Handrick. Fighter pilots originally received training at Bucharest-Pipera, then at Galati, Tiraspol, and — from mid-1944 — at Ghimbav (Vidombák/Weidenbach), near Brasov. ARR personnel were also training abroad. Bomber crews were sent to Tutow, Germany, in the spring of 1941, for training at *Große Kampffliegerschule* (KFS) *1*. Rumanian airmen also studied at the Luftwaffe training centers at Wiener-Neustadt, Rostock, and Lemberg (Lwów) in occupied Poland. Over 2000 ARR personnel — 1500 airmen and 500 anti-aircraft crew — were trained in Rumania or the Reich by the Germans between October of 1940 and June of 1941. On 1 September 1943, there were 1973 ARR crewmembers in various schools in the Reich.

By the spring of 1943 conversion training on new German aircraft equipping *Corpul 1 Aerian Român* (C1AR) took place at Bolshoy Fontan (near Odessa), or at Kirovograd and Nikolayev, at the front. Selected personnel, including assault and dive bomber pilots, were sent to Krosno, Poland, beginning in January of 1944. These ARR personnel learned to master the Hs 129B and Ju 87D at *Flugzeugführerschule* (FFS) (C) *20* advanced flight school. Several prominent pilots were sent to Germany during the summer of 1944 to train on the Fw 190F assault aircraft. Rumania's withdrawal from the Axis alliance cut this training short and all ARR personnel in Germany at that time were interned.

This S.E.T. 4 (No. 18) performed a classic 'Pilot's Monument' during the mid-1930s. The S.E.T. Works in Bucharest produced a variety of training and liaison biplanes (S.E.T. 3, S.E.T. 4, S.E.T. 7, and their derivatives) from 1927 to 1937. Over 100 of these aircraft remained in service at the beginning of World War Two. (Bernád)

An I.C.A.R. Universal (No. 3), prepares to take off for a filming session. A portion of the 'Michael's Cross' marking is visible next to the number 3. I.C.A.R. was the third-leading Rumanian aircraft manufacturing plant and originally specialized in the license production of Messerschmitt sports aircraft. It later produced its own models which were largely inspired by early Messerschmitt designs. (Bujor)

This license-built I.C.A.R. Acrobatic nosed over on the soft ground of an airfield during the war against the USSR. This highly maneuverable sports aircraft, manufactured in 1935, was often flown for fun by top ARR pilots, like *'Bâzu'* Cantacuzino. (Bernád)

ARR operated 1131 training aircraft by 23 August 1944. Approximately 200 of these aircraft were destroyed in the following days by Luftwaffe aircraft. One hundred sixty-one of those aircraft destroyed were parked on the two airfields of Turda, located in previously safe southern Transylvania. Part of *Centrul militar de pilotaj* (Military Piloting Center) was based at Turda. Rumanian troops, on the other hand, captured over 200 Luftwaffe aircraft including a significant number of trainers. These captured aircraft were put to use in the training, liaison, and courier roles.

Restrictions imposed on Rumanian aviation by post-war treaties resulted in scores of military aircraft being relegated to training duties to avoid being scrapped. Older and fatigued aircraft were either discarded or transferred to civilian use where attrition was high. The last Bücker, Nardi, Fleet, Klemm, and other older types remained in service until the early 1960s. Soviet rule and technology had by then reigned for more than a decade.

Two original wartime trainers, a Fleet F-10G and a Nardi F.N. 305, have been preserved and are exhibited today at the National Military Museum in Bucharest. These are the only surviving genuine Rumanian World War Two training aircraft existing today.

Liaison and Courier Aircraft

In late 1939, the ARR's ambitious *Ipoteza* (Hypothesis) *32* plan envisaged the existence of six *escadrile de legătură* (liaison squadrons) and two *escadrile de legătură îndepărtată* (long-range liaison squadrons), each equipped with eight aircraft. This plan was completed by the summer of 1940. During June of 1940, the ARR inventory listed 48 liaison aircraft — primarily Fleet F-10Gs, supplemented with a few S.E.T. 7s and Fi 156s. Sixteen twin-engine long-range liaison aircraft were in service — composed mainly of Lockheed 10s and 14s, along with a few Potez 651s. These aircraft, however, were primarily transports rather than courier aircraft.

The structure of the liaison squadrons was standardized around the Fleet F-10G when the attack on the Soviet Union began in June of 1941. An F-10G was also regularly issued to each combat squadron as a unit hack. The two long-range liaison squadrons were disbanded and their multi-engine aircraft relegated to transport duties. The six liaison squadrons (Nos. 111-116) were assigned to a main ARR unit for use in both front and rear areas. A total of 2883 liaison and courier sorties were flown in under four months, regardless of weather conditions or intensity of flights. Attrition of these light and unarmed aircraft was high, although they did not take part in direct combat. Twenty-six liaison and courier aircraft were lost during the second half of 1941, primarily to accidents. This total included 23 Fleet F-10Gs, two S.E.T. 7Ks, and one Fi 156C. These aircraft lacked armament beyond the pilot's sidearm and were easy prey for enemy fighters. A Fleet F-10G, assigned to *Escadrila 114 legătură* and flown by *Sergent elev aviator TR* Marin Clinciu, was hit by Soviet I-16 'Ratas' and forced to land near Salz airfield. Both Clinciu and his passenger, staff officer Lt Nicolae Vlastov, were gravely wounded. A pilot from the 114 LS pulled Cliniciu and Vlastov from the wreckage before it became engulfed in flames. Aircraft deliveries to the liaison squadrons remained steady to replace these losses.

Courier units were less involved in the Stalingrad Campaign than in the Bessarabian Campaign. The Rumanian 3rd Army began offensive operations in the Caucasus Mountains during the summer of 1942. ARR provided the Fleet-equipped *Escadrila 112 legătură* to *Comandamentul Aero Armata 3,* the air element of the Rumanian 3rd Army. A similarly equipped squadron later joined *Comandamentul Aero Armata 4* in support of Rumanian 4th Army operations south of Stalingrad. Twelve Fleet F-10Gs of *Escadrila 113 legătură* were assigned to *Corpul Aerian Român* when the Corps was sent to the Stalingrad area in early September. By the end of the disastrous campaign in mid-January of 1943, ARR had lost 15 liaison and courier aircraft. These losses included nine Fleet F-10Gs, two S.E.T. 7Ks, two Fi 156s, and two civilian-marked R.W.D. 13s.

During 1943 an effort to replace the Fleet F-10G biplane with the superior Fieseler 156 was underway, however, the Germans could not supply the Storch in sufficient numbers. License production at the

The pilot of an I.A.R. 27 trainer (No. 24) runs through his checklist prior to take off from a Rumanian airfield during the war. The I.A.R. 27 was the only domestically-designed trainer used in large numbers during the war, with the prototype first flying on 8 June 1937. Production was undertaken by S.E.T.-Bucharest, and the first I.A.R. 27s were delivered to ARR flight schools during late 1939. In addition to the standard aft fuselage band and lower wingtips, the upper wingtips of this I.A.R. 27 have also received a coat of yellow paint. (Moisescu)

This Fleet F-10G (No. 268) cruises over wheat fields on a training flight. Beginning in 1936, over 330 US-designed F-10Gs were built under license by all three major Rumanian aircraft factories. These aircraft were used for a variety of tasks, from primary flight training to liaison and courier duties. Additionally, Fleet F-10Gs were usually allocated to the headquarters of each infantry division or other main Rumanian Army units. The F-10G was well-liked by both Rumanian pilots and students. (Bernád)

A Miles Hawk (No. 7) is parked at Salz airfield, Trans-Dnestra, in the fall of 1941. This popular British trainer was also employed as a courier aircraft early in World War Two. (Greceanu)

This Messerschmitt Bf 108B Taifun (Red 1118) was used by *Lt. c-dor av.* Gheorghe Miclescu to visit Mamaia airfield on the Black Sea shore. The aircraft features blue-yellow-red rudder stripes painted in an unusual diagonal pattern and silver-painted cockpit frames. The Bf 108 was employed for training, as well as for the personal transport of high-ranking ARR officers. This Taifun's serial number was identical to the aircraft construction number. (Bernád)

This camouflaged Klemm Kl 35D (W.Nr. 2079/YR-BUG) was assigned to the Rumanian-administered Trans-Dnestra Government in 1943. The products of *Leichtflugzeugbau Klemm* were a common sight in Rumanian skies for more than 20 years after their first appearance in 1931. The Kl 35 was imported in the largest numbers and primarily used by civilian flight schools. (via Petrick)

A Rumanian officer guides a Bücker Bü 133 Jungmeister (W.Nr. 1036/YR-AHN) past a Heinkel He 111 of KG 51 *'Edelweiss'* and towards the taxi strip. This light sports aircraft was originally owned by *Asociatia Sportivă CFR* (Rumanian Railway's Sports Association). The Bü 133 retains the original Bücker livery of overall cream with a green cheat line. The aircraft has been given a 'Michael's Cross', however, no yellow rear fuselage ring or blue-yellow-red stripes are worn on the rudder. (Crow)

I.C.A.R. Works was also slow, with the first Fi 156Ca-3 not being delivered until late 1943. This resulted in only some of the Fleet inventory being replaced before Rumania's August 1944 defection from the Axis alliance. On 23 August 1944, C1AR's liaison strength included *Escadrile 112, 113, & 116 legătură* with 27 Fi 156 and Fleet F-10Gs. *Corpul 3 Aerian Român* employed *Escadrila 114 legătură*, equipped

This anonymous R.W.D.-14b Czapla was one of the few Polish light aircraft retained by ARR after it sought refuge in Rumania in September of 1939. Most of the over 130 light aircraft from Poland — primarily P.Z.L.s, R.W.D.s, and P.W.S.s — were handed over to civilian flying schools and to individuals. These civilian aircraft were later impressed into military service in 1941. (Bernád)

with six Fi 156s and Fleet F-10Gs, while *Escadrile 111 & 115 legătură* were assigned to the two army high commands. An unnumbered liaison squadron with ten Fleets was based at Sura Mică (Kiscsür/Klein-Scheuern), in southern Transylvania, and served with the Rumanian 1st Army on the Hungarian border. By August of 1944, an F-10G was also assigned to each army corps and selected divisions for liaison purposes.

In early September of 1944, sixteen freshly re-painted liaison and courier aircraft, including some captured from the Luftwaffe, were assembled for the beginning of the anti-Axis campaign. These aircraft were consolidated in *Escadrila 114 legătură* and redeployed to Sura Mică, in southern Transylvania. Additional Fleets and Fieseler *Störche* served with army corps and division headquarters. Liaison aircraft flew 820 sorties totaling 1765 flight hours by the end of 1944 while losing three aircraft in combat. A Fleet F-10G flown by *Adjutant aviator* Ioan Simulenciu was shot down by a Bf 109G in mid-September, while two P.W.S. 26s were destroyed on the ground. Prior to the anti-Axis campaign in early September, at least one S.E.T. 7K and an unidentified Bücker had also been shot down. Luftwaffe aircraft destroyed dozens of ARR non-combat aircraft on the ground at Turda (Torda/Thorenburg) and Câmpia Turzii (Aranyosgyéres) airfields during the same period.

In mid-October 1944, the 114 LS was divided into three *sectii* (sections) with four aircraft each. *Sectia 1-a legătură* was assigned directly to C1AR Headquarters, while the other two *sectii* went to the I.A.R. 39-equipped *Grupuri 1* and *2 observatie*. C1AR operations shifted from Hungary to Slovakia in late December of 1944. The weakened C1AR received long-overdue reinforcement from the 112 & 113 LS in mid-February 1945. These two squadrons arrived at the front equipped with 15 Fi 156s and Fleet F-10Gs each. The three liaison squadrons' 40 aircraft flew 833 sorties totaling 1701.5 hours over Slovakia by the end of the war. Among the liaison aircraft lost was a ski-equipped Fi 156C (No. 15) on 20 February 1945. This aircraft was sent to rescue the crew of a downed Ju 87D Stuka and overturned in deep snow while attempting to land on rough terrain at Vel'ká Lúka (Nagyrét), near Ocová (Nagyócsa). The fighter escort leader circling ahead of the Fi 156 notified his base of the accident. A two-seat (!) Fleet F-10G, also mounted on skis, was sent to evacuate the three downed airmen. The Fleet pilot spotted the two wrecked ARR aircraft, however, he could not see the crews in the area. The Rumanian Ju 87 and Fi 156 crewmen had been captured by German *Gebirgsjäger* (Mountain Troops) before they could be rescued. The captive airmen immediately offered to join their captors to fight against Soviet troops, however, this offer was rejected and the untrustworthy Rumanians were held until released after the war.

Liaison units flew 1713 sorties totaling 3466 flight hours during the nine-month long anti-Axis campaign. These missions were flown on behalf of the Rumanian 1st and 4th Armies, C1AR, and the main Soviet units.

The first of 30 Piaggio-built F.N. 305-IIs were delivered to Rumania between February and August of 1938. The aircraft were finished in a two-tone olive and dark green upper camouflage scheme. The Nardi-designed F.N. 305 was one of the most common intermediate flight trainers used by ARR. Former Rumanian airmen remembered this aircraft as requiring constant attention due to its sometimes erratic handling. Nevertheless, the F.N. 305 shaped the skills of hundreds of ARR pilots from the late 1930s to the early 1950s. (Bernád)

ARR units were restructured and reduced in size after the war. This process included the liaison and courier aircraft. These aircraft were consolidated with the transports into *Flotila 4 transport-legătură* during June of 1945. This mixed unit was renamed *Flotila 7 aerotransport-legătură* and reduced to group strength during August of 1946. Only a handful of Fleet F-10Gs and Fi 156Cs remained in military service by the end of 1947, when the 'reactionary' *Aeronautica Regală Română* was officially disbanded. These surviving aircraft were augmented by so-called 'new Soviet technology' — the ancient Polikarpov Po-2 biplane. The majority of Fleets and Fieselers received civilian registration and were assigned to non-military or paramilitary units, schools, and aeroclubs. The last surviving World War Two-era aircraft soldiered on until the 1960s.

This unnumbered Arado Ar 66C was captured from the Germans, hastily repainted, and then used by ARR as a courier aircraft. The exhaust flame dampeners indicate this aircraft was formerly part of a Luftwaffe night harassment unit — believed to be *Nachtschlachtgruppe 5*. ARR took over this Ar 66C before Rumania's new masters — the Soviets — could seize it in accordance to the armistice convention, which stipulated that all captured Axis men and equipment be handed over to the Red Army. (Bernád)

The Fieseler Fi 156C Storch served with *Escadrila 114 legătură* on the anti-Axis Western Front from September 1944 to May 1945. The flexible machine gun has been removed from its mount in the rear cockpit canopy due to the lack of Axis fighter opposition during the last months of World War Two. The Storch was both imported from Germany and manufactured at I.C.A.R.-Bucharest. (MMN)

This anonymous Focke-Wulf Fw 44 Stieglitz is believed to be an ex-Luftwaffe machine captured by the Rumanians during the confusing days of late August of 1944. The ARR roundel and white rear fuselage band were applied after the Fw 44 was confiscated by the Rumanians. (Bujor)

List of Rank Equivalents

ARR Ranks	Translation	USAAF Ranks
Elevi	**Students**	**Cadets**
Elev soldat av.	Student Private Av.	Cadet Private
Elev caporal av.	Student Corporal Av.	Cadet Corporal
Elev sergent av.	Student Sergeant Av.	Cadet Sergeant
Subofiteri	**Sub-officers**	**NCOs**
Adjutant stagiar av.	Junior Warrant Officer Av.	Staff Sergeant
Adjutant av.	Warrant Officer Av.	Technical Sergeant
Adjutant major av.	Major Warrant Officer Av.	Master Sergeant
Adjutant sef av.	Chief Warrant Officer Av.	First Sergeant
Ofiter echipaj clasa a III-a av.	Deputy Sub-Lieut. Av.	Warrant Officer Jr. Gr.
Ofiter echipaj clasa a II-a av.	Deputy Lieutenant Av.	Flight Officer
Ofiter echipaj clasa I-a av.	Deputy Captain Av.	Chief Warrant Officer

ARR Ranks	Translation	USAAF Ranks
Ofiteri	**Officers**	**Officers**
Sublocotenent av.	Sub-Lieutenant Av.	2nd Lieutenant
Locotenent av.	Lieutenant Av.	1st Lieutenant
Căpitan av.	Captain Av.	Captain
Locotenent comandor av.	Lieutenant Commander Av.	Major
Căpitan comandor av.	Captain Commander Av.	Lieutenant Colonel
Comandor av.	Commander Av.	Colonel
Generali	**Generals**	**Generals**
General de escadră av.	General of Air Squad Av.	Major General
General comandant av.	General Commander Av.	Lieutenant General
General inspector av.	General Inspector Av.	General
Maresal de aviatie (Regele Mihai I.)	Air Marshall (King Michael I)	N/A

[Note: 'Av.' means 'aviator'. Ranks of technical NCOs are not listed]

Trainer, Liaison, and Courier Aircraft

Aircraft Type	Manufacturer	Start of Service	Total Number	Serial Nos.	Notes
L 25a, d; Kl 25* A,D,J	Klemm	1931 (*1936)	66+ [45]	Civilian	
S.E.T. 4	S.E.T.	1931	10	N/A	
S.E.T. 31	S.E.T.	1931	10	11-20	
S.E.T. 7	S.E.T.	1932	50	1-50	
Fleet F-10G	Consolidated	1934	20	1-20	Powered by a D.H. Gipsy Major of 130 hp.
Universal	I.C.A.R.	1935	10	9, Civilian	
Acrobatic	I.C.A.R.	1935	3	0, 1, 2, Civilian	Delivery of last two units unconfirmed
S.E.T. 7K, Kb, Kd	S.E.T.	1936	60	101-160	
Kl 35, B, D*	Klemm	1936	67+ [63]	Civilian	Version with enclosed cockpit included
Fleet F-10G	I.A.R., S.E.T. & I.C.A.R.	1936	330+	21-351+, Civilian	Powered by an I.A.R. GI of 130 hp (license-produced Gipsy Major)
J-12 PCLM*	Porterfield	1936	2	Civilian	*Probably Model 35 Flyabout
M2H, M2Y, M7, M11A	Miles	1936	14+	1-10, Civilian	
Bü 131A, B, D Jungmeister	Bücker	1937	25+ [40]	Civilian	
Bü 133A, C, D Jungmann	Bücker	1937	9 [6]	Civilian	
Fw 44J Stieglitz	Focke-Wulf	1937	1 & 5* [1]	1-6 (?), no s/n, Civilian	*Ex-Luftwaffe, captured
Fw 58B, C Weihe	Focke-Wulf	1937	32* & 3**	1-32+	*2 for Trans-Dnestra Government, included into ARR **Ex-Luftwaffe. 36 additional a/c ordered in May 1944
Bf 108B Taifun	Messerschmitt	1937	13 & 5* [13]	1-10, c/n & Civilian	*Ex-Luftwaffe, captured
Bü 180 Student	Bücker	1938	1 [1]	Civilian	
Nardi F.N. 305-II	Piaggio	1938	30 [31*]	1-30	Powered by an Alfa Romeo 115/1 of 200 hp. *Italian sources give sub-type as F.N. 305A
Ba-122	Avia	1938	7+ [12]	Civilian	
Go 145A	Gotha	1939	15 & 5* [15]	1-20, Civilian	*Ex-Luftwaffe, captured
M 35b	Messerschmitt	1939	1 [1]	Civilian	
I.A.R. 27	I.A.R., S.E.T.	1939	80	1-80, Civilian	Prototype built by I.A.R., series production at S.E.T.
Lublin R-XIII	Plage & Laskiewicz	1939	23 [17]	Polish s/n	
P.W.S.-26	P.W.S.	1939	69* [9]	1-27+ & s/n, Civilian	*27 delivered by the Germans in 1941
R.W.D.-8/8a	D.W.L., P.W.S.	1939	59+ [61]	Civilian	

[list continued on inside cover]

Five top ARR fighter pilots — each awarded the prestigious *'Ordinul Mihai Viteazul'* (Michael the Brave Order), 3rd Class — are assembled at Mariupol, Ukraine, on 28 August 1943. From left: *Cpt. av.* C. Cantacuzino, *Lt. av.* T. Greceanu, *Slt. av.* I. Di Cesare, two generals, *Cpt. av.* A. Serbănescu, and *Of. ech. av.* I. Milu. By that time these aces had claimed over 85 Soviet aircraft. The five combined to score over 200 victories by the end of World War Two. All these men — except Serbănescu, who was killed during the last clash with USAAF aircraft — survived the war. (Bernád)

Prince Constantin M. Cantacuzino was Rumania's champion aerobatic pilot before the war. Cantacuzino later became the ARR's leading ace during WW II. (Bernád)

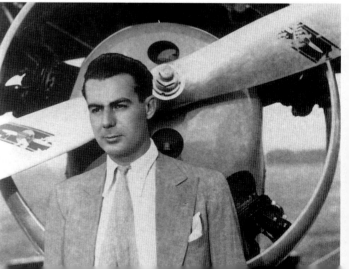